Jungle Breezes

Jungle Breezes

From Amish Farm Boy
to Jungle Doctor
The Life of Elam Stoltzfus

Based on a True Story

By Dara Stoltzfus

VMI Publishers
Sisters, Oregon

Published by
VMI Publishers
Sisters, Oregon
www.vmipublishers.com

ISBN: 1-933204-77-X
ISBN 13: 978-1-933204-77-2
Library of Congress Control Number: 2008943815

Unless otherwise noted, scripture quotations are taken from the New American Standard Bible. © Copyright 1960, 1962, 1963, 1971, 1972, 1973, 1975, 1977, 1995 by The Lockman Foundation. Used by permission.

Printed in the USA.

Cover design by Kara M. Elsberry

TABLE OF CONTENTS

DEDICATED TO…

…my children, grandchildren and beyond, that you may know
where you came from and the legacy that your father and
grandfather left behind…

…my husband, for being the kind of man a father can be
proud of and who inspires a wife to want to write
down your story…

…my mother-in-law, Barbara, for being a woman who has
dedicated your entire life to serving God in every
aspect of your life…

…and to God, for being You.

· · · · ·

THANK YOU

I want to give special thanks and recognition to Ethel Rutt,
and to Jim and Millie Maust, for all of their research and
organizational skills, which laid the foundation for this book
to be written.

Thank you to my Uncle Gwyn for saying something once that stuck in my
head and motivated me to finish this project.

And thank you to everyone at VMI Publishers for all of their work that is
making it possible for this story to be forever captured
this way for my children and grandchildren's sake.

ENDORSEMENTS

I met the Stoltzfus in 1980. Elam and Barbara, along with their children have been always an inspiration for us. To see them come to our country as missionaries. The devotion to our people, even in the hardest of circumstances has always been a source of motivation for us. I will never forget that the very first day I went to into full time ministry; I traveled to "La Anchura" the mission they had founded in the jungles of Petén. I saw their faith in action. I witnessed their unconditional commitment to Guatemala and I saw Jesus' mercy in their ministry. It is with great joy that we salute today this book that celebrates God's love in the form of a family that came to Guatemala to show God's love.

Dr. Harold & Cecilia Caballeros, founder and Senior Pastor of El Shaddai Church in Guatemala City

If you want a real life story of excitement, hardship and faith, this book fits the category. The story of a family who lived in a foreign country with nothing but each other and a faith in God will inspire you to believe that "God and family are a force to be reckoned with!" What was accomplished through this family is nothing short of MIRACULOUS!

Anne Beiler, Founder of Auntie Anne's Soft pretzels

What motivates a young Lancaster County couple to move young children to the jungles of Guatemala, to set up a clinic, to provide vital services for people in great need, only to see the efforts of 20 years be burned to the ground by the Marxist guerrillas? It must have been Jesus. Elam Stoltfus' legacy is indeed "…a life worth remembering."

Vernon Myers, Pastor at Andrews Bridge Christian Fellowship, Oxford, PA

Thank you for an all-inspiring story of the Christian faith and obedience of Elam Stoltzfus and his family by believing God for protection in the midst of satanic pressure. I am reminded as with Abraham, God always keeps His promises. Elam has used one of my favorite verses, Psalm 37:4—"Delight thyself in the Lord and He will give you the desires of your heart."

Jim Herr, Founder of the Herr Foods Company, Nottingham, PA

INTRODUCTION

The book you have in your hands is not the first book I have ever written. No. Anyone who has ever received an email from me when I am fired up about something will attest to that! But, this is the first book that I have ever written and not clicked "send" when I was done.

Sometimes when I meet new people and begin to tell them about my husband's life and family here in Guatemala, I almost short-circuit because there are so many thoughts going through my mind all at once and I want to be able to tell them everything at the same time. There is just so much to hear about this family that even after eight years of being part of the family and asking countless questions, still, out of nowhere, my husband, Elam Stoltzfus' son, will casually tell me something that happened when he was growing up that will send me upstairs to the computer to try to see where I can fit that tidbit into the story!

It wasn't even like I had a say in this, because this book almost demanded that it be written. The life that Elam led tells a story of a person in our own day and age who would have been in Hebrews chapter eleven had he lived before it was written. And the thing that gets me the most excited about this story is that it is not a story that was born. It is a story that was chosen. Elam was not born a hero. He was not born set apart from the rest of us. No. He was a normal, average person in every aspect, except in how he chose to live his life.

He chose to live by faith. And, because he did that, he changed the history of a whole country. Guatemala is not the country today that it would have been had Elam never come here. There are people every day getting married, having babies, and living life who would never have been born had he not come here. How many people can say that about someone in their family? Not many, but how many people should be able to? We all should! There is nothing that Elam had or was that none of us cannot be if we only choose to follow God with our whole heart. If we would only choose to run the race that is set before us, keeping our eyes on Jesus! We, too, can have a life worthy of a novel. A life that is worth remembering. A life that will have us standing before God someday hearing the words, "Well done, my good and faithful servant!"

I want everyone to know what Elam, his wife Barbara, and children did here in Guatemala. I want all of you to be challenged to look at your own life and see areas where maybe you have said, "Well, that doesn't seem like a wise thing to do," and instead choose to say, "OK, God! I'll do it!"

One day I suggested to one of my homeschooled children that he pick out one of the biographies I have on our bookshelves and read it. His response was that they are boring and he prefers to read interesting stories. So, I have done my best to make this story true to life and interesting. I have listened to the stories about Elam over and over and have done my best, usually after midnight after all the children are asleep and often with a baby nursing on my lap, to paint a picture of Elam as I have come to know him through his son and wife, as well as his other children.

As I began to write it was apparent that the number of people who actually contributed to this ministry over the years would be impossible to include. So rather than try to include everyone and then end up leaving someone out, I have stuck to just a few names of people and churches as I found direct references to certain events in Elam's newsletters. Names of Guatemalans have been changed because of the sensitivity and seriousness of the war stories.

My hope is that once you get to the end of this book, you will know what a life lived for God can look like, and that it looks like fun. If you already have a relationship with God, I hope that it inspires you to listen more closely for God's still small voice telling you things you never heard before from Him, and that you will be more eager to live life on the wild side with God. Even if the farthest place from home in the world that God ever leads you is the grocery store, I hope you would begin to go there for Him. And if you don't know or even like God, I hope that this book inspires you to see God in a different light, and maybe you can dial Him up, say hi, and see where things lead.

—Dara Stoltzfus

Chapter 1

Amish Farm Boy

Children are a gift of the Lord, the fruit of the
womb is a reward. *Psalm 127:3*

A malaria-filled mosquito buzzed around the jungle looking for a snack. It was late. She hadn't eaten in days. She spied a bunch of humans hiding out in the trees and made her way toward the tastiest-looking one. She landed on a nice warm patch of bare skin and began drinking. As her belly expanded, something about the snack started to change. It fought back. Suddenly, the human noticed it was involuntarily giving a blood donation. A hand was raised, and Miss Malaria's lights went out.

But Miss Malaria Mosquito would not soon be forgotten, as she left behind a prize that would begin to cause this feisty snack some pain and high fevers in a few weeks. The most unfortunate part would be that after tonight, there would be no free clinic nearby to get the malaria treatment from.

Unless you were equipped with the human-seeking sensors of a hungry mosquito, looking out upon the jungle all you could see were trees, trees, and more trees. But beneath the trees, watching and waiting, were the men whose sole purpose tonight was to steal, kill, and destroy. They sat thoughtfully, silently, as they prepared to carry out tonight's orders.

Off in the distance they heard the sound of the power plant shutting down. The leader looked down at his watch and thought to himself, "Eight-fifteen. Just like clockwork. Time to shut down the power plant. Time to shut this place down for good."

Silently, using hand motions, he told his men it was time to move out. They started their approach of the mission compound. At home in the thick jungle, they didn't make a sound as they crept toward the house. As they got closer to their target, the sleepiness of the hours of waiting and swatting mosquitoes wore off as adrenaline started to flow and the men became nervous. Whenever they set up an ambush or did a raid, there were no guarantees that things would go as planned. There was always the chance that the army would show up or that someone would fight back. There was always the chance that this was the end.

They reached the handmade mahogany front door of the house and pounded on it.

Elam and Barbara were accustomed to emergencies and women in labor showing up at the clinic at all times of the night—babies, it seemed, didn't know how to tell time. And so Barbara instinctively hopped out of bed and ran to the door, with Elam following. When she reached the door, even before Elam could see who it was, her reaction made it apparent that it was no lady in labor. Something was wrong.

"What?" Jean thought, hearing the voices all the way from her bedroom window in the guesthouse across the lawn. The army base was nearby, so the army guys came around a lot, even sometimes at night. But they were normally very polite and respectful, and that was not how she would describe the voices she was hearing outside. She peeked out her window and could see a large group of armed men standing around the house. Having lived in this war-torn area of the Petén since she was nine, Jean recognized the men immediately.

"It's the guerrillas!" Her heart raced. They had been raided by the guerrillas before. What did they want this time?

"Outside! All of you!" the guerrillas shouted and pointed with their guns.

Elam, Barbara, and five of their six children—Jean, Virgil, Anita, Maria, and Lisa—spent the rest of the night held at gunpoint, watching as the communist guerrillas who had been at war against the Guatemalan government for over thirty years whooped and hollered while they raided their home, the medical and dental clinic, the new cannery, and all the apartments. While they watched, they prayed, sang, and witnessed to the guerrillas, and just waited. Though they had lived in the center of the war zone for years, God had always seemed to have a hedge of protection around them. Tonight, something seemed very different.

Elam watched as the guerrillas loaded box after box of their family's belongings into the mission's boat. After it was loaded, for some reason they took the younger of his two sons, Virgil, with them down the river and off into the night.

In the distance was the sound of gunfire. The guerrillas were apparently also attacking the nearby army base in Pipiles at the same time. That made sense. What the family didn't know was that the shots they heard were also a signal to the guerrillas at the compound that it was time for the next step of their raid.

"Mom, Dad...." Jean was looking toward the house, which the guerrillas were now dousing with gasoline.

· · · · ·

Deep in the jungle at the guerrillas' campsite, the commander had just been informed by radio that it was now time to complete tonight's mission. The mission compound had been raided, and now it was time for the second part of the orders: the elimination of the mission's pilot. The commander leaned his M16 machine gun up against a tree, and drew a 9mm from his holster, cocked it, and said to Virgil, "Let's take a walk."

· · · · ·

"Elam, I want you to help your sisters to take these snacks out to the men," Elam's mother Priscilla Stoltzfus said kindly.

She was busy preparing food and drink for the men working in the field on their eighty-five-acre farm in Lancaster County, Pennsylvania. She had already prepared gallons of homemade root beer, which she stored in the big ice-water cooler they kept out in the milk house. All morning she and a bunch of other ladies had been mixing and baking cookies and preparing food for lunch.

"Mom, can I help Dad?" Elam's blue eyes looked up at her hopefully. "Please?"

What he meant was, "After I take the cookies and root beer out, could I please stay in the field and help the men with the threshing?" Being inside doing girls' work was no fun! What he really wanted to do was be out there working with the men.

"Elam, you're a good boy, but you're still too little just yet to help with that. You can help your sisters and me with the meal. Now, hurry out there with the snacks! The men must be hungry!" His mom smiled and shooed him and his sisters out the door toward the field.

Elam wanted to plead with his mom, but he knew that arguing with Mom was not an option. The kids made their delivery, and the girls turned and were off back to the house "right quick," giggling about something as they went.

Elam lingered a little while the girls headed across the field. "Dad, what are you doing?" There was just something about the smell of the plants being cut and the dirt everywhere that called to this little boy in a way that baking cookies and setting the table didn't.

His dad looked down at his son, knowing how much Elam wanted to be outside. "We're threshing the wheat, Elam."

Elam paused for a moment. "Can I help?"

A smile spread across Israel Stoltzfus' tired face. "Son, when you're bigger, you can help. Now, get back to the house."

Elam looked up at his dad, let out a little sigh of disappointment, and then having already learned that Mom and Dad meant what they said he sighed, "OK." Finally, he turned and headed back to the house.

Back at the house, instead of getting to grab handfuls of dirty things and get all sweaty and help his dad, Elam helped to set the nice clean table for his mom.

That night, after the excitement of the day, Elam sat on his dad's lap. He looked up at him and said, "Dad, when will I be big?"

His dad just smiled. "Soon, Elam."

· · · · ·

"Huh? What?" Jonas Stoltzfus muttered to himself, half awake. He opened his eyes. The room he shared with his little brother Elam was dark. It wasn't time to get up yet, but something had woken him up. He looked around the room and noticed Elam's bed across the room was empty.

"Hmm, what is he doing out of bed?" he asked himself.

Then the noise that had woken him up came again. It seemed to be coming from outside their bedroom window. He looked out of the window and said, "What in the world?"

There was little Elam walking on the slightly slanted porch roof, holding out his hands as though he were driving the horses. "He's sleepwalking!"

Jonas stared out the window, trying to think of what to do! Elam walked along the roof almost to the edge. Jonas' eyes grew even wider as he expected to see him go right off the edge, but then he heard, "Gee!" and Elam turned and started back the other direction. Elam got all the way to the other side of the roof and said, "Haw!" and turned and went the other direction again!

Jonas wasn't sure whether to laugh now or not! He was still trying to figure out how to get Elam back inside when he saw his chance. As Elam was heading back toward the other edge of the roof again, he walked close to the window. Jonas reached out and grabbed him just as he got to the window and pulled him in.

Elam startled awake, and noticed he wasn't in his bed. He was a little bewildered. "What?" he said.

Now that Elam was back inside and safe, Jonas thought again of little Elam out on the porch roof "sleep plowing," calling out commands to the horses, and he burst out laughing!

"You…" his brother began and then started laughing uncontrollably, holding his belly, "you…" and the laughter kept coming.

"Jonas, come on, tell me. What? What's so funny?" Elam, confused, whined a little as he climbed back into his bed.

"You just about drove Dad's horses right off the roof!" and Jonas fell on his own bed laughing and laughing.

"Huh? What are you talking about?" Elam didn't get it.

Just then, a shadow appeared in the doorway, which ended Jonas' battle with the giggles. He sat up on his bed, alert. "Um, Dad. I um, just found Elam sleepwalking. He was out on the roof, and I um, he was um, looked like he was driving the team. And, it was, um, kind of funny."

He waited for his father's response. Goofing around after bedtime was not tolerated and usually was punished by a whipping. In a house with no electricity, there were no sounds of fans running at night or the sound of a refrigerator or gentle hum of a furnace in the basement to muffle any little sounds anyone might make. Jonas had been clearly heard on the other side of the large farmhouse.

After a pause, which to a nine-year-old boy can seem like an endless, painful eternity, his father sighed and replied, "I imagine that was a bit funny. Now that you've taken care of your little brother, I think it's time to get back into bed and get to sleep."

Not hesitating for a moment, Jonas pulled his covers up and laid his head on his pillow. "Good night, Dad."

"Good night, Dad," Elam followed, also getting covered quickly.

"Good night, boys," their dad said as he turned to walk back down the hall to his own room, thinking to himself how funny that would have looked. A grin spread across his sleepy face.

As soon as Elam heard the sound of his father's bedroom door click shut, he turned and whispered to his brother. "I was out on the roof sleepwalking?"

"Yes, and you had your arms out like this," Jonas held his arms up in front of him, "like you were driving the horses in the field!" Then, it was Elam's turn to giggle, only very quietly under his covers, then quickly he was off to sleep.

· · · · ·

In the morning, Elam was up before the sun. Today was a school day! He hopped out of his bed and got himself dressed as fast as he could, and ran out to check the traps before his brothers got there. He and his brothers liked hunting and trapping muskrats and skunks during the winter to sell their pelts. Now, who it was that would buy skunk fur and for what remains a mystery to this writer, but they actually sold them. Dad and Mom would let them keep the money, and they would split it and could buy penny candy and five-cent candy bars at the corner store.

Sometimes they would go out at night with flashlights and hunt for them. If they found a skunk, they would try to pick it up by the tail. The trick was that if they kept its feet from touching the ground, the skunk couldn't spray them. To these young Amish boys this was a great challenge and adventure, because for them this was living life on the edge! All boys love danger, and the danger in this was the risk of not being so lucky and getting sprayed. Elam would experience that misfortune a number of times, but since it earned him a day off school to play around the farm, he didn't think it was too bad, really.

It was always fun to be the first one to get to the traps in the mornings to see what they had caught. Sometimes there was nothing, just an empty trap and rotting bait. Sometimes there was a cat in the trap, and that was kind of gross. It was always best to keep that news from his sisters. A few times, Elam had been the first to find a skunk, and assuming it was dead just ran right up to it and ended up getting another day off school.

This morning, Elam reached the traps first, but to his disappointment there was nothing there. All hope for adventure was gone now, so he turned and ran out to the barn to help his father with the milking.

Elam came in and started helping his dad. Israel looked down at his little blond-haired blue-eyed boy with those tiny hands reaching up under the cow, and a smile went across his face.

"He's so cute," his dad thought to himself.

After a few minutes, Elam said, "Dad?"

"Yes, son?" his father replied, while keeping his eyes on his work.

"Why are all our cows black and white?"

"Well, because that's the color of this breed, and that's the breed that gives us the best milk."

"Do the colors make the milk taste better?"

His dad laughed a little. "No, it doesn't have anything to do with their color. That's just what color this particular breed happens to be, and they are good milk producers."

"Oh. What's a producer?"

"That means they make a lot of milk each day."

"Oh. I like milk. I like chocolate milk a lot, too. Do you like chocolate milk?"

"Yes." Israel smiled.

"Do policemans take baths like us?" Elam asked.

Israel chuckled. "Yes, Elam, policemen take baths just like us."

"Oh." Elam pondered that.

"They live in houses, too?" Elam asked.

"Yes, they also live in houses," Israel answered.

They went on milking a few more minutes. "Dad..."

"Yes?"

"Why do all the other kids at school look so different from me?" Elam had entered school this year for first grade at a little red public schoolhouse nearby. The Amish were still another year from having their own private schools authorized and opened, so for now all of the Amish went to their local public schools with the "English" children.

"We are God's people, Elam," his father replied, thinking to himself how funny it was to go from one subject to the next like that.

"Why are my clothes so different from the other kids' clothes?" Before his father had time to reply to that he added, "Sometimes, the kids tease me. Why do they tease me?"

Taking his eyes off of his task, Israel looked down at the bright innocent blue eyes of his son, and searched for the right answer. He, too, could remember being a small child and being teased by the English children in school. He had memories of his own, and it made him sad knowing that his son was having the same experiences.

"Elam, we are God's chosen people, and we are called to be set apart from the world. The Bible says that we are to 'come out from among them and be ye separate, saith the Lord.' This is why we are different."

"Is that why they don't talk Dutch, either?" Elam added.

"Yes, son, that's why they don't speak our language." His father hoped that would be the end of the questions. There was a moment of silence again.

"Dad," Elam said.

"Yes?"

"Do some cows make chocolate milk?"

Israel smiled. Elam was one cute little kid, that was for sure.

· · · · ·

Although the dialogue you just read was in English, Elam didn't speak English very well yet. The language that Elam and his family spoke was a German dialect called Pennsylvania Dutch, which was brought over by their ancestors from southern Germany. This was the language all Amish families spoke at home. At church, which met every other week at someone's home, Elam heard the other language his forefathers spoke: High

German. So until Elam went to the little red public school, he had only heard English spoken when they had English houseguests and when he was out in public at the store with his mom.

On Elam's first day of school, as he sat in his new classroom surrounded by new and strange things and people, trying his very best to be a good boy, he ended up in a bit of a predicament. Elam needed to visit the outhouse but didn't know how to ask in English.

He looked around at the room. It seemed so big, and it was full of strange faces, many of which were looking back at him because he was different and new. When they spoke they only said, "Blah blah blah," and he had no idea what was going on. The teacher was busy at the chalkboard teaching, and she too only said, "Blah blah blah," and his older siblings who knew English were too far away to whisper to. Elam knew better than to be disrespectful in this kind of environment, and knew no other option than to wait till recess. So he sat quietly in his seat and tried to hold it. He really did try.

"Aw, Elam, why didn't you raise your hand?" one of his brothers poked at him fondly as they walked home from school.

"Poor little guy," Fannie said to Priscilla, pointing to her cute little brother whose blue eyes were filled with embarrassment and shame.

"I just didn't know right what to do," Elam replied, relieved to be able to speak to his siblings in Dutch now that school was out.

"Yeah, but you could have said something to the teacher," Rachel toyed at him.

"I didn't want to get into trouble," Elam said with his head down as he pushed himself slowly along on the one roller skate he'd found in the neighbors' trash.

"You don't get in trouble at school for asking to go to the outhouse!" Lizzie smiled.

"I didn't know!" Elam said still looking at the ground.

"You're so silly," Fannie added. Priscilla tussled his hair, and they all continued home to the farm.

Chapter 2

Questions

"For I know the plans that I have for you," declares the Lord,
"plans for welfare and not for calamity to give you
a future and a hope." *Jeremiah 29:11*

The lady in the passenger's seat just couldn't believe her luck. Just a few miles back they'd spied the most peculiar thing in the middle of the road and stopped right there in front of it to get a picture.

"Now would you look at that, honey?" she said to her husband as she snapped the picture of the fresh land mine—recently left behind by one of those Amish buggy horses. "Right here in the middle of the street! Isn't that funny?" Her husband was a little embarrassed, actually, but he politely nodded and smiled at her in agreement. She was having a good time taking pictures on this trip to "*Lan*-caster" County, Pennsylvania.

The kids were having a great time, too. "Wow! Mom! Did you get the picture?" they asked as she hopped back in the car. They continued on their drive out through roads that cut through farmlands and cornfields that reached like oceans out to the horizon.

"It is just beautiful here, isn't it, honey?" she said again, with her camera still in her hand. They rounded a curve, and then they saw him: a lone Amish boy working in the field with a team of five huge horses.

"Oh, honey! Stop! Stop! I have to have that little *Aay*-mish boy's picture!" So Honey stopped and looked at his wife. She handed him the camera and smiled expectantly. He started to protest but was informed, "Well, he's on your side of the car; go take his picture!"

Elam saw them watching him and wondered how long they would wait, as he figured he knew what was about to happen next. Finally, after working up the nerve, Honey got out of the car, crossed the road, and awkwardly approached the little boy.

"Excuse me, son, my name is Ed," he began with a funny accent Elam had never heard before. He extended his hand to Elam, who in turn shook it and smiled at the man.

"My family and I are from Texas," he said, motioning awkwardly back to his car where the eager faces of the rest of his family watched, "and I was hoping that maybe you might not mind if I took your picture?"

He hesitated for a second, then quickly reached into his pocket and brought out what he had. "I am willing to pay you for it," and he offered Elam a quarter.

Elam looked around the field, and could see that no one was around. He imagined what his father's response to this man's request would be. His dad would not have approved. In the Amish church, photos were strictly forbidden, but Elam didn't really mind when people took his picture.

"Sure," Elam said shyly.

"Thank you very much," Ed from Texas said. He nervously started backing off to get a good shot of the little Amish farm boy. "Say, uh, cheese," Ed called out from behind his camera, and then there was a little click.

"Thanks again," Ed said, and began making his way carefully through the clumps of freshly plowed soil to his car.

As the man and his family from Texas drove away, Elam was puzzled. The car had a Texas license plate. Texas? Elam had often thought that it would be fun to go around the world to tell people about Jesus, but travel in a horse and buggy is not like travel in a car or an airplane. You can't just go and go and go and keep refilling the horse with hay. No! For Elam, his world had never been bigger than forty miles from home.

He watched as the car from Texas stopped again, just up the road. Someone hopped out of the car and seemed to be taking pictures of a herd of cows. Elam wondered, "How did that man ever get his car across the ocean?" Elam glanced back up just as the car from Texas was going out of sight and felt a surge of excitement well up inside him. "Someday *I am* going to go tell the world about Jesus."

. . . . .

It was a cold day. The team captain stood in the yard of the new Amish one-room schoolhouse and thought for a minute. They were picking teams for a game of Prisoner's Base. The fastest and oldest boys always got picked first. Everyone's breath was easy to see in the schoolyard, and most everyone was bundled up warmly with scarves and gloves and had a red nose. The captain lifted his arm and pointed to his next choice. "Elam!" he said, and Elam ran from the pile of boys in the corner of the play area over to his team.

Elam was just twelve years old, a sixth grader, and he wasn't one of the fastest, but the captain who had just chosen him was his big brother. Elam knew that by picking him his brother had passed over the chance to get one of the better players on his team, but his brothers were all that way with him. Elam looked at his brother with pride and love inside. "I'm going to make him glad he picked me," he thought to himself.

Another few rounds of choosing went on, and Elam waited to see if his two favorite buddies would be on his team or not. Then his brother made another choice, "John!" John Fisher came running over to Elam's side.

The two boys smiled at each other a smile that said, "Yes!" and then waited as the other team captain made his choice.

"Oh no, he picked Ephraim," Elam sighed, disappointed that his other best bud was going to be on the other team.

"Oh no is right!" John said. "We haven't been able to play together out here at recess for months."

Elam got a puzzled look on his face. "I think it was just a week, wasn't it?"

"A week, a month, what's the difference when you're trapped in the schoolhouse all day every day for all the recesses while everyone else is out here having a great time, right?" John said.

"Yeah, you're *probly* right," Elam agreed, watching the next choice for their team come rushing over.

"Don't say that word!" John said, looking serious.

"What word?"

"Write," John said, looking scared and tired.

"Oh yeah, 'write.' Right, I get it now. I guess not. I was having dreams every night about that." Elam finally caught on.

"Me, too. I'd see myself writing on huge pieces of paper with huge pencils, 'I was a naughty boy, I was a naughty boy,'" he said while making huge writing motions with his arms.

Elam laughed. "How many times do you think you wrote it, anyway? I think I wrote it a million times." Elam then caught sight of the next boy to come their way. "Oh great, we got Amos on our team!"

"Good, he's the fastest boy in seventh grade," John agreed, and remembering the eight terrible days stuck inside writing and writing with Elam and Ephraim he added, "A million and one times, I think."

"Next time you get the idea to go throwing snowballs at cars, why don't you just leave me out of it anyway?" Elam chided.

"Me? No way. You were the one who started it."

"Did not."

"Did too," John replied, giving Elam a friendly punch on the arm. "I just wish that guy had just driven on past instead of stopping at the school and telling on us."

"Well, at least Mrs. Thompson stuck up for us when our dads came to school to talk to her," Elam added, rubbing his hands together and stuffing them down into the pockets of his coat.

"I guess. My dad was pretty angry when he got home that night." John shuddered just thinking about the look on his dad's face as he walked into the living room that night.

"Mine, too," Elam said, "but at least I didn't get a whipping for it since the teacher said that she was going to see to our punishment."

"Yeah, same here. Guess we owe her thanks or something." John looked up. "Hey, we got Arlen, too!" He pointed as another teammate was chosen.

"Know one thing else I wonder?"

"Huh?" John was still watching as the last two boys were waiting to be chosen. Soon the game would begin, and the cold air wouldn't seem so cold anymore.

"What do you suppose Mrs. Thompson does with all those pages of paper that say, 'I was a naughty boy' anyway?" Elam said with a mischievous look in his eye.

"Cheap wallpaper?" John replied, and both boys laughed as they ran off into the pre-game huddle.

. . . . .

It's customary for Amish children to finish with their schooling at eighth grade, so at the ripe old age of fourteen, Elam was free from school-work to spend his days working in the fields. He was out working with his father today. They worked silently side by side for a few hours tossing ears of corn into the wagon one by one, row after row.

Elam enjoyed these times, especially working with his father. He loved the work. He loved being outdoors. He loved being near his father. And it gave him time to think. Lately, he seemed to have found a lot of things to think about, though he didn't realize it was a "struggle" at this point. It was just a lot of things he'd thought of. Things he wondered about. It seemed the more he wondered about, the more there was to wonder about. It just never ended! The frustrating thing was that he didn't seem to have a way to come up with any answers for the things he wondered about.

Although he had spent years listening to the four-hour sermons at church, and had heard much about Jesus, there just seemed to be some-thing missing. It nagged at him all the time.

"How about we take a break *once*, Elam," his father suggested, taking his hat off and wiping the sweat from his brow.

"Sounds good to me, Dad," Elam replied.

They sat down at the side of the harvester and pulled out some beef jerky from a little sack. They sat silently together for a few minutes.

"Father," Elam began respectfully, speaking in Pennsylvania Dutch, "Dat, favach misa mia so untershiet sae fon di undre lait?" *(Dad, why must we be so different from the other people?)*

Always he had the same questions! "You know the answer to that question already, son," his father began. "We are to be set apart from the world."

"I know that, Dad, but I just don't understand why. I mean, like, what is wrong with using machines? What is wrong with rubber wheels and gasoline engines that we must reject them?" he motioned toward the neighbors' fields across the road.

The neighbors used mechanical harvesters and accomplished in days what it took them weeks and even months to accomplish by hand. "What does God dislike about machines? I don't get it."

His father answered quickly and definitely, "The Bishop has the answers. You must ask him."

"But Dad," Elam said, shifting his position to be facing his father, "I know that we are taught to accept the word of the Bishop as the Word of God, and that this is what our church teaches us, but I don't understand why these things are? I mean, Dad, why do *you* feel that these things are wrong?"

It was almost as though his dad couldn't understand the question. "Elam, it is our way. The Bishop teaches us everything that has been handed down by our forefathers, and we aren't to question it. He speaks for God."

Elam slowly shook his head, "But I just don't understand that. Why does God give me opinions and a mind if I am only supposed to obey the opinions of the Bishop?"

"Elam, the Bishop speaks for God. When you are obeying the rules of the church, you are not obeying the opinions of a man, but God Himself." His dad seemed almost horrified.

The Amish believe that the Apostle Peter had been given the authority to make all the rules in the church, and these rules were equivalent to God's Word.

> *"I also say to you that you are Peter, and upon this rock I will build My church; and the gates of Hades will not overpower it. I will give you the keys of the kingdom of heaven; and whatever you bind on earth shall have been bound in heaven, and whatever you loose on earth shall have been loosed in heaven."*
> *Matthew 16:18-19*

Therefore, since the Bishop of the Amish church is Peter's spiritual descendant, his word is considered unquestionable, the same as if God were speaking Himself.

"I am sorry, Dad, but there is just something about all that I just don't understand. What is the basis for all these things? How are we to know that the Bishop is really speaking for God?"

"The Bishop explains these things from the Holy Scriptures for us. That is how we know." Israel was feeling irritated by these questions. "Why are you asking so many questions? Whom have you been talking to?"

"No one, Dad. Just today," he motioned across the street to the neighbors' field, "I was watching the neighbors working as we worked. I know they are good people. They get their work done twice as fast as we do. I just wonder why that displeases God?"

"Elam, our elders and our forefathers have clearly defined for us what pleases God. We all must," he stammered for words, "bear the cross."

"But Dad, is all that is necessary to please God wearing an untrimmed beard, having long hair, dressing by church standards, plowing with horses, and not owning or driving a car? I just don't understand that! Jesus did all that suffering for these things?"

"Elam, Elam, you need to ask these things of the Bishop." His father was starting to feel trapped by the questions, questions he never dared to even toy with in his own mind. Sure, he had noticed how much faster his neighbors could work in the fields. He had spent years working long, hard hours in the field while his neighbor worked his machines, but never did this make him question his faith. He was concerned by his son's discontentedness. He had seen it before in others and knew where such questioning could lead, and he could almost not bear to think of one of his own sons heading down that road.

A few minutes passed, and Elam tried to let it all drop before he really made his father mad. But these things were tormenting him all the time, more and more the older he was getting. He had great respect for his father, and he just wanted to know what his father thought. They didn't often have time alone, so he continued, "Dad?"

His dad raised his eyebrows.

"We don't study the Bible much," Elam began. "Aren't the answers to all these questions in the Bible somewhere? I mean, don't they have to be if the Bishop can find them?"

They didn't spend much time in church studying the Bible, didn't have weekly Bible studies, or listen to Bible teachings on the radio or TV, so to Elam the very book which was the guide for his life was still a mystery to him. On the Sunday mornings when they didn't have church services, Amish families stayed in their own homes, and the parents taught the children to read the High German Bible. It was the parents' duty to teach the children to read High German, and this was the way it was done. But as they read the Bible they were also taught that if one studied the Bible too much they might become mentally disturbed.

"Yes, Elam, of course the answers are in the Bible, but it is necessary to discuss these things with the Bishop in order to fully understand them. He is there to protect us from deception. We cannot understand the Bible on our own. It is dangerous for us to attempt to figure things out on our own. We should always trust the word of the Bishop," his father replied.

Elam wanted to find peace in his father's words. He wanted to be satisfied with his answers, but like always the answers just led to more questions—more nagging questions. He couldn't understand why God would have written and left a Bible for man that could not be understood by everyone who was interested in reading it.

"Dad, I really mean no disrespect with my questions, and I really want to respect the church law, yet it is a terrible thing to know that there is a heaven and a hell but still not know for sure where you will spend eternity. It is a terrible thing to know that there is a God who desires to be pleased, and not to fully understand what pleases Him and what displeases Him," Elam finished with a sigh.

Elam's father offered no response this time. Now the conversation was over. Without saying anything further, they both got back up and began working again. Elam's mind was flooded with questions, while his father's was filled with concern.

Chapter 3

Leah's Tarantula

God made the beasts of the earth after their kind, and the cattle after their kind, and everything that creeps on the ground after its kind; and God saw that it was good. *Genesis 1:25*

Not too many miles from where Elam was, there was a young girl screaming in her bedroom on a Mennonite farm. Terror was rippling through her veins, and her desperate cry could likely be heard for a mile. Would anyone come to her rescue?

Leah tried her best to get away, but it seemed of no use! There was nothing she could do but scream, "Ahhh!"

Barbara pulled up her skirt a little and went tearing up the steps two at a time to her room. "Leah! What are you screaming about?" she asked as she entered the bedroom she shared with her two younger sisters.

Leah was standing up on her bed looking as though she'd seen a ghost. She could barely talk, but she could point. "It's a, a, a..." she said.

Barbara looked down into the corner near the bed where Leah was pointing, knowing what she'd find. "What is it, Leah, another, um, what do you call them? A tarantula?"

She leaned over a little to get a better look and finally saw it. Leah's eyes widened even farther as she saw her sister approaching this huge creature!

"Oh, Leah," Barbara said with a chuckle, "it's just a Daddy Long-Legger!"

Leah was not convinced, and remained safely perched on top of her bed. "Are you sure it's not a tarantula? It looks like one!" Leah's eyes were just popping out of her head as she watched Barbara reach down and pick up the horrible creature with her bare hands!

"No, Leah, it's not a tarantula!" now Barbara was laughing. "You know, I've never seen a tarantula, but I'm sure this isn't one, OK?" Still laughing, she headed for the hallway.

"Barbie, aren't you going to kill it?" Leah shouted from her perch on top of her bed.

Barbara just smiled to herself as she played with the harmless spider. It crawled around her hand and arm while she carried it to a safe place outside, away from Leah. Leah didn't care for bugs. Whenever she saw anything creepy-crawly anywhere in the house she would just lose it! Those things, no matter how creepy or crawly had never bothered Barbara.

"What was all that fuss upstairs about, Barbara?" her mother asked as Barbara passed by the kitchen. Barbara turned and faced her mother, who was armed with two potholders and a steaming hot pie, as Barbara got to the front door. "Oh, you know Leah!" She smiled and held up her arm to display the spider.

Anna Stoltzfus laughed and said, "Yes, I know your sister." She turned and set the pie down on the cooling rack on the table and went back to the oven to get the other two.

Barbara headed outside and found a nice spot under some bushes near the house to set the little guy down. The air was crisp this morning. Winter was approaching quickly. "God is so good!" she thought to herself as she looked across the road at the neighbor's cornfield which stood dry, waiting for the harvest that was soon to come.

An Amish buggy came clopping along on the road as she stood there in the yard, so she raised her arm and waved and smiled at the strangers passing by. As they passed, two cute little kids peeking their heads out the back smiled and returned the wave.

Although Barbara's first language was also Pennsylvania Dutch, she and her family weren't Amish; they were Mennonite. They were from similar roots and often shared relatives, but their churches, style of dress, traditions, and beliefs were somewhat different.

Barbara went back in the house and returned to the kitchen where she'd been helping her mom before she'd had to run to Leah's rescue.

"Barbie, were you reorganizing my cabinets again?" Anna knowingly asked her daughter.

Barbara just smiled, "Well, they were a mess."

"Yes, I know they were, but you should warn me before I try looking for things *usually*!" Anna smiled back at her oldest daughter.

It was the girls' job to do the dishes, which was just fine by Barbara. She liked doing the dishes just so long as she hadn't had to be the one to dirty them. Cooking was not her favorite thing, and she was pretty slick at disappearing to avoid that job. On the other hand, her sisters would rather have been cooking than doing the dishes. They especially didn't like putting the dishes away, and so they did it as fast as they could, not usually paying too much attention as to where things were put. After a few weeks of this, the cabinets and pantry were a wreck, and Barbara would wait until she was home alone and then get to work fixing things up and reorganizing.

"What can't you find?" Barbara asked as her mom was opening all the cabinets up and looking inside of them.

"That other cooling rack," she said.

Barbara moved a few feet, opened up a door, and pointed, "Here it is!"

Anna reached over and grabbed it. "Thanks!"

Leah came walking down the stairs still looking a little shaken and peeked into the kitchen. "Did you get rid of it?" she asked, wondering if Barbara was still holding it.

"Yes, Leah, the tarantula has packed his bags and moved on to the neighbor's house."

Relief flooded Leah's face. "Good." She thought for a second, and her eyes got big. Leah liked the neighbors and wasn't sure if she wanted them to have a tarantula in their house either!

Barbara wondered to herself what Leah would do if she ever saw a real tarantula, and the picture she got in her mind was funny enough to make her laugh out loud a little. Leah noticed Barbara's face and asked, "What?"

"Oh, nothing!" Barbara smiled back.

Just then, they heard the sound of a car pulling into their driveway. Leah and Barbara looked at each other with huge smiles on their faces and were ready to race, but six-year-old Edna beat them to the door. She'd seen

Daddy pulling in the lane from an upstairs window and was already on her way down the stairs and to the front door before the girls heard him.

The girls all stood at the end of the driveway waiting the last few moments until the car would come to a stop. The boys, George and Bobby, were with Daddy and hopped out of the car right away. They ran straight for the field to play.

"Daddy!" the girls cried out in unison and gave him a hug.

He had a few bags of groceries he needed help carrying in and also had with him "the usual"—a half a stick of gum for each girl, which was a very special treat they all looked forward to each time Daddy went to the store. Jake looked down at his sweet girls and wished he had more to give them. The girls, looking up at their loving father, never even knew they were poor.

Most of their non-Mennonite neighbors were busy this week setting out pumpkins carved with scary faces, and stocking up on candy to share with trick-or-treaters, and making costumes for Halloween. Barbara's family, and the whole community of Mennonites in general, didn't celebrate Halloween, but they never missed it or felt left out of the fun. This week was harvest week. To them, this whole week was a fun week.

All of the families "on their block" got together when it was time to harvest and took turns going to each person's fields, harvesting each field together until all of them were finished. When it was your turn to have your field harvested, everyone showed up early at your house, and the men headed to the fields to work. The children played, and the women cooked! It was a fun week with everyone working together, eating together, and singing together in the evenings.

Because they were poor and food was rationed because of the World Wars that had been going on, they had to be creative in making the food stretch. One good way to make a yummy meal that went really far and didn't cost a lot was to make a big pot of cold fruit soup. You could use practically any type of fruit you wanted, but it seemed that bananas worked best. The ladies would gather and peel a boatload of bananas, or as many as they had, and fill a pot. They added milk that was straight from their own cow and some sugar. Then, when it was time to sit down and eat it, one would break apart a piece of bread and drop it in, too. Nutritious, filling, and yummy!

Barbara thought her life was fun, and she felt blessed. She didn't know it, but every day just living her life she was learning things she would need someday in a faraway land that she'd never even heard of yet in school. Some of the lessons would get her through some very hard times and teach one of her children to fear bananas. Some of the lessons would even help her to save people from things way more scary than Daddy Long-Leggers.

Chapter 4

Denial

"I love those who love Me; and those who diligently
seek Me will find Me." *Proverbs 8:17*

"Well, look who's courtin' *already*!" Ammon Fisher teased the two seventeen-year-old Amish boys in the two-passenger open "courting" buggy next to him. Elam and Simmie Glick jumped down from the seat and acted like they were going to pound Ammon.

"Hey, quit it!" Elam tried to look threatening. Ammon pretended to plead. The guys all laughed and settled down.

"Where you headed, Ammon?" Elam asked as he hopped back up into the single seat of the buggy he'd had now for just a little over a year. It was the traditional sixteenth birthday gift for Amish boys.

"Over to Isaac's," Ammon replied.

"The singing is going to be there tonight?" Simmie asked from beside Elam.

"Where you been?" Elam looked at Simmie kind of strangely.

"Hey look, gimme a break. A guy can't know everything," Simmie replied.

"Yeah, then, to catch you up on the latest news, the singing is at Isaac's tonight. I'm heading out early. How about you guys?" Ammon asked as he nodded to the buggy with his Uncle Jonah and family inside as it passed him pulling out of the driveway.

The bi-monthly four-hour church service had just let out, and most of the families were packing their kids into their buggies and heading home.

"I'm busy tonight," Elam said, adjusting his new three-and-a-half-inch-brim hat as though he were a wealthy snob.

"Busy? Yeah right!" Ammon said. "Oh, I know what's different," he said, realizing now what looked different on the harness on Elam's buggy, "Where'd your red keepers go?"

Elam looked over his horse's harness and shrugged his shoulders, "I was talking to my uncle the other day out in the field, and he let me know clearly that he disapproved of them and the chrome, too. So I took 'em off."

"I didn't know the red keepers were forbidden," Ammon said, looking thoughtfully at his own and then back over at Elam's harness again. "You let the chrome on?"

Elam nodded. "I figured that since my uncle is a deacon, he would know, and that's what he told me."

"Too bad. They looked smart," Ammon said, wondering what this meant about what he would do with his own harness if any of the elders mentioned it to him.

Buggies were very plain, black and gray with no luxuries—not even rubber tires, which meant they were noisy and tough on Pennsylvania's roads. The adults usually kept their buggies just that way, but the young boys always seemed to find things to do with them to spiff them up and to personalize them. Most of the metal parts of the harness the young boys had managed to come up with a fancier and flashier version of. Whether they were acceptable or not depended on which church district you happened to be in. The final decision on these things came down from the Bishop.

Elam and his family were members of the most orthodox and strictest branch of the Amish. Because he had a genuine desire to honor God, and had been taught all his life that the way to do that was through the church, he was usually cautious not to break any of the church rules, regardless of whether he liked them or not.

"I heard ya just about ran over a state trooper last night?" Ammon said, changing the subject.

"Oh yeah, who told ya that?" Elam replied.

"A little bird," Ammon winked.

"Jacob?" Elam asked. His little brother was good at reporting all his latest news to his buddies.

Ammon nodded with a smile.

"Well?" Ammon raised his eyebrows.

"Well, what? You want to know what I had for breakfast or something?" Elam tried to look confused.

"Come on! Did he write ya up?"

"For eating breakfast too fast?" Elam replied with a slight slur to his voice, still looking confused.

"For your lights!" Ammon laughed.

"How about for attempted hit and run, *already*!" Simmie added.

"Who asked you anyway?" Elam gave an exaggerated look of irritation to Simmie. "Actually," he added, "I think he felt bad for me when I told him how much he'd scared me." Elam remembered how he'd felt when he'd seen the flashlight waving around in front of him.

Often, the English youth had a lot of fun tormenting Amish kids. It was easy to assume that if a buggy was out late at night it wasn't a lady coming home from the market with her kids and a load of groceries. It was the Amish youth, and the English youth knew this. So, on nights when they'd had their fill of hanging around the local hot spots like restaurant or gas station parking lots, they'd drive around with cartons of eggs, looking for buggies out on back roads, and they'd "egg" the buggies. Sometimes they'd start fights with the Amish boys, and most recently there were some kids who'd been stopping Amish buggies late at night and then beating up the Amish boys.

Late the night before, Elam had been on his way home and was struggling with his lights. Though the Amish do not use electric lights in their homes, Pennsylvania state law requires that all buggies used on public roadways have proper lighting like a car would—headlights, turn signals, and taillights. For this, they use a regular car battery that they charge using a generator at home. The battery that ran Elam's lights apparently had not been charged properly, and he barely had enough power to turn his lights on whenever he saw a car approaching. Even then, the lights were very dim. He had just flicked his lights on again, fortunately getting close to home, when a car passed him and stopped. Then someone got out of the vehicle and started waving a flashlight.

Thoughts of the recent attacks went through Elam's mind, and he felt sure that the person had bad intentions. Immediately, a plan for how to get out of the situation entered his mind. He wasn't about to allow himself to get beat up by a bunch of English boys! The thoroughbred pulling the buggy, Bessie, was a high-spirited horse, so Elam gave her the reins and said, "Get away, gal," and she took off. He drove her straight toward the person holding the flashlight, and tried to pin whoever it was up against their car as much as he could without hitting them. Bessie did her part of the plan very well, and the person jumped out of the way as the buggy skimmed past the rear of the car.

At first, Elam felt relief as his buggy flew past, but then he noticed something familiar about the person with the flashlight. As he passed he caught a glimpse of what looked like a large, flat-brimmed hat! The person trying to stop him hadn't been an English teen wanting to make sport of an Amish kid, but a Pennsylvania State Trooper!

"Uh oh," Elam thought. As soon as he could he got Bessie stopped, and right away the state trooper pulled up behind him.

"I just explained to him what I was thinking, and he actually apologized for scaring me," Elam said to Ammon, whose eyes were wide as he laughed a hearty laugh.

"Oh boy, I can't believe you did that!" Ammon was still laughing.

"What else was I supposed to think?" Elam's arms were up in the air.

"Wow. The first time you get pulled over by a cop, and you nearly flatten him like a pancake!" Ammon said.

"Yeah. That's a story for my grandkids someday, ha?" Elam laughed.

"Maybe someday someone will put that in the book about your life," Simmie teased. He had spied a girl he liked across the yard getting into the buggy with her mom and dad and was barely listening to the conversation anymore, but he did hear enough to take advantage of a chance to make a little fun.

"Who asked you?" Elam gave Simmie's shoulder a push.

"So, did he write you up for not having lights?" Ammon moved on with the conversation.

"No, he cut me a break there, I guess since he felt bad for me. He did offer to follow me home then, to make sure I'd get there before my dim lights turned into no lights at all."

Ammon reached over and punched Simmie in the arm, because he was starting to act like he was asleep. Simmie twitched a little, yawned, and looked over at Elam. "Is it morning already?"

Ignoring Simmie, Ammon asked Elam, "So, what's on the agenda for tonight then? Got your lights fixed?"

"I think I need a new battery," Elam said, waving to the children who were peeking out the rear of the buggy that had just pulled out of the driveway.

"Too bad. Well, are you coming to the singing tonight? Rebecca will probably be there," Ammon said, making tiger noises.

"Nya. And give you guys the chance to pin me up against the side of the barn with her? No way!" Elam replied.

"Aw, Elam, come on! You know she likes you!" Simmie piped in.

One tradition among the Amish youth was the Sunday evening "singings" where they would gather in someone's house and sing German and English hymns together. Afterwards, they would have a party out in the barn, which they called a hoedown. The kids would usually sing and do square dancing together. At these hoedowns, they had another tradition among the youth that had to do with courtship.

If a "guy" had a "gal" he had his eye on, he would tell his buddies, who in turn would run and tell the girl's friends. Then the guys and the girls would conspire together, grab the potential couple, and wrestle them over to the side of the barn. The two people, even if they liked each other, would put up a pretty good fight and pretend to not want to cooperate. Then their friends would get the two of them over to the side of the barn and pin them there until they could maneuver them around and put them together with their arms around each other. At that point, they would usually "give up," and the crowd of shepherds would go their way and leave the new couple alone together.

"We're supposed to be keeping ourselves out of trouble now if we're going to be getting baptized as church members here in a few weeks," said Elam. Some young boys didn't join the church until they were older, but Elam had decided that he would start attending baptism instruction class already with some of his buddies. He was only a few weeks away from getting baptized. Once baptized, that would make him an official member of the church.

"Who says we're going to get ourselves into any trouble tonight?" Ammon said, grinning broadly.

"Yeah, I'm always a good boy," Simmie said laughing.

"Remember, we're The Lemons. We're good guys!" Ammon said proudly. The Lemons was the name of the "gang" that the three boys were a part of. As far as getting into trouble went, they got into their share, but they were usually pretty mellow in comparison to some of the other gangs like The Groffies. The Groffies would drink at the hoedowns and listen to loud music. The Lemons pushed their rebellion limit with cigarettes.

"Actually, I'm pretty tired this afternoon. I think I'm just going home," Elam said. What had been about twenty-five buggies parked in the yard dwindled down to just two. "Looks like it's time to make like a horse turd," Elam said flatly.

"Huh? What?" Ammon didn't get it.

"And hit the road."

Simmie smiled, and Elam led the horses out of the driveway.

· · · · ·

This Sunday Elam stayed in bed a little longer than usual. He lay on his back and looked up at the ceiling. The Amish only have church every other Sunday, and this was not one of those Sundays. Last Sunday had been his church day, and it had been a hard day. This Sunday he hoped would be better.

His buddy Amos went to another church in another district, and they did have church this Sunday. The exciting part about today was that Amos was going to be baptized into the church this morning, and Elam was invited to come.

Elam said good-bye to his family and headed off with Bessie to the home where church was to be held. When he arrived, he parked his buggy and walked around, talking with some of the other youth there. After his experience last weekend, he was struck right away when he saw Amos heading in the driveway. He took notice for the first time of Amos' slicked-up buggy and saw all the chrome rings and buckles on his horse's harness. Suddenly, Elam's excitement for his buddy turned to alarm.

"Amos." Elam went right over to Amos as he was tying his horse and whispered, "You will never get baptized like that."

Amos had barely gotten out of his buggy. "Like what?" Amos' eyebrows furrowed with concern for a moment.

"The chrome, and your hair, and…" Elam was pointing, "your brim is too narrow."

Amos looked up at his hat brim. "I think it'll be OK. Elam, what are you looking so upset for?"

"You know what happened to me last week, right?" Elam said.

"Yeah, you were denied baptism."

Even as Elam heard that, it sent a pang of pain through him again. "But you know why, don't you?" Elam said seriously.

"No," Amos said. "I haven't talked to you since then."

Elam leaned in closer to Amos and spoke quietly. "There were three reasons for the denial. My uncle came to me and told me that for one, he didn't like all the chrome on my harness, and I didn't have near as much as you do."

He and Amos looked at the harness. Trying to not make too much of a fuss, Elam pointed to the harness. "Look, you even have white rings, and they're definitely forbidden."

"Yeah, what else?" Amos was starting to feel a little worried.

"The second reason was that my hair is not quite long enough yet. And he said I should have had my three-and-a-half-inch-brim hat for a longer time to prove myself."

"Oh," Amos checked out Elam's hair and then casually checked his own hair. "Your hair is longer than mine," Amos said nervously.

"And your hat is only a three-inch brim." Amos looked up again at his brim.

"And the reason I just know this has to be a problem is that the same Bishop is over both of our church districts. That means that the same rules will apply!" Elam was sad for Amos, knowing that under these conditions, he surely would also suffer denial just as he had last week. He had felt crushed last Sunday when after all his preparation, anticipation, and excitement, his uncle told him the final decision of the elders that he was to be denied baptism.

"Well, I guess if I get denied today, I'll be going to those extra three classes with you then," Amos said, resigning himself to the fact that at this point there was really nothing he could do about it.

Elam didn't expect there to be any "if" about it. He felt sure that Amos would be denied and be attending those three extra classes with him.

He felt disappointed for his friend. It was almost like experiencing last week all over again. His disappointment had followed him around all week, but on his way to church today he had felt renewed excitement for Amos, at least. Now he would have to watch as his good friend was also denied baptism.

But something happened that day that Elam hadn't expected, something he didn't know what to do with that caused him a considerable amount of trouble in his spirit. When the time came for the final decision of the elders to be passed, Amos with all the chrome on his harness and his short hair and three-inch-brim hat was not denied. He was approved, baptized without any complaint. The same Bishop who spoke for God who'd agreed with the three reasons for Elam's denial now approved of the baptism of someone with those very same things. Why?

All morning, Elam had felt sad for his friend because he didn't want him to go through what he had just gone through last week, yet, now that it had turned out that he was to be baptized, Elam couldn't feel happy or relieved for his friend. The rest of the morning, Elam heard none of the sermon and seemed to be far away. He was seeing his church differently than he ever had before, as though a light suddenly had been turned on. He wondered why he had never seen it before.

Elam had wanted to go tell the world about Jesus since he was a little boy, and God had just the place for Elam to go. But in order to fulfill that dream, Elam would have to do like Abraham and leave his family behind. What was about to happen was going to be hard, and many tears were going to be cried, but lives of literally thousands of people in a country Elam didn't yet know existed would someday depend on the decisions that he was about to make.

· · · · ·

Lying in bed that night, Elam could not sleep. Something was wrong. He knew it. "And if something is wrong, then I must see into it to find out what is right," he said to himself.

Although he had had many questions over the years, Elam had never doubted that he would be Amish his whole life. He felt strongly about this. Yet now, beyond just having unanswered questions about God, Elam started doubting the teaching of his tradition.

He didn't know what to do or where to turn. He'd asked his father questions and had been told that the Bishop spoke for God, but he'd just seen the Bishop contradict himself. He didn't know whom he could trust with his questions. As he lay there struggling to think of whom he could talk to, no names came to his mind. Instead, a desire grew strong within him to read the Bible.

"Makes sense," Elam thought. "I'll ask God Himself in the Bible what He has to say."

Back when Elam was still in school, Gideon Bible distributors had come to hand out pocket New Testaments, and he had taken one home to show to his father. His father quickly took it away from him, believing that it would only cause him problems to try to read it and understand it. Besides, the Bible had been in English.

Although English was not Elam's first language, since entering school it had been the language he had learned to read and comprehend best. At home his family spoke Dutch, and there were no Bibles translated into Pennsylvania Dutch at that time. He heard German in church, and even had some of the sermons almost memorized, but still, his reading comprehension in German wasn't what it was in English.

"Stephen has an English Bible." Elam remembered the offer his brother-in-law had made him to borrow his Bible any time he wanted it, and suddenly felt excitement well up within him. "As soon as I can get over there, I'll ask him if I can borrow his Bible!"

• • • • •

Elam didn't waste any time getting that Bible in his hands, and he lay in bed for long hours into the night reading. He found verse after verse that seemed to conflict with things that he'd been taught all his life. But how could this be? The Bishop was God's voice on earth, so if he was speaking for God, he would certainly never contradict the Bible. But some verses just seemed to lean that way. It was distressing.

• • • • •

"In my heart I have always had a desire to go into the world and tell others about God," Elam said to his father, "but our leaders say that is not our responsibility."

Israel sat in his chair in the living room, listening to his son speak words he'd hoped to never from any of his own children. The cast iron wood stove was putting out a lot of heat, but still, Israel felt a chill. "Yes." His face was stern.

"Look, here I read that Jesus said, "Go ye into all the world and preach the gospel to every creature."" Elam was kneeling on the floor next to his father, holding open the Bible he'd borrowed from Stephen. He was pointing to the book of the Bible called the Gospel of Saint Mark. He then flipped through some pages and pointed again. "The Book of Acts. It's full of examples of the church going into the world and preaching the gospel."

His father was not really looking. His mind was overwhelmed with fear for his son. He saw a fire in his eyes that he'd never seen before, and along with that fire, now he was questioning the church! He'd known of boys Elam's age who had gone down this road and had ended up leaving the church and going out into the world to be lost forever. This didn't happen too often in this area, but it had happened. Images of the wonderfully hardworking little boy, who'd often been such a source of joy for him and his wife, going off into the world swirled around in his mind. His heart ached, and he felt sick to his stomach imagining losing his precious son, but he held back his tears. Elam had always been a good boy. God willing, he would make it through this time in his life and still be on the straight and narrow path. Israel whispered a prayer to himself, "Thy will be done, Lord."

"The church always tells us that we can only hope that we have eternal life, right?" Elam's eyes were bright as he flipped back some pages to some small books of John. "As I was reading last night, I found this in these epistles of John, where I read over and over again that we *can* know that we have eternal life, and that we are the children of God." He found a specific verse and pointed, "See this?"

His father glanced down where his son was pointing and nodded. He saw the rough farm-worked finger there pointing on that page, and all he could think of was losing his son. He couldn't even read the words.

"Then a few nights ago, I was reading the four gospels, and when I got to the last one, John, I read that I need to be born again." He stopped and looked up at his father, hoping to see some understanding, some agreement.

"Well are you sure that you're understanding what you are reading? Maybe you are misunderstanding it," his father dryly suggested.

"Look here." Elam flipped back to the book of John. "I don't see how I could be confused about this. It's very clear. Jesus is speaking to, um…" he looked through the passage once he found it, "to one of the Pharisees, Nicodemus, and Jesus tells him, 'Unless one is born again, he cannot see the kingdom of God.'"

His father made no reply but kept on looking at him sternly, waiting for whatever Elam had to say next.

Elam went on, "That's what Jesus said, that I cannot see the kingdom of God unless I am born again. I don't even know what that could mean! And even if the church teaches that we can only hope to be saved, how can we even hope if we are not born again when Jesus says we have to be born again to get into the kingdom of heaven?" He paused for a second. "In fact, Dad, if Jesus himself tells us that we have to be born again, and if the Bible is the Word of God, then why is it that we are forbidden to go to the Bible studies with the Amish youth who claim to be born again? I just don't understand this. It just makes no sense." Elam shook his head.

Elam knew that all this would have to be distressing to his father, but hoped that his father could see Elam's heart and know that his son only wanted to know the truth. He waited now, hoping that his father would have something to say. His father, though, had had enough of the whole conversation.

"Elam, you need to take your concerns to the Bishop. I would advise you to stop reading that Bible, also. It is obviously confusing you. It could even make you go insane, you know?" Ending the conversation, Elam's father got up and left the room, leaving Elam sitting there with an open Bible on his lap and an empty chair beside him. Both of them were thinking the same thing: "Why doesn't he see what I'm saying?"

Chapter 5

The Runaway

"Ask, and it will be given to you; seek, and you will find;
knock, and it will be opened to you. For everyone who
asks receives, and he who seeks finds, and to him who knocks
it will be opened." *Matthew 7:7-8*

While most seventeen-year-old boys were thinking about girls and… girls, Elam was thinking about his church. It seemed as though there was nothing else Elam thought about now. It was even worse than a song you can't get out of your head, because there was no other radio station he could turn on to tune that song out. Whether he was working in the field or eating his dinner or driving Bessie down to his friend's house, these questions were stuck in his mind and would not go away.

He began realizing so many things about his upbringing and church teaching that he'd never noticed before, things that just didn't add up. They were forbidden to accept literature from the English people or attend their church services, yet Elam remembered countless Sunday evenings when as a family they would sit on the back lawn to listen to hymns and preaching being played over an intercom from the neighboring Baptist church.

The more he read and the more he thought, the more questions he came up with and the more desperate he became. His cousin had left his Amish home and was living with a Mennonite family, he'd been told. Maybe he could give him some answers. Elam didn't want to hurt his parents, but he felt he really would go crazy if something didn't happen. So he looked for his cousin, found out where he was working, and called him from the neighbors' telephone. After Elam poured out his heart, his cousin promised that he would try to find work for him so that he could get away from home.

But how would Elam leave home without breaking his parents' hearts? This was a problem. He loved his mother dearly, and had always felt very close to her. He had great respect for both of his parents, and knew also what would happen in the community if he were to leave. He didn't want to put his parents through that, either. But he had to get away, even for a little while.

Finally, he came up with a plan that he felt would be the easiest on his mother. He would get up in the morning and leave for work on his brother-in-law's farm as usual, but rather than go there he would go to the Mennonite farm where his cousin was. Since the Amish don't have phones, his family wouldn't realize that he was gone until he sent them a letter to explain. Yes. It was a perfect plan. He might even be able to re-solve some things before his parents really knew what was going on.

Unfortunately, things didn't work out as planned. Monday morning came too quickly, it seemed. Elam's heart raced as he prepared for work that day, running his plan over in his mind as he dressed. All weekend he'd run this morning through his mind and then, when it was still in the future, it had seemed almost exciting. It was no longer in the future. It was right now. He was leaving his home. He was frightened. Why had it come to this? How could it have come to this? He had two parents who loved him, and had taken care of him his whole life. Why was it that now he felt he needed to get away from home?

He felt as though he could cry, but he knew that it was time. It was now or never. Elam headed for the stairs. He reached the top step, and just as his mind was about to take another jog through his checklist of what he had to do, he stopped. Israel stood at the bottom of the stairs looking up directly into Elam's eyes. His face was very stern. He could hear his mother and sister were crying in the living room. His mind came to a screeching halt. Something was wrong. He slowly descended the stairs and stopped in front of his father.

His father quietly asked, "Elam, are you planning to leave us?"

He was stunned. How had he found out? He was not prepared for this encounter. He had not run this scenario through his mind at all, and now he had no idea what to do. Now what? He couldn't lie to his dad. He couldn't tell him the truth. They weren't supposed to know this was happening! This was supposed to be simple, painless.

Israel stood silently over his son, waiting for his reply. He could see by the look on his face that it was true. His son was planning to leave them. How could this be? He hoped that somehow, Elam's reply would explain this, that it was all a weird misunderstanding.

"Dad, I don't want to leave, but something is wrong and I don't know what to do." It was all he could think of to say.

And all he could think of to do now was run. With nothing but his old work clothes on and only a quarter in his pocket, he dashed out the kitchen door. He ran across the yard where he had felt so free and happy just a few years ago. He ran toward the road, away from the fields he'd loved to work in and the barn he'd milked alongside his father in. He ran away from the home he had always known and the people he loved most. His heart was broken, and his mind was in turmoil. He wished it would all just stop. He wished he had an easy way out of all of this.

After he reached the nearest phone and called his cousin, Jonas Lapp, he asked a neighbor lady to drive him the five miles to the farm where his cousin was working. When he arrived, they were still doing the early morning milking. It took just one look at the boy's face, and everyone stopped what they were doing and in turn gave Elam a hug and a word of encouragement.

"Don't worry, we will help you," the boss said. "Come and join us for breakfast. After we've eaten we will go and see another Mennonite farmer and see if he will give you work." Elam's desperation began to settle. He felt love from these people, and thought it was strange. He was surrounded by strangers, yet they were treating him as though they'd known him for years.

· · · · ·

"And that's his story," his cousin's boss finished up. He had been telling the farmer, Harry Kreider, the story of how and why Elam had ended up at his place. The two Mennonite farmers talked for some time, using phrases like, "Praise the Lord," quite a few times and then hugged each other as they parted ways.

"Harry says he'll give you a job here until you get on your feet at least, Elam, and a good home for a while," his cousin told him after everyone finished talking.

Elam had never driven a tractor, but right away his new boss put him on one to crimp hay. Here he was just a few hours after leaving home, riding on a forbidden gasoline-powered tractor with rubber tires! It all seemed just too crazy to be real! But Elam's mind had settled a little, now that he felt like he was moving toward getting answers, and he was concentrating on figuring out how to drive this thing. The farmer sat back and watched Elam, prayed for him, and then started to calculate how much fertilizer he was going to need to order this week.

"Whoa!" Elam shouted.

Harry looked up in time to see the tractor, which did not respond well to verbal commands, going right on through the fence, with a very confused-looking boy on the seat.

"I am sorry, I, uh, it didn't stop at the end of the row," Elam said to Harry with his head low to the ground. He'd seen Harry come running as soon as he'd plowed over the fence, and he was expecting his new boss to send him packing already. How could he have been so stupid? He awaited the harsh words that he was sure were to follow.

"It's OK, Elam! It's OK!" Harry was not harsh. He was not mad or firing him. He was, rather, laughing himself almost silly. "Really, the sight was worth having to fix this fence!"

Harry stood and examined the fence, the young uncomfortable-looking Amish boy still sitting awkwardly on the tractor seat, looking ashamed. Anyone not having a personal crisis today would be laughing at themselves for telling a tractor to "whoa" and driving over a fence.

"You've had quite the day already, haven't you?"

Elam nodded his head in agreement.

"Why don't we let this go for now and go into town?" the kind farmer motioned for Elam to come down from the tractor.

"Into town?" Elam hopped to the ground and brushed off the top of his pants.

"Well, we could get a bite to eat at the restaurant, and we can get you a haircut and some other clothes," Harry said.

A haircut. That would be a serious commitment to his new life and his search for truth.

Harry took Elam to the barber. It seemed to Elam that the barber completely shaved his head. He had never had a short haircut in his whole life. Then Harry bought him some work clothes and a fine suit and tie. That evening Elam sat down and wrote a letter to his mother and told her where he was.

He had not made up his mind about his future, but he wanted to see how other Christian people lived and what they taught. On Sunday morning the family he was living with prepared for church. Nervously, he dressed in his new suit and necktie. To anyone else he would have looked very handsome, but when he looked in the mirror he didn't see a new man who was on his way to church to find answers. He looked at his short English haircut and his English suit, and he saw a worldly young man looking back from the mirror at him. A sense of guilt came over him.

A little later he heard a horse and buggy come down the road and turn into their driveway. Elam's father, brother, and sister had come to see him. His heart pounding, Elam took one last look at himself in the mirror, and went out to see them. He knew how they would react—how they would feel.

He self-consciously approached the buggy, feeling as though he were wearing a costume. For about five minutes, all they could do was look at him and cry. After the stress and change of this past week, tears came into his eyes also as he thought of what they must be feeling.

Finally his sister broke the silence. "Please, please, please come home, Elam!"

"Please, come home!" little Jacob said sweetly.

"Please, son, come home," his father said, sounding much softer than he had the last time they had spoken.

"Please, before you do something you'll regret even more!" his sister added.

They begged him to come home with them. Their pleading was moving, but he knew he had to find answers, and he had gotten this far.

"Dad, for once I want to go to another church to see how they worship. I wish you could understand," Elam said.

Israel looked at his son. With his hair was cut off and having abandoned his Amish clothing, he looked to him like a dead man. With a heavy heart, he said his good-bye and left the invitation to come home open.

With a slap of the reins on the horse's back, they left. Elam watched the sad little face of his younger brother Jacob peeking out of the back of the buggy as the horse slowly clopped out of the driveway and on down the road. Another round of tears fell from his eyes. He did want to go with them, but not until he had the answers he needed.

He went along with his host family to the first church he'd ever experienced outside his own, Mechanics Grove Mennonite church. Everything about it was so different. He was used to seeing his peers sleeping and going out for cigarette breaks during the services, but during the Sunday school class he attended, the youth there had come with Bibles and sat attentively and even asked questions! Then during the church service the pastor read scripture in English and the sermon was focused on explaining that part of scripture. The church service he was used to was usually about the customs and traditions of the Amish church rather than about the Bible, and when scripture was read it was read in German.

By the end of that day, he was glad that he had had the opportunity to have this experience, and he couldn't really understand why it was forbidden to visit other churches like this. Everything he'd seen today had been positive and had been all about Jesus and the Bible. But, though he really enjoyed his first experience outside of the Amish church, he returned to his new home that day with a lot of mixed feelings.

Back at Elam's home that first Sunday he was gone, the large farmhouse was packed, but it was not full of people having a new and positive experience. Family members and relatives came to visit and share their grief with the family. The atmosphere was much like a funeral.

On Monday morning one of Elam's friends and his sister came to see him.

"I went to church yesterday at Mechanics Grove Mennonite," Elam began as he sat down on the sofa in the living room next to his sister. "It is really good to see you," he said then, realizing how good it really was to see her.

"Elam, you must come home," Priscilla sighed, with no interest in the news he had just shared. She clutched a hankie in her hands that appeared very worn and used.

Elam tried to continue. He wanted to stay off that subject and move forward and share what he was discovering out in this new world. "It was a wonderful experience yesterday. The service was in English, and the youth there weren't even bored. They were excited about learning the Bible. The people there were so loving toward me," Elam said, hoping that his sister would hear him and maybe give him some support and understanding. Instead, tears flowed down her cheeks.

"Oh, Elam," their friend Rebecca, who also had tears in her eyes, began, "Don't you know that the Bible says that the devil comes to us like an angel of light and the wolf comes in sheep's clothing?" She was more versed in the Bible than Elam was. He looked at her and realized that he just did not have an answer for her.

They pleaded for some time with him to come home. He didn't have much of a foundation to stand on. He felt condemned and ashamed. Finally, he told them that he would return home.

He told his boss that day that he thought he would like to return home. His boss understood all too well what he was going through, and left him free to make his own decision. He even gave him a ride back to the farm.

As they pulled in the driveway, Elam wanted to shrink into the seat of the car. The whole yard was full of buggies. The mourners were all still here at the house. He looked over at his boss who had been so kind and giving to him. "Thank you for all that you've done for me."

Kind eyes looked into his, "You're welcome, Elam. If there's ever anything I can do, you know where I am."

"Thank you," Elam said again. He got out of the car and shut the door behind him. He looked up at the house. "I don't want to face them," he said to himself. So, passing through the full rooms of very somber people, he made his way back up the stairs which he had fled down just a week before, and locked himself in his room.

He took off his English clothes the Mennonite farmer had bought for him, folded them neatly, and set them at the corner of the bed. After putting on his familiar Amish clothing, he sat down on the bed next to the clothes and cried. What was happening? How could his life have gotten to this point? Just a few months before, he was excited and planning his future around being Amish. Now look at what he'd done. He'd decided to come back home, but he didn't feel like this was finished.

His father came in shortly after he arrived. "It's good to have you home, son." He tried to smile at Elam. He looked down at his son and saw a very disturbed boy. His hair was all cut off, and his eyes looked so sad. And there, next to him on the bed, were the clothes Israel had seen him in yesterday. How awful it had been to see his son that way.

Elam sat there with his head down, unable to look at his father. He held his hat in his hand. "It doesn't fit anymore," he said. Now that his hair had been cut off, his hat was too big. Israel felt compassion for his son, and he hoped that he had gotten over whatever had been bothering him, and had returned for good. He hoped he was sorry for what he had done. Israel offered some encouragement. "Don't worry, son, your hair will grow back." And out the door he went.

Two days later when Elam was ready to come out and face his family, he was treated like the prodigal son. They repainted his buggy and bought him a new buggy blanket, among other things. It was like Christmas, day after day, for a while. His sisters smiled and sang around the house, and his mother made all of his favorite meals and desserts. After all the turmoil over the past few weeks and after all the shame he'd felt this last weekend, this treatment felt very good. He felt forgiven by his family and accepted again. After a while, the treatment he was getting was almost fun, and it didn't take long until Elam was taking full advantage of the situation.

He tried to convince himself that he'd made a mistake in leaving, and that he wanted to be a good Amish boy, but there was still that whirl of questions in his head that wouldn't go away. Though in his mind he was convinced that the right thing to do was be the good Amish boy that his parents wanted him to be, he just didn't want to do it. It just wasn't *him* somehow. And, now that he'd already left once, it seemed that the family was afraid to put too much pressure on him to correct him about anything, so he began to do things that were forbidden right in front of his parents.

"What are you doing? Your parents are right inside!" Ammon whispered sharply.

"Elam, are you lighting that up right here on the front porch?" Simmie looked a little shocked.

Elam often sat on the front porch of his parents' house with his buddies in the evenings after work. Sometimes, when they were feeling rebellious, they'd all take a ride out on a back road where no one would see them, and they'd all light up cigarettes. Or, when they were out in the field where no one would see them, then they would light up. But right here? In front of his parents?

"Why not? My dad and a buncha other men from church smoke cigars," Elam responded.

"Yeah, but…" Ammon said, looking nervously into the house, "Those aren't forbidden, you know that."

"Anyway, Elam, you know cigarettes are," Simmie added, also looking into the house. "Why aren't your parents saying anything to you?"

"They're afraid I'll leave, I think," Elam said, propping his feet up on the porch railing.

"I can't believe you're doing this," Simmie said.

"What?" Elam asked, holding out the pack of cigarettes to Simmie. "Want one?"

"Come on, Elam, this is just too much. This blatant rebellion against your parents, right in front of them. I don't know if I agree with you." Simmie looked away from Elam, out over the farm. He had played many a summer day away with Elam here on this farm. He, too, could not believe what had taken place in their world in the last few weeks. It had hurt him to see his friend going through all this. It had hurt to see Elam's family go through it as well. He wanted to stand by his buddy. Sure, he and the guys would sneak out and do some wild things together now and then, but that was in private and it was just for fun. It was almost as though it didn't hurt anyone, but this…this blatant display of disrespect for authority that Simmie was seeing here on the front porch seemed to be crossing a line that he just couldn't agree with.

"I'm sorry, Elam, I can't go along with you on this. This isn't funny," Simmie said.

"Haven't your parents been through enough already? Do you have to keep throwing things in their faces?" Ammon added.

The fun taken out of his cigarette, Elam stood, crushed it on the ground, and looked off into the distance for a while. He too was thinking about the days when all the boys simply worked and played and had no worries or cares. Those days were gone now.

After a bit, Simmie and Ammon had reasons they needed to get going, and said good-bye. Elam went upstairs and flopped down on his bed. He lay there for a long while, just thinking in the silence of his room. Downstairs, his mom and dad were talking, and as they walked into another room, Elam began to be able to hear them through the vents in the floor. They were discussing their biggest concern, of course: Elam. Elam wasn't really listening, as he'd heard it all before, but one thing stuck out. He heard his father say, "I would sooner see Elam go out into the world than go to a Mennonite church."

Chapter 6

Answers

"…and you will know the truth, and the truth
will make you free." *John 8:32*

"Why would my father feel that way?" Elam asked. He was working on the same carpenter crew again with his uncle.

"Because, well…" his uncle wasn't sure how to answer this one, and now he was almost sorry he had started this conversation. "Elam, are you planning to be baptized in a few weeks with the other boys?" he finally said, changing the subject.

Elam's hair had been an obstacle to baptism before, even though it had reached to the bottom of his ears. Rejecting the things of the world didn't just stop at rubber tires and electricity in the house. It was the reason for the way they dressed and the way they chose to keep their hair and beards. Whatever the world did, they didn't do. This meant that since the world cut men's hair carefully and stylishly, layering it and cutting around their ears, the Amish allowed their hair to grow long all one length, all the way around in a bowl shape.

Now, Elam's hair was as worldly as it got, cut neatly up over his ears and shaved close to his head at the back of his neck. There was no question that his hair was too short this time. As his uncle asked him this question, he could not believe what he was hearing. "There must be a catch along with this question," Elam thought. He replied, "You mean that you would now baptize me with my short, English haircut?"

His uncle said, "If you promise to let your hair grow, we will overlook the short hair."

"I don't understand." Elam stopped what he was doing and looked straight at his uncle. "You would really baptize me with my hair this way?"

"Yes," his uncle said confidently.

This inconsistency rekindled the turmoil inside of Elam that had ebbed for the past few weeks, and he knew he would not be being baptized Amish anytime soon.

· · · · ·

With his insides unsettled again, Elam realized that he had made a mistake in coming home so soon. He needed to get out again, and spent the week looking all over the house for his English clothes. His father had contacted the Mennonite farmer and had paid for the clothes, since Elam had worked only a few days and the clothes had been very expensive. He had intended to then sell the clothes, but for now they were still hidden somewhere in the house. Elam finally found them in the bottom of his mother's hope chest. His sister was taking a nap in the same room, however, and was actually not asleep. She saw that Elam had found them, so in a few days they were hidden again and the searching continued.

The following Sunday Elam stayed at home when the rest of the family went to church, and he searched the house for the clothes again. He found them in the attic in the bottom of a rag barrel.

"Here we go again," Elam thought, looking down at the clothes. He went down to his room and took his Amish clothes back off, folded them neatly, and piled them on the edge of the bed where just a few weeks before he had set the pile of English clothes. He could hardly believe this was happening again.

He went to the neighbors' house and knocked on the door.

"Hi, Elam. How are you today?" Rosemary asked him, noting that he was not dressed in his Amish clothes.

"Well, I'm not sure. Could I use your phone, please?" he asked politely.

"Sure! You know where it is." Rosemary stood aside and ushered him into her kitchen.

He went over to the phone and dialed his cousin, and asked him to take him back to the Mennonite farm. When he was off the phone, he found a glass of water on the table next to where he stood, and he took a drink. "Thank you."

"Anytime."

"Could I please have a piece of paper to leave a note for my parents?" he asked quietly.

She gave him some paper and a pencil, and he wrote a note for his parents telling them about his decision, and hoped that they would understand this time.

His cousin came and picked him up, and took him back to the same farm, where he was received warmly. Again, he tried to make himself believe that he had made the right decision, but it seemed that no matter which side he was on, he felt all twisted up inside. During the following weeks he got pleading letters from his family asking him to come home. And his parents had a reaction that he never would have expected. A few days after he left, his father called from the neighbors' house asking Elam if he was coming home.

"Dad," Elam began, "I hear you are getting the law after me. Is this true?"

There was a pause at the other end of the line. His father had not expected Elam would hear about that but replied honestly, "I will do what I have to to get my son back home where he belongs."

It was true then! How could it be? This was so unreal. One thing that the Amish almost never do is go to court. What was happening?

"Dad, I really don't feel I can come home under these circumstances then."

Again, there was a thoughtful pause at the other end of the telephone line, then his father said, "If that is the case, then I will have to go to the courthouse again."

Elam knew that he was serious about it. His father had never made idle threats—he always meant what he said and said what he meant. So the next day his employer went to the courthouse to see what his father could actually do to him and found out that since he was a minor, the court could return him to his father and also prosecute the employer for hiring him without his father's consent. Elam didn't want to get his employer in trouble, but he also didn't want to go home, either. A solution seemed to be found in a suggestion from another ex-Amish man from the church, who suggested that Elam go to Florida for the next six months until he turned eighteen.

Elam had never been more than forty miles from home in his whole life. The idea made him nervous, but it seemed to be his only option. So plans were made, and soon he was 1000 miles from home. The odd thing was that once Elam arrived in Sarasota, Florida, he found himself surrounded by so many Amish and Mennonites in a little community called Pinecraft that it was almost like being in Lancaster County, except for all the palm trees. And again, just as it had been at Mechanics Grove Mennonite church, he found warm welcome and acceptance into their community.

He found a job as a bag boy in a grocery store for a short time, then found a better job working at an expensive beach club as a busboy waiting on rich tourists. There, he made a surprising discovery. The Amish prohibited the smoking of cigarettes, because they said that the world smokes more cigarettes than cigars. His father himself smoked cigars. But here in this fine dining club full of worldly English people, Elam noticed that most of these rich men were not smoking cigarettes, but smoked only expensive Cuban cigars.

For three months Elam heard nothing from his family, because they didn't know where he was. He missed them, and so finally he wrote to them to let them know that he was alive and well in Florida, and that he still loved them.

Now that they knew where he was, they again set out to try to convince him to come home, but this time with a different approach. One day while he was working at the club, a notice came for him to appear at the Sarasota courthouse.

"I have a summons from the Lancaster Courthouse," the judge said. "Tell me, young man, why did you run away from home?"

"Your honor, I didn't want to run away. I would love more than anything to be at home with my family right now, but..." Elam opened up and told him the whole story.

It was not like the usual stories that the judge was accustomed to being told. This was not your typical rebellious teenager who complained that he didn't like his parents' curfew and wanted to run off and do his own thing. This was a young man full of love and respect for his parents, trying to figure out what was right. The judge was deeply touched by his situation.

"Look, maybe we can help you," the judge suggested. "Here in Florida you are still considered a minor until you reach age eighteen. But if your father doesn't have a lot of money, you don't need to worry. The court in Lancaster would have to send someone all the way down here to take you back to your home, and that would be very expensive. I can see here it will not be too many months until you turn eighteen, so I suggest you just go back to your work and I will let you know if anything more develops."

Elam went back to work and didn't hear anything from the law again. For the next three months, however, he received countless letters from his family asking him to come home. One letter from his sister went on for line after line saying nothing but, "Please come home," over and over. The letters just about broke his heart every time he opened one, but Elam felt by now that he had made his decision: he would never again go back to the Amish church.

· · · · ·

Elam could hardly believe his eyes. It was almost as though it was an answer to a prayer he hadn't even prayed.

"I've been wanting to talk to you for a while now, Sam," Elam said, shaking his cousin's hand.

Sam actually lived pretty far away from Elam's neighborhood, but for some reason today he had decided to come way out of his way to get his horses shod at the very same blacksmith shop where Elam happened to be.

"Hey, it must have been God, because I never come this far just to get my horses shod," Sam said smiling.

They sat down together under a tree outside, and Elam just let it all out.

"Sam, I need answers. I feel sometimes like I could just go out of my mind!" Elam said.

"Well, I'll try to answer your questions, Elam," Sam replied. "Why don't you tell me the whole story?"

Elam poured his whole story out to him. "I wanted to be baptized. I wanted to be right with God, to have peace in my heart. I knew that if I could just be the best Amish boy in the world, I would have that peace."

"But you didn't have peace, did you?"

"No! The closer I got to being baptized, the more confused and stirred up I felt inside!" Elam went on to tell him about his experience with the Mennonite farmer, and about his time at Pinecraft in Florida. "When I got back home here to Pennsylvania, I decided to visit with my family before going back to work on the Mennonite farm. It had been a long time since I had seen them, and I missed them. I even took them a bunch of fresh Florida grapefruits that I had brought back just for them."

"And how'd that go?" he asked.

"Well, they welcomed me back and were happy to see me, but wouldn't take the grapefruit," Elam said sadly.

"I can understand. To accept your gift from Florida would almost be like accepting that you went there," Jonas tried to encourage him.

"I suppose," Elam agreed.

"Then what?" Sam asked.

"Well, I stayed at the farm, and right away my married brothers and sisters came home and tried to persuade me to come back to the Amish. They threw all kinds of unfamiliar scripture verses at me, and I didn't know if they were interpreting the verses right or not, or if they were using the verses to support their own opinions. All I knew was that they were sincere. They loved me, and they were worried for me and so…."

"You went back," Sam smiled.

Elam smiled back at him. "Yup. So, after a few days of wrestling with my convictions, I decided for a second time to come back and give it another try."

Sam sat back and nodded his head in agreement. "I totally understand."

Elam continued, "I let my hair grow and mixed in with the Amish youth again, and I even told others not to do what I had done. But I just couldn't be the very plain and strict Amish boy that my father wanted me to be. It seemed like I was always pushing the limits. So, even though I wasn't feeling very peaceful about my decision, I decided I would go ahead and get baptized. I thought it would help, and it just seemed like the right thing for me to do." He paused a moment and shook his head. "I hoped that after being baptized I would feel differently, but I don't. For more than a year now I have gotten involved with all of the youth activities and have just tried to put my whole heart into this, but it's not helping!"

"No?" Sam asked.

"No. I still have nights I just can't sleep! I will lie there for hours just thinking and thinking and wrestling with questions that just won't go away," Elam sighed.

"So, how can I help?" Sam asked.

"I heard rumors that you believe a strange doctrine and that you've been saying that you were born again and you knew you were saved. When I heard this, I remembered some of the phrases that I had found in the English Bible two years ago. And, in Ephesians I read that you can know that you are a child of God and that you are saved by grace and not by works. But I didn't know what to believe! I just knew I needed to talk to you."

Sam understood all too well what Elam was going through, because he had gone through the same thing. "Elam," he began, "I had this same stirring in my heart that you have now...."

Elam drank every word in that his cousin said. Then for the first time in his life, sitting there in a blacksmith shop, after all the many hours he'd spent in church his whole life, salvation by grace and being born again were explained to him in his first language, Pennsylvania Dutch.

"The Bible says, Elam, that 'I bear them record that they have a zeal of God, but not according to knowledge. For they being ignorant of God's righteousness, and going about to establish their own righteousness, have not submitted themselves unto the righteousness of God'" (Romans 10:2-3, KJV).

Elam sat back and processed that. "So, what you're saying is that what I have been trying to do my whole life is make myself right with God by establishing my own righteousness according to my own standards through a religion, and that God is not interested in my works but that He saves me by grace. That it is all about having a relationship with Christ? I can be God's friend? I can know I'm saved?" Elam was starting to feel like all the lights had just been turned on in a dark room he'd been stumbling through for so long.

"Exactly! So many of us try to 'establish our own righteousness' through our religion or our actions, our good works, but the Bible says that it's by God's grace that we're saved, that it comes through faith, and that it's not a reward based on our works. It is a gift of God."

"But I have been taught my whole life that you *cannot* know that you are saved! That…that is arrogance!" Elam exclaimed.

"Well, the Bible says…" Sam reached into his coat pocket, pulled out a tiny pocket New Testament, and quickly flipped through the pages to the book of first John. "Here, read this," he said and handed it to Elam.

Elam looked at the words and read them aloud:

> *If we receive the witness of men, the witness of God is greater: for this is the witness of God which He hath testified of His Son. He that believeth on the Son of God hath the witness in himself: he that believeth not God hath made Him a liar; because he believeth not the record that God gave of His Son. And this is the record, that God hath given to us eternal life, and this life is in His Son. He that hath the Son hath life; and he that hath not the Son of God hath not life. These things have I written unto you that believe on the name of the Son of God; that ye may know that ye have eternal life.*
> *1 John 5:9-13, KJV*

Elam paused for a moment and repeated, "…that ye may *know* that ye have eternal life." He looked up at his cousin, "That I may know…"

Finally, it was all clear to him. It made sense. The lights were all on! His spiritual eyes and ears were finally opened. It was as though Jesus were standing on the boat in the stormy sea of Elam's heart and He had raised His hand and said, "Peace! Be Still!" Elam began to feel a peace inside him that he'd never felt before, a joy that ended the torment that had been in his spirit now for two years. Not so far away in heaven, a proud Father stood by and watched as his newborn son was born. The angels were rejoicing.

"All my life, I've been basically listening to the witness of men, then, listening to what people had to say about God and trying to get my eternal life through what they said about God. I was trying to get my eternal life through everything but His Son. What I need to listen to is God Himself." He held up the Bible. "Right here, God tells me that for me to not believe I am saved is to make God a liar."

Sam could see the light in Elam's eyes. He remembered the moment when he himself had finally "gotten it," and he was close to tears knowing that God had allowed him to be here for that moment with Elam—that He had used him as an answer to Elam's prayers.

"Sam, I'm saved! I am going to heaven when I die to be with God, to be with Jesus forever!" Elam said with his brilliant blue eyes lighting up. "I'm saved!"

"Praise God, Elam!" Sam said as he reached over and gave his new brother in Christ a hug.

Chapter 7

Peace

But they who seek the Lord shall not be in want of any good thing. Psalm 34:10

Elam had finally put all his questions to rest and had submitted his life to God. Now that God was in control He started to do things in Elam's life that he couldn't have done in his own power. The first thing that God did when He moved into Elam's "house" was to clean the air. In all his rebelliousness Elam had acquired a pack-a-day smoking habit, and as smokers know, quitting is no easy thing. Elam knew that the Amish church disapproved of cigarettes, but no one had told him what God thought of it. Amazingly, that first day of his new life with Christ, God showed Elam His care and awesome power, and Elam completely lost all physical and psychological desire for cigarettes.

The next thing God did for Elam was that He opened up a door for him to get to study the Bible. He was introduced to a group of born-again Amish youth that met weekly for Bible study and prayer.

Then there was the matter of Elam's future. Elam's heart had cried out to go tell the world about Jesus for years, and God was going to grant him that desire and had just the place for him to go. But for that, he would need help—he would want help. God knew his perfect mate, the woman he would need by his side for him to fulfill his mission.

The Sunday after his conversion, Elam took his girlfriend to the Sunday singing and shared his new faith with her. He hoped that she would be as excited as he was, and to Elam's delight she seemed to be thrilled and tried to understand. But soon she was torn by family loyalty. Her father heard that his daughter's boyfriend had gotten mixed up with a false teaching and told her she had to end the relationship. They both cried a lot the night she told him, but they decided that they had no choice but to break up. She was not the perfect mate God had for him.

Elam's family had noticed a change in him recently, but little was said until the second Sunday when he left his buggy at home and went with a born-again Amish friend to a Bible study. Elam's friend pulled into the driveway and picked Elam up in his car.

Israel walked into Elam's room early the next morning, "Where were you yesterday?"

Elam looked up from reading his Bible. "I went to Bible study with some Amish youth." Elam sensed some tension in his father's voice.

"How did you get there?" was Israel's next question.

"One of the guys picked me up in his car," he replied.

"Who picked you up?" Israel didn't sound pleased.

"Jonas Stoltzfus."

Jonas was an ex-member of the Amish. He had already been a member of the church when he left last year after being born again. That meant he was shunned.

"Elam, you can't drive with him. He is in the baun. You know that the Bishop will not allow that."

The practice of shunning or baun was a tradition carried down from the days of Jacob Amman, the founder of the Amish church, around 1690. The rule states that "If anyone, whether it be through a wicked life or perverse doctrine, is expelled from the church he must also, according to the doctrine of Christ and his apostles, be shunned and avoided by all the members of the church, particularly by those to whom his misdeeds are known, whether it be in eating or drinking. In short they are to have nothing to do with him, so that they may not be defiled by relationship with him and partake of his sins, but that he may be made ashamed, be affected in his mind and thereby induced to amend his ways."

In the Bible, 1 Corinthians 5:11 says something similar, "…I wrote to you not to associate with any so-called brother if he is an immoral person, or covetous, or an idolater, or a reviler, or a drunkard, or a swindler—not even to eat with such a one." Elam's new friends were none of those things.

His new friends loved God as much as he did. According to the Bible, these were the people he should be hanging out with.

"But Dad, it doesn't make any sense that I wouldn't be allowed to hang around with kids that want to know more about God and more about the Bible just because they no longer dress Amish, but that I am allowed to hang around with kids who sleep through church and only wake up to take cigarette breaks outside," Elam protested. "Last night, I felt so good going to a youth group that was truly interested in God and His Word."

His dad shook his head in exasperation. "It doesn't matter what you were doing together. You know the rule, and as a member of the church you are obligated to obey the word of the Bishop."

"He is my brother in the Lord. I can't shun a brother in the Lord," Elam protested.

Israel turned and walked back down the hall, worried that Elam's running days were not over. He feared that his son was being confused again by the perverse teachings of those who called themselves, "born again." He went downstairs and pulled the prayer book off the shelf. He found an appropriate prayer and prayed for his son.

The next week was very tense as Elam again struggled to know what he should do. He had no way of knowing that God was leading him away from his home and away from Lancaster County. He had no way of knowing that God would use his Amish upbringing to train him for a very special mission field thousands of miles away.

When we read in the Bible that God told Abraham to leave his home, we aren't told the story of how that happened, how hurtful it may have been for him to leave his home, friends, and family behind and head off into an unknown world. All we're told is that he did it. The mission that God had in mind for Abraham couldn't have been fulfilled had Abraham stayed at home, and neither could the mission that God had in mind for Elam.

Not knowing what he should do, Elam sought council with a Mennonite minister at the same time Israel was seeking the council of the Bishop.

"I don't want to leave the Amish church," Elam told the Mennonite minister. "I have told God that I will gladly stay Amish for the rest of my life if only I can help my family find the same peace that I have found in Christ."

"The decision is yours to make, Elam. You need to pray about it. God will show you what you need to do," the minister advised.

Elam prayed to God for wisdom.

. . . . .

"I don't want Elam to leave home again," Israel told the Bishop.

This had been going on for a long time now with Elam. The family had done all they could. They had forgiven him, exercised patience with him, loved him, and accepted him, and he was still heading down the wrong path. It was time for something different if this boy was to overcome this.

"As long as he is involving himself in these things, he is a danger to your family. He should not be influencing your other children. If you give him a strong ultimatum, it may persuade him to come to his senses, finally," the Bishop suggested.

. . . . .

Both Elam and Israel spent the next week deep in thought. Elam kept praying for God to show him what to do. He didn't want to make the decision on his own this time. He didn't want to leave, but he didn't want to stay if staying meant giving up the peace he now had with God.

Israel didn't want to see his son lost forever. Daily, he searched the prayer book and prayed for Elam's soul. How he loved his son. For the last two years, it had seemed that whether Elam was home or away in the world, he was lost. He needed to do something to help him. He needed to do something to keep the rest of the children safe from any influence that would lead them in the same direction.

The following Saturday night, Elam and Israel finally came to a decision. Elam's mother sat crying in her chair in the living room while her husband talked to her son. Why did it have to be this way? Why couldn't she have her sweet little son back? She didn't want to shun him. She didn't want to see him leave. But she, too, knew that he could not be spreading his false beliefs to her other children, or she might lose them, too.

Israel began, "I have done a lot of thinking this week, Elam, and I have also spoken to the Bishop."

Elam braced himself for the worst. His heart raced, and he felt the tears beginning to well up in his eyes already. "I have been doing a lot of thinking and praying this week myself, Dad."

"Elam, I don't want to have to do this, but you have given us no other options." As Israel took a breath, the only sound in the room was Elam's mother crying. Israel forced the words he now had to say. "If you do not give up your false beliefs, I can no longer permit you to live in our home. I shall no longer consider you my son. I cannot have you living with us and influencing your brothers and sisters with your false doctrines."

Hearing the words spoken out loud between her husband and son sent a rush of emotion through Elam's mother. "Oh, Elam! Please! Please! Please! Don't go!"

Tears seemed to just pour out of Elam's eyes like a river. This hurt more than it ever had before, though at the same time hidden in the pain was a peace that was beyond his understanding. This peace added to the pain of what he was about to say, because he knew the peace he felt had to be from God, confirming to him that it was time to go. That meant there was no turning back this time. He was really leaving for good.

"Dad, I don't want to leave you and Mom." He was unable to go on for a moment. He looked over at his mother. Her eyes were full of pain. He knew her heart's desire was for him to stay. He knew the words he had to speak now would break her heart, but he had to say them. It had to be this way. He composed himself finally and continued, "I don't want to leave, but if it means I have to give up the peace I've found, then I have no choice."

His mother put her face into her hands and wept. His father turned from him and walked away. When he had reached his own bedroom, the man who was had been so strong through all of this sat down on the bed and finally broke down in tears as well. He knew in his heart, also, that this would be the last time Elam would leave and that it would be for good.

The next morning Israel searched for a suitable prayer in the German prayer book. Elam's mother and sisters were crying as Elam calmly and purposefully packed a few clothes in a suitcase. He felt no urgency or need to run. He didn't feel confused. All he felt was sad. He was saying good-bye to his family. For real this time. For good. Israel rose from his chair and met Elam at the door. "I do not want you to come home again unless you come home Amish."

"Good-bye, Dad", Elam said and stepped out the door.

With just three dollars in his pocket, Elam started on his journey of faith. He walked out the front door of his home and away from life as he'd known it without a map for his future, much the way Abraham had done thousands of years before. God had told Abraham that He would bless him and make him to be a blessing to the world. God had in mind the same thing for Elam.

Elam found himself at the door of his neighbor's house, once again. "Hi, Rosemary. May I use your telephone again?" he asked when she answered the door. This time she saw a very sad young man, but the desperation she'd seen in him in times past was not there this time.

He used her phone and called his cousin again, as well as another one of his Amish buddies who now went to Weavertown Amish Mennonite church. They came and picked him up and took him to the church. They also put out the word in their prayer chain about Elam's situation, and people began reaching out to him.

A family from the church decided that Elam could stay with them for the first night, and the next day another family invited him into their home until he could find a more permanent place to live. Their son was a building contractor and gave him work. His first day into his new life he had a home and a job.

Soon, he moved to a very small building on a friend's farm. After a few days his father sent word that he wanted Elam to send his clothes home. To anyone not Amish this might seem like a silly thing to request, but it was a big deal to Elam's family. Since Elam had gone out with only a few dollars in his pocket, he hadn't had money for a new wardrobe yet, so he was still dressed in his Amish clothes.

His father said, "If you don't want to be Amish, then you must not look like an Amish." Somehow, the pastor's wife found out, and that night when he came home Elam found his cupboards loaded with food and his closet filled with more clothes than he needed. He stood there just staring at his closet full of clothes and thanked God.

That same night he took his Amish clothes home to his father. He knew for sure now that he was not to return to the Amish way of life. It made him sad, and at the same time it made him feel so free—to finally know and to not have to deal with the questions and confusion and uncertainty anymore. Yes, he was finally free.

Even when he was visited by the leaders of his Amish church and officially informed that he was excommunicated from the Amish church, officially "in the baun," he still felt peace. Had he made this decision before he had been baptized it would have been different, but because he was an official church member now, from that day on unless Elam returned to the church, he would be shunned. He would no longer be able to eat at the same table or have any dealings with his family and other church members, along with many other restrictions. His ties with his family were completely severed.

He continued attending the Mennonite church and enjoying his new life. He felt that God was more than faithful and truly had given him a completely new family in Christ. What he had overheard his father say through the floor vent so long ago began to make sense. He didn't understand then why his father had said that he would rather have Elam go to the world than to a Mennonite church. Many Amish youth go out into the world and live a very ungodly life for a number of years. If they do not find peace with God, as Elam had not those first two times he had left home, most of them will in time return and submit to the teaching of their elders. Some will remain Amish for their entire lives. If, however, they find new life in Christ, find peace with God, and join a church that teaches God's Word, as Elam finally had, they almost never return to the Amish fold.

God then began a new work in Elam's life. He had been changing and moving things around, preparing to give Elam the desire he'd had in his heart ever since he was a child. Finally, it was time to bring that most important part of Elam's life into place; her name was Barbara.

Chapter 8

Exploring Guatemala

Now the Lord said to Abram, "Go forth from your country,
and from your relatives and from your father's house,
to the land which I will show you." *Genesis 12:1*

Elam looked out the window at the simple thatched-roof huts with the cute little dark-haired children running around the front yards and the chickens and pigs pecking and rooting in the grass. He felt a smile come across his face. Although what Elam saw outside the bus window didn't look one bit like Lancaster County, something about the scene reminded him so much of home.

"Would you look at that?" Barbara said, pointing out the window. There was a woman walking with three little kids trailing along behind her, all headed to the creek to take their baths and wash clothes. The woman could not have been more than five feet tall and was dressed in just about every color of the rainbow. She was walking along the road with a baby in her arms, and balanced on top of her head was a huge basket of laundry.

"She's just walking along like it's no big deal that she has fifty pounds of stuff sitting on top of her head!" Barbara's eyes were wide with amazement.

"I wonder if she even weighs as much as that!" Elam said.

Once they passed the lady, they saw that not only was she carrying a baby in her arms and walking along balancing this huge thing on top of her head without using her hands, but she also had what looked like a toddler strapped to her back! Elam and Barbara just looked at each other and raised their eyebrows and laughed. "I don't think I'll ever be that much of a woman!" Barbara teased.

Elam laughed and continued looking out the window, watching the beautiful Guatemalan countryside pass by. "This is where I want to serve God," he thought to himself.

The year was 1961. They had left home weeks ago with a small group of thirty-eight young people from all over the U.S. and Canada to do a singing tour throughout Central America. Their intention was to travel through all of Central America, but they had created their schedule in an American mindset, and not in their wildest dreams could they have anticipated the uncooperative conditions of Central American roads. Originally they had planned to head much farther south and visit El Salvador and Honduras, but time was running out. Guatemala would be the last stop.

The main road through Guatemala, which led from the Mexico border to the capital, Guatemala City, was a one-lane, unpaved road that wove its way through the mountains in places even mountain goats might fear to tread. The tall mountains on one side of the road inspired the travelers to say, "Oooh," while on the other side there were ravines that dropped so sharply the only appropriate words were, "Oh dear God, please protect us!" There were no guardrails, and vehicles going different directions could only pass each other at certain designated areas.

At times they had to pass over bridges that had a posted weight capacity that was less than the weight of the bus—without passengers—so they would gather for prayer and have the group walk across first, then the bus would follow. At one point the road was so bad that they had to load the bus on the flatcar of a train and ride 100 miles on the train carrying their bus. What an adventure!

That first night in Guatemala they stopped in a town to the west of Guatemala City up in the mountains called Quetzaltenango. The young Mennonites drew a large crowd as they sang, and afterwards some of them spoke through an interpreter and shared their faith. Little did Elam and Barbara know that they would someday be here in this same town, attending the wedding of one of their own daughters to a man who would be born and raised here.

·····

A year after their trip to Guatemala as boyfriend and girlfriend, Elam and Barbara came together as man and wife at the Weavertown Amish Mennonite church. Elam could not have found a more perfect helpmate. Had he found just about anyone else, he never would have lived the life that fills the rest of these pages.

They began their life together by being fruitful and multiplying, adding three children to their new family in the next five years; Wilma Jean, Miguel, and their *cutest* child Virgil (not that the author of this book would be biased, by any means).

With his mind and heart set on someday going to a Spanish country, Elam focused on missions within the United States among Spanish people. For a while they worked in Florida with Cubans, where Elam picked up a pretty good Cuban accent. Then he worked on his Puerto Rican accent working in Lancaster, Pennsylvania, with the growing Spanish population there.

·····

After seven years of marriage, in August of 1969 Elam and Barbara left the kids with family and took a trip to Guatemala to decide where they were going to settle there. For a few weeks they traveled around the country talking to all the missionaries they knew there. They prayed and just listened to see where God would lead them.

On this trip, as they learned more about the many different people groups in this tiny country that was the same size and population as Pennsylvania, Elam was struck by how much the people reminded him of the Lancaster County Amish.

Elam looked out from his seat in the restaurant as a bus went by with thick black smoke billowing out the tail pipe. They had been waiting for their meals to come for over an hour now.

"Maybe they had to go out and catch a chicken for our meals?" Barbara laughed.

"I did think I heard some squawking coming from the kitchen about a half hour ago; you could be right! I hope they get all the feathers off," he laughed back.

Just then the waitress came out to the table with their drinks. Their meals had to be coming soon.

"I just can't get over how much the Indians here remind me of the Amish, you know what I mean?" Elam said.

"Oh, I know! It's funny! I wonder what it is?" Barbara said.

"I know just how these Indians feel sometimes when they have to leave their villages for some reason." Elam remembered his first days in the English school—how frightening it had been to not be able to communicate with the people around him.

Twenty-three different dialects are spoken across the tiny country of Guatemala, and the villagers most often lived in villages that didn't have any schools. Add that to the fact that many of these villages didn't even have a road that connected them to "civilization" at all, and so it was actually possible to be born, live a whole lifetime, and die in Guatemala and never learn Spanish. That frightening feeling that Elam had had as a six-year-old boy not being able to communicate was a feeling some adult Guatemalan Indians had when a situation forced them to have to interact with the rest of their own country!

"Just watching how they farm, too, reminds me of home." Elam thought of the people he'd seen out working their fields on this trip. "They get out there in the hot sun with long pants on and work the soil without machines, just like we did on the farm when I was a kid." Elam remembered the days riding behind the horse-drawn plows. Then the waitress and two plates of fried chicken heading their way caught his eye. "Food!" he smiled.

The waitress dropped off their food, a little dish that you had to use your fingers to get salt out of, and a little basket of fresh homemade corn tortillas. Then she took off again for the kitchen. Barbara and Elam prayed and dug into their long-awaited meals.

"Any feathers?" Barbara asked.

Elam pretended to look his chicken over. "Nope. They got 'em all!"

They both smiled and kept eating.

"I notice, too, that they are like us in that the villages are like their own individual little communities, separate from the rest of their country, like the Amish." Elam rolled up a tortilla and dipped it in the sauce on his plate.

"You don't have anyone ever coming into the Amish community from the outside, either, like here. I notice how shy the people are when we visit." Barbara tossed a scrap to the stray dog wandering around the restaurant.

Elam gave her a look that said, "You really shouldn't feed the dog," and her look replied, "I know, but he's so skinny!"

The Indians did live in very close communities, and they didn't often get out. Because of the isolation, they had religious practices, superstitions, and traditions that were exclusive to their own groups. Even the clothes they wore, if you knew what you were looking at, would tell you which group they were part of. To an outsider, all of their clothing was simply colorful, bright, and busy, but the patterns were special and specific to their own communities.

"How about that one lady we talked to, how she was telling me that she grew up in a village and that when she stopped dressing the traditional way her parents disowned her for a while because they were so hurt," Elam said in between bites. "I can't hardy believe how that is just so exactly like the life I had, how it is so like what I went through. I mean, even though I'm an outsider and I look so different from them, I can still say I can truly relate to them!"

"That does make a difference! You even know what it's like to live without electricity," Barbara added.

"Yeah! And that! I know what it's like to grow up without a washing machine in the house or electric lights or TV and all that stuff!" He looked over at his wife, "And you know what all that is like, too!"

Yes, Barbara also knew what it was like. It was as though the two of them were trained their whole lives to come live together as missionaries in this country.

"You know, if we are going to end up in one of these villages way out in the middle of nowhere, all the stuff I learned growing up is what is going to make it possible for me to not only relate to the people we'll minister to, but for us to survive, even!" He said.

"I know. I can't imagine how we could survive if we hadn't grown up the way we did." Barbara had actually met a few people in her life that had never even had a garden and had no clue how to can or to cook anything that hadn't come from a grocery store. She knew how to live off of the land and how to get by with little. And she knew how to make a fine banana soup.

Thinking about it, Elam could see why he had needed to grow up Amish, and why he had needed to leave. "It's like my whole life was college." He paused for a second, "But for me graduation and leaving that school behind was not something to throw parties over." He missed his family and often wished he could share with them all the things that were happening in his life.

"Do you realize that if we move to a village, we will have to not only learn Spanish but also whichever one of the other twenty or so dialects that are spoken in this country?" Barbara added.

It was true. If they did end up in a village, they would need to learn two languages. If that were to happen, that would mean they would speak or understand German, Pennsylvania Dutch, English, Spanish, and something else. Five languages. (I don't even know what the word for a person who knows that many languages is, except maybe "no fair!")

"What I wonder is, when the people here can have up to three harvests a year, and no winter to deal with, why in the world are they starving?" Barbara said.

"You're right, there is no natural reason for it," Elam agreed.

There was no natural reason for it. It would seem more logical for the Guatemalan Indians to be rich than the Amish, yet the Amish were exceedingly richer than even their non-Amish neighbors, and the Guatemalan Indians were poor and starving.

"You know, they not only have two fewer harvests a year than the Indians, but they also even have one fewer work day per week," Barbara added.

"You are right." Elam thought about that.

The Indians worked seven days a week, while the Amish did absolutely no business on Sundays. They "honored the Sabbath day and kept it holy." So what was it?

"Our struggle is not against flesh and blood," Barbara smiled as she quoted the Bible.

Elam looked up at his wife as he finished up his plate of food, "You are right again." There was only one reasonable explanation for why, despite the fact that the cards were stacked against the Amish, they would be rich. God.

"You're so right. Everything about the Amish religion is about what they think pleases or displeases God. They do everything they can to put

Him first, so God is blessing them." Whether or not in Elam's heart he believed the Amish had gotten everything right, he still respected the fact that the Amish did center their lives on God and living the way they believed honored Him.

Barbara thought of something else and pulled a dollar out of her pocket. "And here's another reason."

Elam looked down at the dollar.

Barbara helped him out a little, "It says, 'In God we trust.'"

Elam caught on fast and pulled a quetzal out of his pocket and laid it down on the table next to the dollar. There, next to the dollar that proclaimed that "In God we trust" was a quetzal decorated with a Mayan priest and a temple.

"Sure," he said. "They taught us in school that the U.S. government was founded on Christian principles, so not only are the Amish themselves blessed, but they live in a blessed country."

Barbara said, "I remember they also taught us in school that when the United States started, people were sick of being told what religion they had to be. In Europe, every time they got a new king the people had to change religion. Not following the king's religion sometimes landed people in jail. Those were probably just terrible times, especially for the Christians who believed that following the king's orders would lead them to dishonor or turn their backs on God!"

Because of where they came from, as they were starting their new country, the colonists put assurances in the Constitution and the Bill of Rights that they were endowed with certain rights by our Creator, and that the State would keep its nose out of the Church.

"That's the real separation of Church and State, you know," said Barbara. "No more kings telling them how to worship."

Elam let out a little "hmph" sound as he thought about how he had known that kind of persecution. His whole ordeal leaving the Amish was about the leadership trying to tell him how to follow his religion, when his relationship with God got him into trouble.

There really was no reason for people to be starving in the tropics, where sometimes fruit trees would just grow all by themselves without anyone even planting them. They were starving physically, because they were starving spiritually.

When the Spanish arrived in Central America centuries ago, they found the country already inhabited by the Mayans, who are known to have been some of the bloodiest people ever. Their human sacrifices went so far as even cutting out people's hearts and offering them to their gods before they stopped beating. The Mayans were already killing themselves off, as they were constantly at war. Then the Spanish invaded, so the Mayan reign came to an end.

The Spaniards then introduced to the people a new religion: Catholicism. Some converted, and some preferred their own Mayan religion and continued in it even until today—without all the blood, of course. But some of the people decided they liked the new *and* the old ways, so they mixed the two and created their own bizarre form of Catholicism. Elam would someday visit a cathedral in Guatemala that had statues of Catholic saints on one side, and statues of the Mayan gods on the other, with worshippers burning incense and candles to both. According to the locals, animal sacrifices were even offered on the steps of that cathedral.

Elam and Barbara found all this exciting, because they could relate to the Indians in ways not many non-Amish Americans would be able to, and they could see they had a message the Guatemalan people desperately needed to hear.

· · · · ·

There were plenty of missionaries all around the southern and mountainous regions of Guatemala, where the country was the most heavily populated and well developed. But Elam wondered, "What about the Petén?"

"What about the Petén?" would be the response from whomever he was talking to.

Elam remembered reading a newsletter back in the States from a missionary named Don Donaldson who lived in Guatemala City. Don had said there was a need for missionaries in the Petén, which was a state in the northern part of the country where it is always hot.

"Yeah, but it's hot there," people would say.

"Mosquitoes are really bad," was another thing. "Oh, and the scorpions, they've got scorpions up there!"

No one seemed to think the Petén was the place to go. There were only two (very terrible) unpaved roads that led out to the Petén from the capital city. There weren't even a whole lot of people living out there, really. The government of Guatemala had just recently opened the Petén up, offering land at a very low cost to encourage people to move there. So even to Guatemalans who lived in the southern part of the country, the Petén seemed to be another country in itself. Also, the Petén at this point in time was the part of the country where most of the civil warfare was going on. (And it was very hot. Did I mention that part?) Because of this, it wasn't only the American missionaries who didn't want to go there; most Guatemalans were afraid to go there as well.

"'Besides, there's a war going on, you know. It wouldn't exactly be wise for you to take your family up there anyway.' That's what that guy told me today when I asked him about the Petén," Elam said to his wife as they lay down for bed that evening.

"Well, I guess," Barbara shook her head.

"Isn't the safest place to be in the world wherever God wants you to be?" Elam thought out loud, taking his watch off and laying it on the bedside table. He turned toward Barbara again, "What do you think? Should we still go there and see it? I think we should. I just don't feel like we've found our place here yet."

"Me either. We've met some very nice people here. It's very beautiful around here, and the climate is nice, but," Barbara paused, "I just don't feel like we've found our place here either yet."

"If we're not feeling peace yet, then we need to keep looking." Elam was thinking out loud again.

"And maybe that's why we're receiving so much negative advice about the Petén," Barbara added.

"Because that's where God wants us, and we have an enemy who doesn't want us there. Is that what you're saying?" Elam loved the way his wife thought. His wife wasn't swayed by all the stories about mosquitoes and scorpions and lack of conveniences. She just wanted to go where God wanted them to go. "I am such a blessed man." Elam thought to himself, looking at his wife.

"Something to keep in mind, anyway." Barbara smiled and laid her head down on his shoulder.

It was decided. "Then we'll check out the Petén before we leave."

. . . . .

On their way back from Guatemala to Lancaster, Elam and Barbara made their usual stop in at Lakewood Church in Houston, Texas. Although they didn't attend there all the time because they were living in Pennsylvania, they considered Lakewood Church to be their home church and John Osteen to be their pastor. They would be going to Guatemala as Lakewood missionaries.

John Osteen knew all about following God's voice when it didn't seem logical. He had started Lakewood in an old abandoned feed mill on the wrong side of town. Everyone had told him that Lakewood would never make it, yet he trusted God. Eventually he gave up leading crusades in India to commit his time to pastoring this tiny little church that would someday become one of the largest churches in the United States.

"So, where exactly is it that you're going to be living?" Pastor Osteen asked.

"Well, we finally decided we will be living in the Petén, which is in northern Guatemala near the border of Mexico." Elam thought for a second. "When we're at the farthest point in the villages down the river nearest to Mexico, we'll only be fifty miles from the nearest dirt road."

Pastor Osteen smiled. "And how far from a paved road?"

Barbara looked over at Elam. "Two hundred miles I think it is, right?"

"Yeah, just 200 miles."

Pastor Osteen laughed, "*Just* 200 miles! That's great!"

"There are about a dozen villages which have just recently sprung up there all along a river called The Passion River. And there are really no churches there yet, so there is a great need for the word of God in the area." Elam was excited about the life he envisioned living there and getting to take Jesus to people who hadn't met Him yet.

"Well, if you will be ministering up and down the river, where do you think your home base will be?" Pastor Osteen asked.

Images of the houses Elam had seen while visiting Guatemala went through his mind. He pictured Barbara cooking their meals just the way the ladies did in their little thatched-roof huts over the open fires with their kids running around the dirt floor. "We'll probably be living in a thatched-roof hut like the local people, and we figure we'll make our home base in a town there about fifty miles from the border. From there we can use boats to go up and down the river and minister in the villages."

The pastor thought for a second. "But if you're going to be ministering to the villages all up and down the river there," he said excitedly, "then what you need is a houseboat!"

Pastor Osteen might have just as well been suggesting that they buy a gold-plated pickup to drive to Guatemala. A houseboat? Houseboats were luxury items that rich people and presidents bought, not something cabinetmaking missionary families bought. "That would be great, but, Pastor, how would we be able to afford something like that?" Elam said.

"Brother Elam, if you need it, God is going to supply it!" Pastor Osteen had been a great inspiration to Elam and Barbara and the children already. Virgil was just a little kid when they had started going there, but he actually sat still through Pastor Osteen's sermons willingly and had even asked to be baptized before they moved to Guatemala. Over the course of their years in Guatemala it would be countless cases of videotapes of Lakewood services that would keep the family encouraged and growing.

Elam just looked at his pastor. To John Osteen, what did the price of a houseboat have to do with whether or not God would provide it? He was a man with a faith in God that Elam knew right then he didn't have yet. Someday he would.

Then Pastor Osteen, still looking into Elam's eyes, said it again: "Brother Elam, if you need it, God is going to supply it!"

Chapter 9

Missionaries in Lancaster

*Whether, then, you eat or drink or whatever you do,
do all to the glory of God. 1 Corinthians 10:31*

People often have this idea that a missionary is a person who lives across a border in a foreign country, but a missionary is simply a person with a mission. Elam and Barbara were just that: people with a mission. Jesus was their mission, and they didn't have to wait for their geography to change to do something about that. So until it was time for them to go to Guatemala, they settled in Lancaster.

They bought a house, and Elam, who was a very skilled carpenter and cabinetmaker, worked only a full-time job at a furniture shop. Barbara worked as a seamstress, a chef, an accountant, a teacher, a banker, a therapist, a counselor, a nurse, a housecleaner, a masseuse, and a chauffer: she was a mom.

Together, they did what they could where they were to bring Jesus to those around them, and so they started a ministry of home fellowship which they called New Life Fellowship. The group would gather and study the Bible, sing, and pray together. More and more people came. It grew until there were too many people coming for everyone to fit in one home, so they started new groups in several other homes.

They also directed a seminar at the Landisville Campgrounds about the Holy Spirit which over 1400 people attended. Finally, all of the home groups became a church, which was originally called Victory Chapel, in Atglen, Pennsylvania. The church was one of a kind in the area, took off, and was very successful.

Little did Elam and Barbara know that in thirty years Virgil's wife and the author of this book about their life would stand at age twenty-nine by the side of her first husband at his funeral in the lobby of the church they had just started.

After that, Elam and Barbara started attending a Spanish Mennonite church in Lancaster City that was under the direction of a Mennonite Missions board. The attendance was dropping, and the congregation was struggling. Soon the church split, and most of the church left with the pastor and started a church in someone's home. The pastor had gone to a very conservative Bible school and could no longer adhere to the Mennonite church's ways (they were too liberal!). Now there were just a handful of people still coming to the church that had no pastor.

Elam didn't want to see the church die completely, so he met with the missions board and asked if they would license him so that he could continue the church. They agreed, and he took over as pastor. The church continued.

God says that if you're faithful with little He'll give you lots, and that's what happened with this church. Elam and Barbara would show up each Sunday morning at 9:30 a.m. and again at 7:30 p.m., open the doors of the church, and wait. There were times that no one showed up by church-time, so they would then go to the local Assembly of God church or go around and visit neighbors and people they knew didn't go to church anywhere.

Sometimes they would open up the church doors, and just one family would show up. They would have an informal but encouraging time of worshiping God, prayer, and fellowship. But week by week, more people began to show up until in just a few months the church was filling up!

· · · · ·

One night, Elam returned home, parked his car along Pershing Avenue, and headed toward their house. He had been at the hospital for a few hours helping to interpret for the nurses in the ER. The nurses were struggling to take care of a Spanish patient who had recently come in after a car accident. Elam often helped at the hospital and at the police station interpreting for the Spanish people. Today had gone well, and he'd even gotten a chance to talk to the injured person about life and death and what it meant to live your life for Jesus.

Guatemala came to his mind a lot, but he mostly thought about the work he was doing in Lancaster. He was having a good time rebuilding the church and really enjoying the people he was working with. Some of the people who knew of Barbara and Elam's plans to someday go to a mysterious far-off land with jungles and scary things were happy to see them settled in Lancaster where it was safe.

Elam reached his front door and walked inside. Right away he was tackled by his biggest fan and oldest daughter, Jean. "You're home, Daddy! I missed you!" she exclaimed lovingly as she hugged him around his waist.

Elam smiled back at his princess. "I missed you, too!"

Miguel was sitting at the table near the kitchen window and was concentrating on a toy he'd just taken apart. Virgil, now almost three, was playing on the floor by the living room sofa with a few little cars he had, lining them up all in a row.

Virgil looked up, saw his dad, and ran to him. "Daddy! You come back!"

Elam reached down and scooped up his little boy and smiled. "Yes, Daddy come back, little guy!"

Barbara came around the corner from the kitchen and gave Elam a big smile. He put Virgil down and then hugged her and gave her a kiss. He loved coming home to this family.

"Something smells good!" Elam said, taking notice of the smell coming from where Barbara had just been. For a woman who didn't like cooking, she sure knew how to make a man's stomach glad it had come home!

She just looked at him and smiled.

He took his shoes off and left them by the front door and then headed for the sofa to read the paper. He needed to prepare his sermon for this upcoming Sunday, and he thought that he would go out and do some visiting later tonight, but first he wanted to just relax a little.

Relaxing was not on the agenda, however. As he read, he thought he heard something outside that sounded like screaming. It sounded like children screaming. It was getting closer. Soon, there was loud banging on their front door. Elam sprang up and opened the door. He found two of the neighbor's children standing there with terror in their eyes.

"Help, please! Help!" they said in Spanish.

"What?" Elam knelt down to the older child's eye level.

"It's my daddy! He's trying to kill my mommy! Help!" he said frantically.

Just then, Elam could hear the sounds of a man and a woman fighting and screaming from the direction of the children's home. Without even thinking about his shoes or anything, Elam went around the children and took off running toward their house. Barbara told her children to stay put and then followed with the neighbor's children.

Elam approached the couple's house and could see their other children standing out in the street, and then he saw them. The wife had burst out of the house and out into the street. Her husband was right behind her, caught up to her, and she spun around to face him. He raised his hand, and a large kitchen knife was in it. He brought it down in the center of her chest. She crumbled to the ground in between two parked cars. Just then, Elam reached the man and grabbed his arm.

"Julio, give me the knife!" he shouted to the man who was still focused on his wife. "Julio! Julio!" Elam yelled again.

Still Julio struggled. Elam grabbed his arm and the hand with the knife and rubbed his fist over his fingers until he let go of the knife and finally settled down. The knife dropped to the ground, and Elam kicked it away with his foot. By then Barbara and the children had reached the scene as well. Julio's eight-year-old son knelt down and picked up the knife that was stained with his mother's blood. He threw it even farther away from them in anger.

As soon as Elam felt like he could let go of the man and he would not attack again, he went to the wife, Madeline, still slumped on the ground in the same place. She was bleeding profusely from her chest, but she was still breathing.

"Someone get me a towel!" Elam shouted. He applied pressure on the wound to stop the bleeding, but unfortunately the bleeding was coming directly from her heart. The knife had cut into one of her main arteries, and it was a short time until she bled to death.

The next day, Elam went to visit his neighbor in jail. Julio sat on the chair and looked as though he'd been the one under attack by a crazed lunatic yesterday. His eyes were heavy, and he had huge, dark circles underneath as though he'd not even slept since it happened. When he saw

Elam walk in, he seemed to get a glimmer of hope in his eyes. "Brother Elam! Please, tell me I didn't hurt you yesterday!"

"No, you didn't hurt me," Elam reassured him. He seemed relieved to hear that.

"Now, tell me," he began and his eyes grew wider. "Please, tell me I did not kill my wife!"

Elam just looked at him silently for a moment. "I can't tell you that, Julio."

It was as though in all the chaos, his only hope hinged on the words of his trusted friend. Maybe the police were saying he'd killed his wife, but it had to be a lie! When Elam confirmed that it was not a lie, huge tears began to stream down Julio's face.

"You did kill your wife yesterday, Julio," Elam said.

They sat in silence for a long time as the reality set in. Finally, when they started talking, Elam asked him the obvious question: "Why did you do it?"

He had no explanation as to why he'd done it. He claimed that he didn't even remember it happening. Madeline's sister had been there at the house when he'd come home. She said that he had come home drunk but they hadn't really gotten into a fight. He'd just blown up at her and gone after her with the knife.

Elam felt sad that he'd not been able to get there fast enough to save her. It was so frustrating! He'd been right in the street and seen Julio lunge at his wife and had seen his arm raised to give the fatal blow. If Elam had arrived just a few seconds earlier he might have been able to stop him! Just a few seconds!

It was too late to save Madeline, but now another life was in danger: Julio's. Julio's brothers-in-law had been in Philly that night at the bull fights when they heard about it and were on their way back to Lancaster. The family was crushed by the loss of Madeline, but they didn't want any more bloodshed and knew what Madeline's brothers probably had on their minds. They called Elam and asked him to be there when her brothers arrived.

The family's own pastor from the Methodist church and Elam were both there when they arrived. It was around 1 a.m., and just as the family suspected, they wanted to go straight to the police station and "take care of him." This time, Elam was there in time to stop the madness before someone got killed.

He lay in bed that night thanking God for using him to spare the family more pain. Elam thought of his future—of Guatemala. He saw the need for Jesus right there in Lancaster, yet the desire to go to Guatemala never went away. He had no way of knowing that in Guatemala he would be in situations like this many more times. There would be many more deaths that Elam would see and be helpless to stop, but there would also be many, many more deaths he would be able to prevent.

· · · · ·

It wasn't long after that that finally it felt like it was time. After so many years of dreaming and talking about "someday when they would go to Guatemala," someday had arrived. Although the missions board knew that Elam and Barbara were planning to leave to go to Guatemala back when Elam had taken the position as pastor, in all that time they still had not found a replacement for the pastoral position in the church. Elam didn't want to just leave the church high and dry, but he just knew it was time.

They had just one month before they were going to leave when Elam ran into the former assistant pastor of the church. He too had left the church with the former pastor, but that had ended up not working out and he had just started another church. Elam invited him to come to a service. He did and returned another time, bringing along the whole congregation that had left with the old pastor.

Everything seemed to be working out perfectly. They went to talk to the missions board, and the former assistant pastor now became the new pastor. Sunday he was "installed," as church people put it, and Elam "passed the baton" to the new pastor. He'd taken his turn running this race and had run his leg well. He'd stuck by the church even when it seemed all the life was gone out of it. Now the church was alive again, and it was someone else's turn to run this race. Monday morning, Elam and Barbara got in their car with their children, said good-bye to Lancaster, and headed off toward Texas and the border beyond. It was time for a new race to begin!

Chapter 10

The Dream is Real

"And I will bless you, and make your name great; and so you shall be a blessing; And I will bless those who bless you, and the one who curses you I will curse. And in you all the families of the earth will be blessed." *Genesis 12:2-3*

People talked. "Have you heard that Elam and Barbie are taking their children to Guatemala!"

"Are you serious?"

"Oh, it's true! Isn't it horrible?"

"He says God is calling them there!"

"Oh, get real! What does he think, that he can hear from God?!"

"When are they going?"

"I think they've already left!"

"Isn't that an island somewhere? How are they getting there?"

"Oh, I mean it! There's a war going on there!"

"I think it's over near the Philippines or something like that."

"Oh, like you mean over by the Middle East! Isn't it dangerous there?"

"I think it's child abuse, plain and simple. No one who loved their children would take them to a place like that! It's just terrible!"

"Who knows what the natives will be like in an uncivilized place like that."

"Oh, I know, it's just awful. Especially not with children!"

"Those poor children."

· · · · ·

Headed for Houston, Elam, Barbara, Jean, Miguel, and Virgil pulled out of Lancaster and drove down through Maryland to West Virginia. For the family, traveling didn't mean watching DVDs, listening to their iPods, stopping at fast-food restaurants, and swimming in hotel pools for days on end. It meant spending hours in the car singing and talking and looking at the scenery and getting to visit with old friends and new ones.

In West Virginia, their first stop, they visited with Paul and Ruth Willouer, whom they had met at Eastern Mennonite University in Harrisonburg. They spent the evening catching up on old times and talking of their plans and dreams for the Petén.

"There are a few Catholic churches here and there, but for the most part there are no churches in these villages at all yet, no representative for Christ whatsoever," Elam explained. "So we want to have a ministry to these villages that are just scattered for miles and miles along the Passion River from a town called Sayaxché down as far south on the river as Mexico."

"How many miles would you say it is you will be traveling?" they asked.

Barbara looked at Elam and cocked her head a little. "Oh, about fifty, we figure. Isn't that right?"

"Yep. About fifty," Elam agreed.

Paul got an idea. "Sounds like what you need is a houseboat!"

Elam and Barbara smiled at each other. "That's what Pastor Osteen told us, but houseboats are only for rich people who can afford yachts. We don't even own a motorboat!" Barbara said.

Elam continued, "But God says that He will give us the desires of our heart when we delight in Him, and He knows the desire of our hearts is to go to Guatemala to spread His word. He knows our hearts and our needs, and He will make it all possible!"

Paul gave his wife a look that said he had an idea, and she knew what it was and smiled.

The conversation continued on into the evening, and Elam and Barbara didn't give the houseboat another thought. All they knew was that it was God leading them to Guatemala, and they knew that He would take care of the rest. Sometimes it didn't seem logical to set off on such a mission with so little money, to have a ministry along a river without even a speedboat, but Abraham setting off for Mt. Moriah to sacrifice the son God told him He'd bring him descendants through wasn't logical either.

Abraham didn't run what God had told him past his elders board or pray over it for weeks on end, he just did it trusting God and was called the friend of God. Elam and Barbara, too, knew that God was calling them to go to Guatemala and that as long as they did all that they could, He would do what they couldn't.

The next morning at breakfast, Paul and Ruth seemed excited about something. Ruth was busily getting dishes out of the cabinets and dipping fresh eggs out of a pan on to each one, which she then passed over to the table. Paul received his plate of food and sat down at the table. Then he looked to his friends. "Last night we talked about your need of a boat."

Elam reached out and took the plate Ruth was handing to him. "Thanks." He was not at all expecting what came next.

"Elam, Barbara, the Lord has blessed us richly in our business, and we have some money that belongs to Him." Paul glanced at his wife, who was smiling broadly over by the kitchen sink and watching Elam's face as her husband spoke. "We believe the Lord has entrusted us with that money to buy you that boat."

Elam and Barbara's eyes met as both of their hearts beat faster. "Are you serious?" Elam was astounded!

Paul smiled. "I'm serious, Brother Elam! Go find the boat you need and send us the bill."

· · · · ·

It had to be a dream, but it wasn't. It was better. It was God. There before Elam and Barbara was their Chapel of the River. This was all really happening.

It was a crisp Texas Sunday afternoon in November 1971. Several friends and members of Lakewood Church had traveled to the Nassau Bay Yacht Club to dedicate the new boat. The Chapel of the River was a $16,000, thirty-four-foot houseboat with only eleven hours of use and the unbelievable price tag of just $7,500. While by today's standards one could buy only half a car for that price, back then that was actually the equivalent to the average person's wages for one year! This gift was almost incomprehensible! Today, the average American needs a five-year loan to pay for a car that costs a fourth of a year's wage…and Elam and Barbara had just been given the title to this boat that was valued at a whole year's wages free and clear. It was amazing!

The houseboat would wait in Texas until after Elam and Barbara were settled in Guatemala and could bring it down, but it was there. It was bought and paid for and dedicated for service, just like they knew they were bought by the blood of Jesus and dedicated to His service! They were both too excited for words at times! This was really happening!

· · · · ·

"What was that?" their truck had just made a thump and something seemed wrong. Elam stopped their pickup truck, put the emergency brake on, and hopped out.

"What is it, Elam?" he heard Barbara call from the passenger's side of the truck now parked in the middle of the road. They were stopped in Northern Mexico, pulling an overloaded trailer that was barely hanging on by its broken hitch!

"Oh, just a little, uh, hitch in our plans," he chuckled to himself. Elam looked over the side of the mountain he now realized he was stuck on. It was beautiful but dangerous, dropping off very sharply on one side.

Barbara laughed a little. Her hand slid over her large belly as she got out of the truck to see for herself. "What?"

Elam met her at the door, and put his arm around his wife. "Maybe we'll just set up and minister here? See that spot over there?" he was pointing to a slightly clear flat spot with a little patch of grass. "You could have the baby over there."

"What?" she laughingly asked again, walking around to where her husband stood. She looked at the hitch and realized the trouble they were in. "Sure, maybe that spot would make a nice place to have a baby," she laughed. "But where will we put the crib?"

This was just the beginning—just the beginning of a seemingly never-ending river of inconveniences they would encounter over the course of their life in Central America together. What a woman Elam had chosen to be his bride. Here she stood, seven months pregnant, all of her belongings being hauled in a trailer, which was now stranded in the middle of a dangerous road in Mexico—a country where she couldn't even speak the language. So far, the whole trip, her pregnant bladder had never had the luxury of a nice clean toilet or soft toilet paper, yet she smiled and trusted God. She never complained and never cried that she wanted to go back home to Lancaster County. He could never have even made it this far if she were a worrier or a complainer. "It is better to live in a corner of a roof than in a house shared with a contentious woman" (Proverbs 21:9).

He loved her so much. "I am going to achieve my dreams and fulfill Your plans for me, Lord, thanks to the help I'll receive from the wonderful woman You chose for me," he prayed in his heart.

The two then joined hands by their trailer and prayed, "Lord, OK, we're helpless here. We need you to get us out of this."

Virgil and Miguel, being properly equipped for such a time as this, had run off across the road to use the rest area. Jean was just waking up in the back of the pickup under the camper top. Within five minutes, even before they all really had a chance to get bored, a car slowed down and pulled over in front of their truck. Two American guys hopped out.

"Having a little trouble?" the taller man asked Elam.

"We have a broken hitch."

The shorter man approached and offered Elam his hand. "Name's John. And you?"

"Elam," he replied and then motioned toward his wife, "and this is my wife, Barbara."

"My name's Derrick," the taller man offered his hand to Elam.

"So what did your wife swallow, a watermelon seed or something?" John chuckled.

Elam and Barbara both laughed.

"Roads are pretty bad down through this way. We've got about three more hours left till we get where we're going. How far you headed?"

"Guatemala."

"Whooo wee, my you have a long way to go, then!" Derrick said.

"Yeah, and we knew the roads were going to be bad, so we did a lot of work on these vehicles before we left. I would have thought we could have made it the whole way to Guatemala without much trouble, really." Elam told them about the weeks he'd spent at the home of the High family in

McAllen, Texas, working with Melvin High many hours into the night getting the truck and trailer in shape for the 2,000 mile trip to Guatemala.

Another missionary had told Elam that he had had fifteen flats on one trip through Mexico, so special attention was paid to the tires. They made sure their tires were in shape, and put in all new brake linings on the wheels and new seals and bearings on the rear.

The roads in Mexico were very deceptive. They were paved, but they were actually worse than if they were unpaved because of all the potholes—potholes that had sharp edges and deep drops that would blow out even a brand-new tire if it was hit just right.

"Well, funny thing is that we had trouble then even before we hit Mexico! We worked and worked and worked on these vehicles, and when we were sure we had everything as ready as it could be we headed off for the border. We got ten miles down the road when we smelled something hot," his eyebrows rose. "A brake drum had burned the new seal and bearing and ruined the axle."

"No!" John said.

"Did you have any trouble when you finally made it to the border, then?" Derrick was leaning on the hood of the truck considering whether or not he needed to use the rest area now that he was stopped.

"No, we went right on through, without a hitch."

John and Derrick stopped and looked at each other. One of them said, "Without a hitch, huh? I get it."

The four new friends shared a laugh.

"And even after all that preparation we have actually already ruined a couple of perfectly good tires," Elam said.

"Yeah, we usually try to bring at least one spare along," John agreed.

"Yeah, we have had some bad experiences on these roads ourselves," Derrick added. "We usually get to know several of the vulcanizadores on the route."

Elam would become all too familiar with those as well. Vulcanizadores were the little shacks all along the route through Mexico of people who would fix your flat tires.

"We tried bypassing the Mexican roads altogether earlier this year, but that didn't work out." Elam then told the men about his adventure just a few months back trying to sail The Chapel of the River through the Gulf of Mexico. It had been one thing after another on that short journey.

"I don't know what I was thinking. I guess it was just a childish excitement really, but without knowing exactly what lay ahead for me, I just set sail in that houseboat and tried to head for Guatemala through the Gulf." Elam laughed a little at himself.

"So how'd that work out for ya?" one of the men asked.

"Almost right away the weather just got terrible. We figured we'd find a safe place to dock for the night and set sail then later, and it was then that we ran into some experienced fishermen and they kindly informed us there was no way on earth we were taking that trip!" He laughed again just thinking of how eagerly he'd just jumped into that boat and taken off, not knowing what was ahead of him.

"God must have stopped you," one of them men said matter-of-factly.

"I have no doubt that it was God now," Elam agreed. "We also found out then that the rivers we had planned to enter into Mexico and navigate through to Guatemala had too many falls and were too shallow at other places. There was no way we'd be able to get the boat through."

"So, where's your boat now?"

"Waiting for us in Texas. We're gonna head on down to Guatemala and get settled, wait for the baby to come, and then in a few months I'll be going back up for the boat. We'll bring it down on a truck."

"Hey, Dad!" Miguel pointed toward an approaching tractor-trailer. "I think he's pulling over!"

The large truck with a bumper sticker that read, "Jesus Saves" slowed to a stop, and a burly man hopped out of the driver's seat. "Would you happen to need any help here?" It was another American.

Barbara smiled up at the man's wife still in the cab, who returned a wave and started getting out of the truck. "My wife and I pass a lot of cars parked along the road," the truck driver started to explain. His wife eagerly finished his sentence, "But we both felt like God was telling us not to pass by but to stop and help you."

"That's funny," John said looking at Derrick, who was nodding his head, "we had the same experience when we came along and saw you here."

The truck driver offered to tow the trailer all the way in to the nearest town, which was eight miles away, and helped them find a place to have it repaired.

Sometimes, people tend to look at inconveniences as, well, just that: inconveniences. They look at trouble in their path, and they grumble and complain and wonder, "God, where are you?" But "blessed are those who persevere under trial, knowing that the testing of their faith produces endurance." Many of us learn from infancy that there are times that when we feel distressed we are basically on our own to deal with it, and that we had better have a good reason to cry out. But God never leaves us to deal with our troubles on our own, no matter how big or small the problem is and no matter when we cry. He is always there. But, because we all know from experience that "man" will let us down, we have to be trained to believe that God is not like man, that His ways are not our ways, and He is never too busy or too tired to come to us in our time of need.

Elam and Barbara were entering a world where inconvenience and trouble lay waiting around nearly every turn. Many situations would arise that would be out of their control. Some of those things would be small and some would be larger than they could even imagine. They would need to be able to trust God in ways they'd never had to before, even with their very lives. They needed to have full confidence even in their small troubles that God would not leave them on their own, that He would always be by their side.

Chapter 11

The Stillbirth

... pray for one another so that you may be healed.
The effective prayer of a righteous man can accomplish much.
James 5:16

It only took a dozen or so visits to vulcanizadores to bring them to their final destination: the border of Guatemala. As they came around that last curve approaching the border crossing out of what was then still called British Honduras (which now is Belize), they could see it just over the trees. There it was, a big billboard-sized sign that read: "Bienvenidos a Guatemala." Welcome to Guatemala.

In their first few months they had settled in a town called Santa Elena, which was about forty-five miles east of what was to be their final destination in Sayaxché. They got this far and stopped because of rain. In the States, sometimes our roads in the North are impassable for a few hours or in extreme cases even days because of ice or snow, but here the dirt roads became impassable for months at a stretch because of rain. The dirt roads would literally become huge mud pits in places where nothing could get through.

So, being the rainy season, they stopped in Santa Elena and decided it was just as well that they would settle in here until the baby arrived and Elam was able to go back for the houseboat. They'd found a house to live in after spending a few weeks in the back of their pickup truck and had moved in. It was not a terribly comfy house like houses in the States—it had a concrete floor and no screens or glass in the windows—but it was better than the back of the pickup and the whole family was thankful for it.

The children all soon found friends and things to do in their new world. Elam began making connections with the local churches and working toward his goal of getting to the villages along the Passion River. Barbara prepared for the arrival of her fourth baby, who would be delivered in the local government hospital and become their family's first Guatemalan citizen.

· · · · ·

The time came in March, 1972. Elam had been waiting in the delivery room for a while now. Barbara's contractions had never really started, but there had been signs that the baby was soon to come. Bad signs. They'd gone in to see the doctor because she had started bleeding a little here and there. It wasn't constant, but it just kept happening. Dr. Baldison examined her and felt that her placenta was very low, but that the baby's head was down in position. Because her bleeding had come and then gone, he felt that the baby would be delivered safely. He sent her home and told her to come back to the hospital when she felt it was time or if the bleeding got any worse.

What was happening inside of Barbara that was causing the bleeding was the position of the placenta. Sometimes the placenta will attach itself completely over the birth canal opening or cervix, which is an obvious problem because as the cervix begins to open it detaches the placenta completely and is in the way of the baby coming out. This was not what Dr. Baldison felt Barbara had. But he did believe that her placenta was low and near the cervix, so as labor approached and the cervix area began to change it was disturbing the placenta, causing it to bleed some. Because it was not a lot of blood, he felt it was not a serious problem.

A day later Barbara and Elam arrived at the hospital late at night. The nurses admitted her. Unlike what we are accustomed to in the United States, that meant they showed her to her cot, and that was it. No one took her vitals or took her information and made a file for her. No chart. No fetal monitor. They didn't call the doctor.

To say that the government hospital in San Benito was lacking in technology and personnel with adequate training would be an understatement. But it did serve a dual purpose in serving both as a hospital and a roach motel.

So why did Elam and Barbara choose to go there? It was the only hospital around. The local doctors who had their own offices took turns being on call at the hospital, and that was the reason there was no doctor at the hospital when they arrived. The doctor would only get up out of bed and come rushing to the hospital if it was an emergency, and although Barbara was in late term pregnancy and bleeding, according to the nurses whose education was not impressive by U.S. standards, this didn't seem to be one.

When last Elam and Barbara had spoken with the doctor, he had said to keep an eye on her and if she started bleeding that she was to come to the hospital and he was to be called immediately. They had done as the doctor ordered. Elam kissed his wife good-bye and planned to be back the next day as soon as visiting hours allowed him, trusting that his wife was going to be taken care of. But all night the nurses ignored the problem, and Barbara lay there bleeding while the doctor slept, not even knowing she was there, and while her placenta, the life-support system for her unborn baby, was detaching.

Barbara expected the doctor to at least come in the morning, but he never showed. Patiently she waited and prayed. Elam prayed for his wife, expecting that she was already having her baby, and he prepared to go visit "them" at 1:30 in the afternoon as soon as visiting hours started. But when Elam arrived, he found his wife not looking so well, still pregnant, and now she was bleeding a lot. He left the hospital and rushed over to the doctor's office across town.

As soon as Dr. Baldison looked up and saw Elam's face, he jumped up and took off for his car and the hospital. Elam made it there just after he did, but already the doctor had Barbara taken off into the delivery room so Elam went to the customary place for those days: the waiting room. Daddy and the camera crews would have to wait a few decades to be welcomed into the delivery room.

"Are you having any pains?" Dr. Baldison asked Barbara.

He had checked her, and she was fully dilated. She had to be having contractions.

"Well, no not really." Barbara smiled at him weakly.

"Well, if you have any, even small, pains I want you to start pushing, alright?" the doctor told her.

She nodded at him and prepared to start pushing.

"You know this is going to be a boy," he said confidently with a little smirk.

Barbara smiled again. "What? Well, we've already decided it's supposed to be a girl."

The doctor moved into position as the nurses prepared for the baby to arrive. "I only deliver boys."

Barbara finally felt a pain and began to push. It didn't take much, as the head was right there. Dr. Baldison was hopeful that he was going to get this baby out fast, but he was very nervous as there was a lot of blood.

In only a few pushes the baby was born.

Barbara breathed deeply and thanked God under her breath for helping her. She watched the doctor and the nurses then as they worked with the baby.

The doctor was very busy but said, "Well, I was wrong. It's a girl."

Barbara smiled. "See? I told you."

It was a relief to hear that bit of normal news, but the doctor didn't have anything more to say and wasn't smiling. The baby was not making any sounds or moving and looked very blue.

"Lord, is she going to live?" Barbara asked God, suddenly aware of how very serious this was. She watched them work, realizing that the baby was not breathing yet. She was no nurse, but she knew enough to know that the longer that went on, the more likely it would be that the baby would have brain damage. She imagined herself trying to raise a brain-damaged child on the mission field and how difficult that would be. "Lord, I know I should tell You that 'Your will be done' but…" Barbara couldn't say that. She looked at her newborn baby lying there lifeless, and her heart broke.

"Lord, if she's going to be brain-damaged, I want You to just take her," she prayed.

The nurse then took out a needle and injected the baby with something. Barbara wasn't sure, but it looked like the baby moved.

· · · · ·

Elam tried to listen to what was going on inside the delivery room, but it was too quiet. He tapped his foot as he sat on the mint green plastic chair praying, "Lord, we have committed this baby to You, and we trust You to bring her safely into the world!"

He stood and paced around the room a bit, still trying to hear what was going on. He was no doctor, and he had learned not to worry, but he just sensed it. Something was wrong with the baby. He continued to pace and talk to God about this.

Finally, there were some sounds. Some shuffling, and sounds of the nurses moving around rapidly, and the doctor talking to a nurse were all he could hear coming through the door. It gave Elam the impression that the baby had been born, so he waited for that other sound, the sound of the baby crying, but nothing came. At least fifteen minutes had passed since he thought the baby had been born, and still there were no sounds of a baby crying. Then the door opened, and the doctor came out, looking distraught. Elam's heart sank.

The doctor approached Elam and stood a few feet from him, eyes downcast, and spoke quietly, "Your wife is fine, but I am sorry, your baby is dead." He paused for a moment, a look of genuine remorse in his eyes. He sighed, "I'm sorry."

The new father's heart was broken, but even in the face of this great tragedy, he trusted God. He looked up at the doctor and told him, "We have already committed the baby to God, and we trust Him."

· · · · ·

Someone in the States was talking on the phone with her best friend. "Oh, I know, I still can't get over it, them taking those kids down into that God-forsaken jungle."

"And with Barbara being pregnant, too. What in the world is Elam thinking? I mean it, what if something happens to her or to her baby?"

"Right, and what if they can't get good medical care there? Do they even have doctors in South America?"

"And he calls himself a Christian!"

"I just don't understand what someone like that is thinking!"

"You know, I heard that Marvin's wife wore a sleeveless dress to church last week."

"Are you serious? Well I heard that she used to…"

. . . . .

The three ladies in Texas met for coffee in the afternoon often to talk and pray together. Nothing formal, just something they liked to do. Today they sat at the diner and talked about the weather, their grandchildren, and their prayer concerns. One of the ladies opened up a devotional book and read the passage that focused on Ephesians, "For our struggle is not against flesh and blood..." Before they downed the last of their coffee, they took a few minutes to pray together. One of them prayed for her favorite missionaries, Elam and Barbara, down there in Central America, in Guatemala.

. . . . .

Looking at the gray tile floor, the doctor was wondering what would be appropriate to say next. He had just told this man his child was dead, the worst news a doctor ever has to deliver. He was about to start speaking again when he thought he heard the sound of a gasp coming from the room where the baby had been taken.

"It couldn't be!" he thought. His eyes lit up, and he flew off to the room. There on the table was the baby he had given up for dead, just where they had left her, only now she was moving.

"This can't be! She's been dead since she was delivered!" the doctor thought as he rapidly spoke orders to the nurse for oxygen to be brought and for more nurses to come help. As they worked on her, her chest heaved as she began to breathe, and color began to come into her skin. Her eyes even tried to open. It was just not possible.

They worked with her for over a half hour until they felt they had her stable, and then the doctor stepped aside for a moment, "for a drink of water" he had said, but really he wanted to think. He could not believe what had just happened. There on the table lay a newborn infant whom he had given up for dead less than an hour ago. "She was dead," the doctor said again to himself under his breath as he watched one nurse stroking a tiny pink hand.

Over in the other room were two people hugging and smiling, to whom he had just given the bad news less than an hour ago that their baby was dead. "But their baby is alive." He shook his head and walked out into the hall to be alone for a minute.

He had heard of miracles on TV but had never bought that whole healing thing that the TV evangelists did. It all seemed like such a show. He knew how to heal people, because he had gone to medical school; and there were just things that you had to do for healing to happen, simple as that. And there were things that just didn't happen—that had just happened right before his eyes. There was no medical explanation for what he'd just experienced. There had been no loud dramatic evangelist with a religious accent and TV crew putting on a show, just two humble people praying and trusting God. He knew what had just happened. "Their God saved their baby."

He walked into the room to Elam and Barbara, who smiled at him. "Thank you for all you've done, doctor." Elam was sitting at his wife's side, holding her hand. Both of them were smiling.

The doctor just shook his head. "Don't thank me. I did everything I could to save your daughter. God gave you your baby."

Elam and Barbara were not medical doctors, but they too knew that what had just happened had no medical explanation. They knew it was God, and they were so excited to have had the opportunity to see Him work that way. It was just like when Jesus raised Lazarus out of the tomb. He could have healed Anita right away, or even prevented the problem from arising, but through this situation He showed this couple who'd just taken a huge step of faith out into the scary jungles of a foreign country His power even over death. Elam knew before they left for Guatemala that God was going to watch over them, that He would be a shield around them; but now, more than knowing it, he'd experienced it.

No amount of Bible study could teach them what they had just learned that day—the day the Lord of heaven and earth who gives all men life and breath gave them back their baby.

Chapter 12

Houseboat Arrives

*...make it your ambition to lead a quiet life and
attend to your own business and work with your hands,
just as we commanded you, so that you will behave
properly toward outsiders and not be in any need.*
1 Thessalonians 4:11-12

Their family now was now up to six people. Little two-month-old Anita was growing normally and showed no signs of any brain damage from her traumatic birth. She was often referred to as "our miracle baby" by her parents. Of course, once she was a grown-up and making a habit of cooking cotton balls inside of cupcakes she prepared for visiting missionary groups, some would doubt that, but that's another story entirely. And besides, as of yet no studies have been done to prove that oxygen deprivation during birth can cause ornery streaks. They always looked at her as a living example of God's love and care for them.

The small house they were renting happened to be near a school, so during the day the children started sitting in on classes and quickly picked up Spanish.

"Ma, meh, me, moh, moo, la moola eres tu," the children would recite while they played.

"What's that mean?" Barbara finally asked one day.

Virgil giggled.

Jean giggled.

Mirna giggled.

Miguel answered, "That means that a,e,i,o,u, the mule are you!"

Barbara giggled. Learning a new language was always quicker for the little ones than the older ones!

"Lunch is ready!" Mirna announced to the children who all ran in and sat at the table eager to eat the fresh corn tortillas Mirna was so good at making.

"Thank you, Mirna." Barbara smiled as she put Anita down in the play-pen and made her way to the table also to eat.

She was feeling good after the delivery of Anita, and the baby was doing great! She was gaining weight and seemed to be a happy, normal baby. Having Mirna around was working out great as well. Not too long after settling into their house here in Santa Elena, Elam and Barbara had decided to hire a "muchacha" or a young lady to help with the housework. This way the family would have a native Spanish speaker in their home most of the time to help them learn Spanish, and Barbara would have someone to help her with all the household chores after having her baby, now that her washing machine was a thing of the past and she had to scrub the clothes by hand. Also, with Mirna around there was someone to help with the children when Elam would have to leave to go to the States to get the houseboat.

Mirna had fit in with the children right away and had made a hit especially with Virgil with her cooking: he loved her beans and tortillas. Mirna had worked for a missionary family before and so even knew a little English already. But there was one thing that she thought for sure was weird about this new family she was working for.

"The first time you have me sit right at the table with you when we eat meals I was very surprise!" Mirna told Barbara one day, practicing her English.

Barbara thought that was very strange. "Why?"

Apparently, the other family she had worked for made her sit in the kitchen whenever they ate meals. It was the customary way of the Guatemalans when they had a maid in the house that she would eat apart from the family, and the other missionary family had adopted that same practice.

"You two treat me very well, make me feel like family." She smiled at the both of them.

Elam had felt comfortable with her right away and quickly made a habit of teasing Mirna almost as soon as he met her. "Oh, you just watch!

Both of our daughters are going to marry American men, and so someday we'll even bring you a husband from the States!"

· · · · ·

Settling into the community so far had been fun with the kids in school, and with Mirna being added to Elam and Barbara's family Guatemala was quickly starting to feel like home. They also started attending many of the local churches and just started to get to know people, which was very easy. While the Indian people in the villages were very shy, the people who lived in town were more curious about these newcomers and really wanted to meet them and get to know them. They were being asked to people's houses for meals all the time, and visitors showed up often at their door as well. It didn't take long until the children were chattering away in Spanish just like their little Guatemalan friends!

Elam got to know a pastor in a town halfway between Santa Elena and Sayaxché, called La Libertad (The Liberty), and soon he was even invited to preach at some of their services.

By May, it had been two months since Anita's delivery, and everyone seemed to be settled in well enough. Barbara had Mirna to help her, so Elam decided it was time to head back to get the houseboat. It was a six-week trip altogether, and things went well both for him on his trip and for his wife and kids back in Guatemala. Although he tried to be prepared, just like his first journey through Mexico he still had flat tires and many delays, but nothing extraordinarily inconvenient. Then, finally, the end was in sight! He had made it all the way back through Mexico, and had passed through the border into British Honduras without much hassle. He was almost all the way through the country, could almost smell the border of Guatemala, when a very small obstacle stood in his path.

"Can't we just pray for God to widen the bridge?" Virgil, who was almost five, asked in all sincerity. Barbara looked down at him and wondered if God would. She and Virgil had driven over to Belize City to meet Elam when he arrived with the houseboat, leaving Jean, Miguel, and Anita with Mirna. All had gone smoothly from there, until they reached this little bridge. It was such a small obstacle, and that was the problem. It was just an inch or so too narrow for the boat riding on its trailer to fit through.

"This definitely would be in the 'you have got to be kidding me' category," Elam laughed.

Finally, after much thought, they ended up putting the houseboat, and the trailer it was riding on, on top of another flatbed to get it up high enough to pass through the narrow part of the bridge. It took a few days to accomplish this, but once they did they were home free.

At the border, the customs agents didn't even know what to do with this, this, thing. Was it a house or a boat? There was nothing in their books !like it. They finally decided to call it a house on wheels and sent it through. And, when it finally came down to it, the customs agents decided not to charge them any duty for it at all, which for this new missionary family of six living off of donations was definitely in the "major blessings" category!

Then, as they approached Santa Elena, again so close to their final destination, they pulled into the driveway at the home of the Crafts, who were also new missionaries in the area. Since they were passing by they were excited to visit and show them the houseboat. Once they put the rig in park they heard a loud noise. They turned and looked at each other and almost had to laugh. A spring had just broken on the trailer. "Guess we're not going to be going anywhere fast, now will we?" Elam said.

Around here there was no such thing as getting things fixed fast, so the boat was parked and there it stayed for the next month.

· · · · ·

The loud boom startled everyone in the house.

"What was that?!" Miguel sprang over to the front window of the Crafts' house to look outside. Virgil was right behind him trying to get a look, too.

When they'd arrived in Santa Elena with the houseboat, everyone had packed up and moved out of the house they'd been living in and into the houseboat. Yes, with it still perched on top of the broken-down trailer right there by the side of the road. What an adventure this was already! They spent most of their time in the home of the Crafts, and today they were entertaining the governor of the Petén, who had stopped in out of curiosity. Who were these strangers from the United States, and what in the world was this thing they were living in? He had come without any security people, and so because he was a government official, and there was a war going on between communist guerrillas and the government, loud booms always got his adrenaline rushing!

Elam turned from the front window and started to laugh.

"What?" Barbara looked out the window. At first she wasn't sure what she was seeing. The houseboat wasn't too far from the house, and it appeared that there was something dark dripping down the sides, but what was it? "What is that?" she asked, and then, as the words exited her mouth, she realized what it was and started to laugh, too.

Now everyone was curious, and even the governor had relaxed a little and sat back down in his chair. "Remember a couple of days ago I made a batch of root beer?" Elam began. Now the Crafts were laughing, too. The governor didn't know what root beer was, so he needed a longer explanation.

Root beer was something the Mennonites and Amish often made at home. Although it isn't an alcoholic beverage, it still has to go through a stage of brewing, a state in which it does produce some gases that expand—gases produced at a certain rate Elam was accustomed to when his root beer was brewing in the nice sane Lancaster County sun in Pennsylvania. He had forgotten that he was in the Petén now and had filled a five-gallon water jug with his mixture and let it sit on the roof of the houseboat…sealed…brewing…out in the insanely hot Guatemalan sun. Boom!

The boys ran outside to check it out and marvel at their dad's mess up close. Jean went back to reading her book, and little Anita opted for a nap.

· · · · ·

After a month living in the driveway of the Crafts, Elam and Barbara's trailer was finally fixed. They said good-bye to all their new friends in Santa Elena, including Mirna, and headed out to Sayaxché. The forty-five-mile trip *only* took five hours, no springs broke, and no tires went flat! Finally, they were at their destination. After all these years, they were here. Elam backed the trailer down into the water and released the houseboat into the Passion River. They were home.

. . . . .

Elam took a few trips on his own downriver in a cargo boat to check out the villages. He found there were about seven on the route from there to the Mexico border. Once into Mexico, if he took a right up into the Usumacinta River, which flows north, there were five more villages along there. Some of the villages were made up of families from southern Guatemala who had immigrated north for the cheap land, and some were Indian villages. None of the villages had a Christian church already established. He had a lot of work to do!

They began making connections and friends wherever they could, and their supporters backed them up from the U.S. with prayer, finances, and supplies for their work. Someone sent them some equipment to show movies in the villages, and this was a big hit. Even before making their way down the river to visit all the villages, they met a man who invited them to come to his village to preach and show movies.

So one day the family headed the opposite direction upriver from Sayaxché a few miles until they reached the closest place to their destination and docked their boat. Barbara strapped tiny Anita to her with a sling, and all the kids piled onto shore. The villagers had sent some people out to greet them with a few horses to help carry the equipment and so that Barbara wouldn't have to walk with the baby. A few of the men grabbed up the little white kids, whom they called "gringitos," and put them on their shoulders, and off they all headed into the jungle. They fought their way through the mud, which seemed hungry for some shoes that it was good at sucking off their feet, for an hour at least to get to the village.

Once they arrived at this tiny isolated village with nothing but thatched-roof huts, little pot-bellied children smiling shyly at them, and quite a few topless ladies with babies strapped to their backs, they knew their efforts to bring Jesus out here were not in vain.

Soon thereafter the locals assured them that the river was high enough for their houseboat to get through everywhere, so they set sail toward Mexico and headed for the first village, Manos Unidas (United

Hands). They pulled their boat into shore and docked it. Soon everyone came out to see who in the world these gringos, these white people, were with their very strange boat that looked like a house, and they just started talking to people.

They asked if it was alright for them to dock there for a week or so, and they received a wholehearted "yes" from the village leader. The people wanted to know all about them and offered to make them meals and brought them food. Barbara kept a big tub on the deck of the houseboat to put all the food in that they received, and they did their best to eat it all! The people were so kind and generous to them!

In a few of the villages, rather than showing up as Christian missionaries they simply stayed there and made some friends for a week and began building relationships. Some of the villages were normally very hostile to strangers, especially Christian ones, so it was worth taking some time to get to know the people first. But in many of the other villages the people, hearing that they were Christian missionaries, would ask them to hold church services. So from the deck of the Chapel of the River Elam would preach to the people, sometimes every night of their stay. At services like this in a village with no electricity and no television shows to compete with, the entire village would come out to the service. Even the town drunks would swagger in and listen. Elam would preach, and the children would sing. The whole family had a lot of fun with it.

Sometimes they would have a special treat for the village and show a video with the equipment that they had been given. That was even more of an attention getter than just a normal church service! Sometimes the town drunk would even come to the movie before he was completely toasted so he could actually watch the movie! Most of the people had been living so isolated their whole lives that they'd never even seen a TV before, and so to some of them, these movies of Jesus were amazing in a way we cannot even relate to. On occasion, they even had a hard time understanding that they were watching actors and that what they were seeing wasn't real.

The entire trip from Sayaxché down the river to the last village into Mexico and back again would take about two months. They would stay at the villages again on their way back up the river, too, so in that time they would visit each village, except the last one, twice. Even before the end of their first year in Guatemala, they saw many people converted and heard many pleas for churches to be started in their villages. They were just at the beginning of this new life, and it was turning out to be just awesome!

· · · · ·

After a few of these long trips, they decided that a more central home base would work out better for them. Often, after they would complete a two-month trip, Elam would want to go back by speedboat to visit with the villages. Already, they had planted six churches, and they needed help and attention more than just a few times a year. The churches and villages on the far end of the route were not so convenient to visit, especially for a guy with a wife and four children! If their home base were more in the middle, it would be easier for Elam to go out and visit all the churches on a regular basis without having to be away from home for so long.

Because the government had just opened up this entire area for settlement, all you had to do was "squat" on a piece of land and then petition the government for it, and usually it was granted to you for the price of maybe four dollars an acre. On their trips they'd already had their eyes on a nice piece of land about halfway between "here" and "there" where there was a large wide spot in the river and an island with thick dense jungle all around it. As it turned out it also had several buried Mayan temples and other buried ruins on the property, too.

They stopped on one trip and asked at a nearby hut if that land had been claimed by anyone yet, and it hadn't. So, although they would still spend many more years traveling up and down the river and living on their houseboat, they began the process of squatting on this land and petitioned the government for the 400 acres.

Part of what squatting entailed was working the land, or doing improvements on it. With the use of one little chainsaw that had been donated to them by Victory Chapel, and a few locally bought machetes, Elam with his two boys began the tough work of clearing the land by hand.

"I'm glad those trees are already gone!" Miguel said, looking around at all the huge tree stumps that were scattered throughout the land. They had been mahogany trees, likely hundreds of years old. Some lumber company had already been by and taken them.

"Normally, I might think that's not a good thing," Elam smiled looking at their tools, "but in this case, I think I agree!" He looked out into the dense jungle ahead of them, leaned down to Virgil's eye level and pointed. "OK, Virgil, you go to that tree…that one and that one."

Virgil looked at the six-year-old-sized square of jungle that his dad had just pointed out. "OK," he replied.

"Miguel," he looked toward another patch, a little bit bigger since Miguel was three years older, "you go to that tree over there, then to that tree and that one." He pointed out all the trees, and Miguel nodded his understanding and began chopping.

Each boy had a certain amount they were expected to do each day. It wasn't a lot, but it was enough that they worked up a big hunger by lunchtime. The boys were free to go play after they either finished their portion or worked until 3:00 p.m. This was one thing that really started to get the attention of the local people. These gringos worked hard. Elam wasn't just a preacher who sat in his room and read books and then told them how to live; this guy worked as hard as they did.

Together, father and sons worked to clear the land that would someday be their home, the land that would someday be known to all the locals and even be printed on official maps as La Anchura (pronounced Lahnchuda) or "the wide spot."

· · · · ·

Because of growing up Amish, hard work was not something Elam was afraid of or unfamiliar with; it was something that made him feel good. He knew how to work with the soil. The soil here in Guatemala was a bit different than the dark, rich Lancaster County soil, but he knew how to farm nonetheless, and soon he got to work with planting a garden.

There were a couple of things about clothing in the jungle that the family soon learned were important. Mosquitoes and pickers were less irritating if you had on long pants while working, for one thing. For another, the culture here was a little funny about shorts. It didn't matter if it was 104 degrees in the shade outside and 101 percent humidity and all the ladies in the village had no tops or bras on; the men wore long pants. The only men who wore shorts were tourists, and the only women who wore shorts in those days were the prostitutes.

If Elam wanted to fit in and be accepted by the people, it was important for him to not offend them with what he and the children wore. "Whether, then, you eat or drink or whatever you do, do all to the glory of God" (1 Corinthians 10:31).

For a non-Amish person who had grown up living in a world where the minute-markets have to post signs that say, "No Shirt! No Shoes! No Service!" during the summer, this would have been a hardship. It's no small thing to get used to wearing "winter clothes" out in the hot sun working in the field. But for Elam, working hard with long pants on in the hot weather was something he was used to. All summer long he'd worked out in the field while the English neighbors would drive by and sweat just watching him working in the sun wearing those long black pants. Again, his Amish upbringing had prepared him for a big part of his life in Guatemala.

He also thanked God for his wife's upbringing in the Mennonite culture. She was not suffering living far from a grocery store. She was not suffering living off of what they could grow in the garden. She knew how to can and garden and how to make bananas stretch meals. She wasn't afraid to sift bugs out of her flour and keep on cooking. She was used to making the most with what she had, not wasting anything, and appreciating what she had.

As a young adult, Elam had come to a place in his life where he thought he'd had to put everything he loved from his childhood behind him. But already, over and over, they had seen that far from leaving the Amish way of life behind him, Elam's upbringing and roots were with him, helping to get him through every day.

Chapter 13

Christmas Dinner

...eat anything that is set before you without asking questions for conscience' sake. 1 Corinthians 10:27

Barbara's sister, Leah, looked down into the wobbly wooden boat and noticed water coming into the back. This wasn't as bad as finding a tarantula in the boat, of course, but still it started her heart racing. "Elam, the boat is filling up with water!"

He took a few steps over and had a look. "Oh, I guess we forgot to check to make sure the drain plug was in." He started to get back to what he had been doing and said to everyone, "Try to look around the boat for the plug."

"Oh, sure, he just forgot to put in the drain plug, is that all?!" Leah thought, horrified.

Everyone looked around in the dark trying to find the plug. Flashlight beams darted around the little boat's bottom. No luck.

"No oars, and our boat has a big hole in the bottom," Leah thought to herself. "I can do this!"

It was late at night, and they had just pulled into Sayaxché where the Chapel of the River was docked. It had taken them all day on an awful mud road to get here. Now they stood at the river's edge with all their luggage sitting on the muddy ground, staring at this tiny boat that was supposed to take them across this dark river to the other side where the houseboat was. The boat had no oars, so they had just finished hunting around for pieces of wood to use and were about to pile in, and now this!

"No problem." She shivered a little, both from cold and a little from nervousness.

Elam had gone to the States a few weeks ago to visit with some churches and bring back some equipment, and he had planned his trip so that he would be able to pick Dave and Leah up in the airport in British Honduras on his way home. Because Elam had no telephone, Barbara and the kids really only had a general idea as to when he was coming back. Sometimes flat tires and things would bring him home even weeks later than originally planned, so they had learned not to worry.

"Guys! Guys!" Jean called to her brothers from her bed. "I think I hear the boat coming!" Not only was her hero coming home, but Jean was so excited to be getting visitors from home come for Christmas this year that she hadn't been able to sleep for the last few nights. She ran out to the edge of the boat and strained her ears to hear.

"Maybe you can hear *a* boat coming, but you don't know if it's *the* boat, Jean. It's awful dark out there," Miguel piped up sleepily from his bed across the room. She ignored him and kept listening.

Virgil stirred from his sleep. "Hey, what are you guys doing?"

"I hear Dad talking!" She jumped out of her bed. "It *is* them!"

"Maybe you can hear *a* dad talking," Miguel began and then snickered a little as he ran outside with Virgil and Jean to the edge of the boat to see.

· · · · ·

Two-year-old Anita was already sitting at the table happily smearing oatmeal all over herself when Dave and Leah and the girls got up in the morning. It was Christmas Eve. Who would have thought years ago, when Leah and Barbara were just little Mennonite girls playing together in their yard with their younger sister Edna, that someday they would be sitting on a houseboat in a third-world country that was in the middle of a cruel and violent civil war on Christmas Eve?

"This is not like any Christmas Eve we ever had at home, is it?" Leah said.

Barbara looked over at her sister from the stove where she was stirring something she was whipping together for breakfast. "Nope, it sure isn't," she said with a laugh.

Dave and Leah had had a talk with their two daughters, Wanita and Charlene, before they left home to help encourage them and prepare them for this visit to a third-world country to see their cousins. They told their eight- and five-year-old daughters that "things would be very different, and maybe even scary." They all agreed that while they visited their cousins they would not complain about anything they saw, smelled, or felt.

"I can do this," Leah told herself again.

Dave was still fishing around inside the boat looking for the plug. In a more advanced part of the world, what else would you use to plug the drain plug hole in a boat but the drain plug, right? But, in the jungle you need to be a little more flexible, or you don't get anywhere. Elam quietly distributed sticks of gum to everyone.

Leah received her piece and automatically said, "Thank you," then at the same moment wondered why Elam was passing out gum when the boat was sinking. Everyone stood there chewing on gum, watching Elam rearrange some things in the boat. Leah was really feeling nervous. "What is he doing?"

"Now give me your gum," Elam finally said as he turned and held out his hand to everyone.

"But I'm not done," thought Charlene as she glanced at Wanita, who had a look on her face that said the same thing. Charlene pulled her gum out of her mouth and held it up to put it in her uncle's hand. She giggled a little at him when he actually took it. "Gross," she said to her sister. Elam stuffed the gum into the hole, and the hole was sealed.

"Cool," Wanita said to Charlene.

Leah looked down at what Elam had just done. That wasn't a real seal! They were going to get in this boat! The river ahead of them was wide and so dark and deep, and there was a big wad of gum stuck in a big hole at the bottom of the boat. "Are you sure that'll stick?" Leah asked with her brow furrowed.

"Yeah. That'll do just fine," Elam replied nonchalantly.

Leah glanced at the girls and then at Dave with a cautious smile across her face. "I'm not complaining, if that's what you're wondering."

"Sure." Dave smiled as he looked at his wife, who was holding h flashlight near her chest and had it aimed right at the plug. "You just ke an eye on it for us."

At Christmastime at home in Pennsylvania, there was a lot of very yummy homemade food, the houses had Christmas lights neatly and symmetrically hung along their rooflines, and it was cold outside, sometimes even snowing. In Sayaxché it was hot, and the closest they got to snow was the frost that built up on the inside of freezers. As far as yummy food goes, they were miles, OK, more like days, from the nearest grocery store that would sell anything like what they would have known from home. This was a very different Christmas Eve, indeed!

Leah sat down next to Anita and started helping her out a little with her breakfast and talking to her. "You sure are having fun with your food, aren't you?"

Anita smiled from ear to ear. "Yes! This good!" she said plainly.

"She speaks so clearly!" Leah noted.

Just then Barbara looked over at her sister playing sweetly with her baby and caught sight of something just beyond the high chair in the corner by the wall. Ever so casually, she slipped past the high chair, and Leah watched as Barbara scooped something up off the floor.

"How did you get in here?" Barbara whispered to the little visitor in her hand.

"What is it, Barbara?" Leah asked with a calmness that said she didn't suspect anything.

"Oh, just something that maybe one of the kids brought in that should be outside, is all." From her tone she could have been talking about a rock.

Leah went back to wiping up Anita's hands and talking to her, while Barbara went outside. Barbara leaned over the side of the houseboat and gently dropped the tarantula onto the ground and nudged it to walk away. She smiled. "If Leah had seen this, all the neighbors within screaming distance would have wondered what was going on here!" she thought to herself.

Sounds of splashing came from the river side of the boat. Pancho, the family's spider monkey, was squealing up a storm from the deck as Virgil and Miguel showed off for their cousins.

"They're just showing off," Jean told her cousins.

"We're not showing off, Jean!" Miguel shouted.

Jean laughed a little at herself. "I guess he heard me!"

"Yeah, Jean, we're just taking our morning bath!" Virgil yelled and then disappeared under the water.

"You guys wanna swim with us?" Miguel asked.

"It's almost Christmastime!" Charlene replied with her eyebrows in an arch shape that said, "We can't go swimming at Christmas!"

"Are there scary things in the water?" Wanita asked.

"Yeah. There's crocodiles and stuff, but they don't bite us," Virgil piped in.

Charlene shook her head. "What?!"

"What is that?" Wanita asked, pointing toward the black chatterbox on the deck of the boat.

Jean went and picked Pancho up and brought him over to the girls. "This is Pancho. He's a spider monkey."

"Mom doesn't like spiders," Charlene said matter-of-factly.

"Yeah, I know," Jean laughed.

"Is he a real spider?" Charlene asked.

"No! He's a monkey! He's just called a spider monkey because, well, I don't know why!" Jean laughed. Virgil came up close to the boat and gently splashed some water on the girls' feet.

"Hey!" they cried out.

"That's not too cold," Wanita noticed.

They only ever went swimming in the summer and never in December, but the water here was pretty warm for December. So was the air. Maybe swimming would be fun at almost Christmas?

Miguel got out onto the side of the river and grabbed an overhanging vine. "Watch this," he said. He ran, swung out over the river, and dove into the water.

"That was cool," Charlene said to Wanita, giggling a little. Both of them were now a little more interested in swimming at almost Christmas than they had been a few minutes before and had already forgotten about the crocodiles that don't bite.

"Let's just go over there to the bank where Miguel is swinging from and get a better view," said Jean with Pancho still by her side, headed for the plank to get off the houseboat. The girls followed.

Later that morning, Elam announced that everyone was to prepare for a boat ride; it was time to do the "shopping" for Christmas dinner. He grabbed a gun and handed one to Dave, too. Sure, why not? Dave had been hunting before. Deer, wild turkey. They were probably heading out to get one of those, or maybe a wild boar or something.

Everyone piled into the family's cargo boat. Miguel drove the motor while everyone else was looking for something in the trees. Charlene looked around the boat at everyone who was looking up into the trees and wondered, "What are we looking for?" She tried looking in the trees for birds.

Just then, Miguel pointed insistently but silently toward a tree. A gun went off. Something that was two-thirds tail fell like a rock into the river.

"What was that?" Wanita asked, whipping her head around toward her parents.

Dave and Leah just smiled at each other a smile that said, "Should we tell her?"

Miguel had his eyes glued to the place where the odd-looking creature had gone into the water. Something began to surface, and quickly Miguel's hand was in the water. He pulled out Christmas dinner.

· · · · ·

The hunt had gone well yesterday—so well that they had a few kills to spare—so Elam had given one to one of the neighbors along the river. This man, in turn, had invited Elam and everyone over to their house for dinner to show his gratitude.

Their house was a one-room thatched-roof hut with stick sides and a dirt floor a few hundred yards from where Elam and Barbara normally docked the houseboat. The hammocks the family used for sleeping were tied up to the ceiling out of the way. A metal tire rim filled with pieces of wood gathered from the jungle was used for cooking food. The family had prepared their best for their guests and were very excited and honored to have them in their home.

For Elam's family, this was normal. They had eaten in many village homes since arriving in Guatemala, and had even adapted to being served, at times, by ladies who were not wearing tops. For Dave and Leah's family, this was an awesome experience, being treated so wonderfully by someone who had so little—and fortunately was wearing a top. Not being able to communicate with their hosts, they did a lot of smiling and saying, "What?" to Elam for interpretation. Looking around the home they were now in gave both Dave and Leah more appreciation for the things they had at home.

"Dave, we're eating our Christmas dinner this year by candlelight, isn't that romantic?" Leah said with a quiet giggle. The candle, which was not a decoration but the kitchen light in this home with no electricity, was a cloth wick stuffed into a glass coke bottle.

The girls were getting something out of this experience, too. Charlene and Wanita looked at the Christmas dinner before them. Both of them were thinking about their promise their parents had just reminded them of to not complain no matter how weird or gross anything they experienced was, and this was pretty weird and gross. Seated at the table made of sawed-off tree stumps and a board, they looked at the plates on the dinner table and looked silently at each other, both thinking, "I can't believe we're about to eat lizards."

They bowed their heads to pray. The girls listened to Elam praying in Spanish and prayed one of their sincerest prayers in English themselves, "God, help us eat this." Amen.

After the amen, Elam and Virgil just dug in. They and their host family all grabbed tortillas from the center of the table and piled the fried iguana onto them and ate.

Wanita and Charlene watched their cousin in awe. Virgil looked as though he really liked it! They looked at their plates again, at the lump of lizard and rice. They gave each other a glance and then looked at their parents and did their best not to look the way they felt.

Dave and Leah gave each other a look, quietly laughed a little, and started eating. Both of them took note of how normally Elam and Virgil were acting, as though they hadn't noticed they were eating lizard! Elam just sat there and chatted away with the man of the house about all that was going on with the churches and his plans for La Anchura. Leah told herself after taking a few bites that it wasn't the worst thing she'd ever eaten. Yes, positive thought would get her though this meal. Dave had another technique.

Charlene took note of how much meat had been on her father's plate in the beginning, and it seemed to be disappearing rather quickly.

Dad was enjoying his meal, also! "No fair," she thought as she opened her mouth to take bite number two. What she didn't see as she chewed and chewed on the cooked weird green lizard in the dim romantic candlelight was the dog sitting at Dave's feet under the table—the very happy dog licking his chops sitting at Dave's feet.

By the time their visit to the jungle was over, the girls were already starting to get used to all the weird things around them. They were even posing for pictures with the iguanas. They still thought that their aunt Barbara's dozen or so jars full of canned iguana meat in the pantry was gross, but they couldn't wait to tell their friends they'd eaten lizards once they got back home and to school.

Chapter 14

Midnight Flight

"Are not five sparrows sold for two cents? Yet not one of them is forgotten before God. Indeed, the very hairs of your head are all numbered. Do not fear; you are more valuable than many sparrows." *Luke 12:6-7*

"I want a chocolate cake," Virgil said happily.

"Chocolate. I should have guessed." Barbara smiled.

"Uh huh! Chocolate!" Virgil said again, smiling broadly.

Tomorrow was Virgil's seventh birthday. He wasn't picky about anything. He ate anything that was set before him and even peacefully swallowed his cold banana soup three days a week over breakfast even while his mouth was screaming, "Oh, yuck!" So for him to specify that he wanted a chocolate cake meant that he really wanted a chocolate cake.

"Are you sure I couldn't make you something else?" Barbara asked. She looked at her cute little boy sitting there at the kitchen table swinging his legs.

"That's really what I want, Mom," he said smiling.

Barbara sighed a little. "I'm sorry, Virgil, but I can't make you a chocolate cake."

He didn't argue, but the look on his face said, "Why?" so she continued. "It takes an egg to make a chocolate cake, and I haven't got even one egg on the boat."

The expression on Virgil's face was sad but uncomplaining. They had set out just a week or so ago from La Anchura making one of their regular trips with the houseboat up and down the river to visit the newly planted churches in all the villages. Right now they were docked miles away from any place where Barbara could buy eggs.

In fact, they were docked pretty far away from the nearest K-Mart or Wal-Mart or anything of the sort! Living on a missionary's income didn't leave a whole lot of extra money for taking trips to go shopping to buy birthday presents, either. So, usually there were no presents—just a special dinner or a cake. Virgil wanted a chocolate cake for his birthday, and it looked like he wouldn't be getting it.

Barbara looked at him and suggested, "If you want a chocolate cake, you will have to ask the Lord to send us an egg."

So, when Virgil climbed the ladder and headed to bed that night, that's just what he did. In his childish innocence, he had no doubt that God would send him an egg. "Dear God, Mom needs an egg because I want her to bake me a chocolate cake for my birthday," he told God matter-of-factly, and added his request for God to please send one. He prayed for his mom and dad and for all the people in the churches his dad had started, and then he went to sleep with a smile on his face. Tomorrow was his birthday. He was going to get a chocolate cake!

· · · · ·

The duck wasn't sure, but for some reason, her roost seemed uncomfortable tonight. She fussed with the twigs under her bottom for a bit and then finally decided to go out for a midnight fly. Maybe that would help her sleep?

· · · · ·

About 5:30 in the morning, just as the sun was peeping its head out over the horizon on August 9, 1974, Elam got out of bed, grabbed a towel, and headed for the deck of the houseboat which had now been his home for two years. Growing up on the farm, Elam had always enjoyed the early morning. Here in the jungle, living right on the river, he especially enjoyed the early mornings. He would awaken each morning to the sounds of parrots screeching and howler monkeys hollering just as the sun was lending a warm red glow to the sky. The river water would glow a warm golden color, and the air was still cool from the night. It was the best time of the day!

Elam stood on the deck and tossed the towel over the railing. He looked out over the tranquil water of the river and could see a turtle silently swimming by. There was a little mist rising off of the water. "Thank you, God, for all your blessings!" he said. "Thank you for another day that you have made!" He turned to head toward the end of the edge of the deck to dive in for his morning bath when something stopped him in his tracks.

Virgil groaned a little and opened his eyes. His dad had awakened him many times when he'd overslept in the morning, but the look on his dad's face right then didn't look like his "get up, you've overslept" face.

"What is it?" Virgil sat up still feeling a bit fuzzy.

"Virgil, did you pray for an egg last night?"

It took a few seconds to process the question. "Yeah, Dad, I did."

Elam's heart warmed intensely, and his face shone with the biggest smile as he lifted his hand up toward Virgil's face. "Look what God brought you." There in his hand was one white duck egg. "I found it just lying out there on the deck just now when I went out to take my bath."

Virgil's eyes focused on his birthday present direct from God. "Yeah! Now mom can make me my cake!" Virgil said, as he bounced out of bed.

What a happy birthday. To a seven-year-old boy, it was a no-brainer. Virgil needed an egg, God can do all things, and getting an egg is pretty simple. Virgil asked for an egg, so of course he got an egg. But Elam knew what had just happened was a miracle.

God tells us that we can "move mountains" with our prayers, but often people are afraid to pray or they just don't because they don't think it's something God would care about. But if God cares about what flavor of cake a little boy gets for his birthday, how much more does He care about the really important things in life? This was a lesson that Virgil would really take to heart as he got older, and one that the whole family was going to need to remember as long as they lived in the jungle in the middle of Guatemala's civil war.

· · · · ·

"Amen!" Barbara said as she finished thanking God for their lunch, and they all really meant it. It wasn't like the standard saying grace or blessing the food, it was like for-real thanking God. The whole family dug into the food on their plates, and no one complained that this was the seventh day in a row that they'd eaten the same thing. Up until this week they had always called them "catfish," but now they knew they were actually manna.

Elam had been gone to the States on a quick and unexpected trip and had been gone a little longer than planned. Somehow the family had managed to run out of food. The day that she realized that soon all they would have was white rice to eat three meals a day, Barbara had prayed and knew God would provide. She just wasn't sure how.

The next morning when the boys were out taking their morning baths in the river, Miguel was in the inner tube pulling himself along with the fishing line that was strung across the river from one side to the other. At this time of the year it was just lying there on the bottom of the river with no bait. He felt something wiggling and pulling on the line, and his eyes got big. "Hey, Virgil! I think there's something big on the line!"

When they pulled it in, it was a huge catfish.

The next morning there was another catfish on the unbaited line. They then caught some minnows and started baiting the line, and every morning there was a huge fish waiting on the line for them until Elam finally returned. Manna.

· · · · ·

It wasn't long after that that Virgil began to have headaches and stomach pains, and he gained a lot of weight even though he had no appetite. At first he seemed to just be gaining some weight, but then all of a sudden he swelled up overnight. Over the next four days or so not only did he not want to eat banana soup, he didn't want to eat anything.

They decided to take him out to see the same doctor who had delivered Anita. Dr. Baldison wanted Virgil to stay for testing and treatment but didn't have his own clinic where he could intern patients, so they stayed at a hotel and went in to the office every day. For several days Virgil got three injections and some pills, which he was barely able to keep down as he had gotten to the point he vomited up absolutely everything that he ate or drank. He was not having a good time. Finally, the doctor decided that Virgil needed to go to Guatemala City to see a kidney specialist.

"It's my opinion just based on my observations that your son has a form of nephritis that's commonly called Bright's Disease," he said, pronouncing the last two English words with a thick Spanish accent.

"OK," Elam was calm. "What does that mean?"

"Well, there are various forms of it, but it basically means that your son's kidneys have stopped functioning. Now, depending on the severity of his case, that can be temporary and he can either get better on his own over the course of several months or it could progress to complete kidney failure and in that case he would have to have a transplant or else…" the doctor paused, catching himself when he almost said the "die" word.

"Or else he could die?" Barbara finished his sentence.

"Yes," the doctor said apologetically, "but he really needs to see a kidney specialist and have the proper tests done in order to make that diagnosis."

Barbara was not naïve. She knew that the doctor knew what he was talking about. But she had seen God bring her baby daughter back to life, and she knew that Virgil's life was in His hands as well.

Elam and Barbara left the doctor's office and took off on the twenty-four-hour journey on the dirt road through the mountains that led to Guatemala City. They admitted Virgil right away at the Methodist Hospital.

Back in those days, parents were not welcome to stay 24/7 with their children in the hospital. If you weren't a patient, you had to stick to the hospital's visiting hours, so each night Virgil was left at the hospital alone.

For two nights, Virgil felt so sick he was scared. He just cried and cried. The nurses, who perhaps had failed "Compassion 101" in nursing school, were tired of all the noise and scolded him. He looked out of the window in his room and thought to himself, "The next time the nurse comes in to change my IV bag and she unhooks me, I'll just take a run for the window." He didn't know where he'd go from there, and he was afraid that his dad would be mad, so he gave the idea up. All he knew was that this was just no fun at all. He was lying in a hospital bed, still getting three shots a day in his hiney, which was surely as perforated as a spaghetti strainer by now, hooked up to two uncomfortable IV tubes, and although his swelling had gone down he was still unable to eat anything without vomiting it back up. He felt just awful. What he really wanted to be doing was playing in the river with Miguel back home. It seemed to him like forever since he'd gotten to swim in the river.

The second day the test results were in which confirmed what Dr. Baldison had suspected: Virgil had nephritis. They told Elam and Barbara that Virgil would need three to four months of bed rest and weekly penicillin injections for up to four years. Poor Virgil was released from his bed and IV tubes and left for home.

Over the course of the next two days, however, Virgil still seemed to show no signs of improvement and lost eight pounds! Now rather than retaining too much fluid he was dehydrating right before their eyes! After all the shots and all the treatment he'd been having they felt desperate and made a phone call to the States.

The public phones were extremely expensive and complicated. In order to make a call they had to go to the main telephone company office, give the attendant the number they wanted to call and the name of the person they were calling and pay for the time they wanted. Then they took a seat and waited until their names were called. They splurged on a whole three-minute call to Barbara's mom and took a seat to wait. After a few minutes their name was called, and they went to the booth where Anna was already waiting on the line.

Elam picked up the phone. "Mom?" was all he could get out, and he broke down and started crying and handed the phone to Barbara.

"Hello! Mom!" Barbara said.

"Hello! Is everything alright down there?" Anna did not like the sound of Elam's voice a moment ago. What was wrong?

"Mom, we only have a few minutes, so listen carefully!" Barbara then told her as much of the story as she could in the remaining two-and-a-half minutes she had.

"Alright, I will call the churches! We will be praying!" Anna promised, and then the line went dead. Time was up.

That evening, Virgil started to perk up. "Mom," he said in a pitiful voice, "I'm hungry." He hadn't said that for almost two weeks now!

"What do you want to eat?" Barbara smiled down at him.

He thought seriously about it for a second, and seriously, just a second: "I want a Big Mac and a chocolate milk shake."

Elam and Barbara just looked at each other and stifled a laugh. "Honey, you can't eat that. It's been so long since you ate anything if you eat that it will just make you get sick and throw up," Barbara said apologetically.

"And besides, food like that can kill perfectly healthy people!" Elam thought to himself.

"Please?" his eyes seemed to say.

Elam crouched down to Virgil's height. "Are you sure that's what you want to eat?"

Virgil's eyes brightened then. "Yes!"

Elam stood up and looked at Barbara. "Alrighty, then, McDonald's it is!"

• • • • •

Elam just sat there across from Virgil watching him suck the last few drops of his chocolate shake down, delighting in the loud slurping sounds that said the shake had been completely consumed and had not come back up. The kid was not getting sick. He looked across the table at Barbara and smiled and shook his head. Anita's birth. The egg. Now this. He thought watching God do things in other people's lives was one thing, but when He would reach down right into your own family and do things it had a way of really building your faith.

Once they got home to the houseboat the next day, they began their doctor-prescribed regimen of bed rest. They had stocked up with some toys and coloring books, but Virgil was not cooperating at all. Instead of coloring he watched out the window and begged and begged to go out and play in the river with Miguel. They tried to explain to him that he was still sick and that the doctor had said he needed to rest, but Virgil disagreed.

"But God healed me! I'm not sick anymore!" Virgil insisted.

After a few days of a very persistent little boy insisting that God had healed him, they finally let him out to play. And he was just fine. His appetite was back to normal, and he showed no signs of having been sick at all. Four months of bed rest and four years of penicillin shots didn't seem to be necessary at all. Like Virgil said, God had healed him.

Chapter 15

Houseboat Explosion

Therefore they said to Him, "What shall we do, so that we may
work the works of God?" Jesus answered and said to them,
"This is the work of God, that you believe in Him whom
He has sent." *John 6:28-29*

"Watch it!" Elam smiled at his wife, "You could hurt someone with that thing!"

"Well!" Barbara laughed as she squeezed her nine-month-pregnant belly past her husband to get on the houseboat.

It was March of 1975, three years after their arrival in Guatemala. Barbara was just shy of her due date for their fifth child, so it was time to get going to the hospital in Sayaxché. The whole family was going along on this adventure, of course.

Butch and Diane Coleman, long-term missionaries who had come to help work with the village churches for a few years, would be going along on this trip also. They had been staying at La Anchura for a while but would be moving to Sayaxché into a house-trailer they had set up there that had been donated by a good friend in the States named Dallas Darling.

It was a beautiful morning. Everyone was excited about the arrival of the new baby, and riding in a boat along the Passion River is a very enjoyable thing. Even on the hottest day the breeze feels cool, and the steady hum of the motor is relaxing. Really it is something everyone should have the pleasure of experiencing at least once.

The children always enjoyed coming home at night from church in the speedboat. Once the hot tropical sun was down, being on the river actually felt cold, so the children would cuddle up at the bottom of the boat away from the wind. They would pull a blanket or a sheet of plastic over top of them to keep the wind off them and then usually would fall asleep.

On today's trip in the houseboat everything was going well, and there was no reason to expect anything but smooth sailing all the way to Sayax-ché…except that this was Guatemala. About fifteen miles up the river, the motor started sputtering.

When Elam noticed that the motor was having some trouble, he quickly pulled the houseboat to the water's edge and anchored to be able to check things out. Then the motor died completely.

"Oh well, guess we'll stop here for a while!" Barbara laughed. By now she was used to life in the jungle. In her few years here, there were two things Barbara had learned to count on. One was that unexpected things happened all the time. Two was that God was always there to help. So this was no surprise, and it was not a worry.

Elam tied up to a tree and got out his tools, and set them out on top of the motor's hatch. All the while he did this, he forgot to turn off the master switch to the motor. That meant that for the five minutes he was preparing to work on the motor, the gas pump had still been pumping gas into the covered motor area, which was still hot. He knew better, but he just didn't think of it. When he went to open the motor hatch, he stepped on it; and a second later it exploded.

Barbara's smile turned into a frightened scream as tools went flying everywhere. Elam was thrown several feet, and flames shot up all around him. Even in all the confusion he knew he had to get the fire out before it reached the gas tank. He found the fire extinguisher and put the flames out. Then he sat down almost in a daze.

"I can't believe that just happened," he said as he looked across the deck of the boat. There above the opposite hatch, hanging onto the second floor ladder, was Virgil. He had been sitting on the hatch but had just gone up to the second floor where the rest of the kids were to get something and was on his way back down when the explosion happened. The hatch that Virgil had been sitting on just moments before had been torn off its hinges and thrown upside down. For at least the second time that Elam knew of, he'd been given Virgil back from death. For a few minutes everyone was shocked into silence.

"Hon, are you alright?" Elam finally asked his pregnant wife, who'd been sitting only a few feet away from him when it happened.

"Yeah, I'm fine," she said, looking him over.

She was alright, but she could see that he was not. He had burns on his hands and arms, and one of his legs had what turned out to be second-degree burns. He also had first- and second-degree burns on his face.

The boat was definitely not going anywhere now. Whatever had been the problem that Elam might have fixed before was nothing compared to the damage that was now waiting for repairs. The impact of the explosion blew out all four back doors, and most of the screens throughout the boat went blasting out into the river. Elam looked over his tools and noticed that many of them had apparently been thrown into the river. "Oh no! Tell me the chainsaw is on the deck of the boat here somewhere?"

Everyone looked around the deck for a minute. Barbara made a face that said, "Sorry. It's gone."

The new chainsaw had just been brought down from the States. Later, Elam spent two days at that spot diving for that chainsaw, trying to retrieve it, but it was just gone!

There were no cell phones at this time and no nearby homes with phones to use to call for help. They had no other choice now but to dock here for the night and wait for a boat to pass by. Fortunately for them, since there were no roads in this part of the world, the river was the main highway. Cargo and passenger boats traveled up and down the river all the time. There was bound to be a boat coming by within a day or so, but there was no telling how long of a wait they had ahead of them. They did what they could to prepare some food for dinner and went to bed. A trip that started off as a relaxed ride to the hospital for Barbara was now a trip to get help for Elam.

Almost twenty-four hours passed by as they waited and waited by the river's edge in the middle of the Guatemalan rainforest, with nothing but the sounds of screeching parrots, howling monkeys, and the occasional distant gunfire to entertain them. Finally, a small boat came by, and they flagged it down. The people agreed to take Elam with them to the hospital. The rest of the family waited for a larger boat. The Chicsoy Oil Company barge usually came by every other day, and it did come. They were more than happy to give the stranded houseboat and its passengers a tug the whole way to Sayaxché.

· · · · ·

Four days after the explosion, Barbara sat beside Elam on the houseboat, docked in Sayaxché, and fed him oatmeal. His hands and much of his face were wrapped up like a mummy, and he was pretty helpless. His wife was about to have a baby, and he had groups of volunteers scheduled to come in the upcoming months to help with the construction on the property at La Anchura and do ministry projects in the villages. He needed his body to be in working order to take care of all these things!

Thoughts raced though Elam's mind about the explosion: "Why didn't God protect me? Or was this an attack of satan?"

He thought about the fact that they had just entered a world where God's Word wasn't preached in most of the communities. Up until now, satan had had full reign of all these villages. It could have been an attack. But then the obvious conclusion to that would follow: "I can't blame satan, because I was the one who didn't turn off the switch; it was *my* mistake! *The devil didn't make me do it!*"

Elam had already seen God do amazing things. There were so many other times that bad things had almost happened to them but hadn't—harder things than this, such as bringing Anita back from the dead and curing Virgil! This would have been so much easier to prevent! Why hadn't God stepped in this time? He didn't like to think that he was doubting God, but he just couldn't help but keep wondering why God had allowed this to happen when it was totally in the way of him serving God like he had planned. He had so much to do! God knew he was busy! The sun was coming up and going down every day, and Elam was not able to do any work in between! Why had He allowed this to happen?

Barbara winced, and he caught it. "Are you having contractions?"

"Well, yes, I think I am. But the pains aren't very bad yet; don't worry about it." She smiled and offered him something to drink. She was never worried about herself.

Finally, Barbara did what most pregnant ladies do and decided that at 1 a.m. it was time to go to the hospital. The houseboat was docked on the opposite side of the river, so Butch offered to drive them across in the small runabout boat. The three of them reached the hospital side of the river. Barbara was first to step out of the boat onto the muddy shore. She turned around and reached out her hand to help Elam out of the boat. She could walk better than he could. Butch almost had to laugh.

They walked the few blocks along the dirt streets to the hospital. Elam, noticing that Barbara didn't seem to be in too much pain, told Butch he might as well go on back to the boat because this would probably take till morning. Fifteen minutes later, just shortly after they had arrived at the hospital, Elam and Barbara's second baby born in Guatemala as both a Guatemalan and U.S. citizen, Lisa Reina, was brought safely into the world with no problems.

· · · · ·

The next day, Barbara and the new baby were home safe and sound. Elam knew he should be happy that everything was OK, but he was still not at peace with what had happened. He lay in bed and wondered why God had allowed the explosion to happen. He had so many things to do, so many plans. All he could do was lie there, helpless, and wait until he was healed. He couldn't help Barbara out with the new baby, and he couldn't even hold the baby, for that matter. Sweet little Lisa was so precious, and he couldn't even hold her! He was frustrated.

Elam got out of bed and turned on a light. He started to read in his Bible. "And we know that God causes all things to work together for good to those who love God, to those who are called according to His purpose" (Romans 8:28).

Elam thought about that verse. It was a favorite of most Christians because it gives hope in any situation; it means that no matter what happens, no matter how bad a situation gets, God is a master at working it for good. Still, why hadn't God just skipped the part of having to work this mess for good by simply preventing it from happening in the first place? What about verses like, "When you pass through the waters, I will be with you; and through the rivers, they will not overflow you. When you walk through the fire, you will not be scorched, nor will the flame burn you. For I am the Lord your God" (Isaiah 43:2-3)?

Where had God been? It all just seemed like such a stupid waste of time. In their marriage vows, Barbara and Elam had pledged to have no goal but to do the work of God and His will for them. Elam thought about that. "How can I do that in this situation?"

And, as he lay there in bed, finally the answer came as though Jesus were speaking to him, "This is the work of God, that you believe in Him whom He has sent" (John 6:29).

Then, Elam's whole outlook changed. He realized that he had gotten wrapped up in doing things for God rather than just being wrapped up in Him. The work of God was not the *things* he did for God, it is just knowing Him, believing Him without question or protest. Like Mary and Martha, he needed to be able to sit still and realize that doing all the work is not the better thing.

For Elam, a man who never stopped, to be forced to lie around and do nothing while his body healed seemed so impractical, but he had heard God. And he believed Him. The next morning he felt refreshed, and even smiled when he tried patting little Lisa on the head with one of his bandaged hands.

· · · · ·

"You put what on it?" the doctor asked, marveling over the fact that Elam's burns were almost completely healed. After his release from the hospital, Elam was supposed to return every day for the nurse to scrub his burns clean and dress them. Only two days of that and he'd had enough. On the third morning, he asked Barbara for a big pan. He put creolin in the water and soaked his arms for about an hour. Then he used the blunt end of a butter knife and slowly rubbed it up and down his arm to clean off the dead skin. Each day, he would return to the hospital and show them that he was already all cleaned up, and they would just check him and send him on his way back home. But they just couldn't understand what in the world he was doing to get his burns so clean.

"Creolin!" the doctor thought. "That's for cows?"

"Yeah, we always used it back on the farm for our animals, and we also used it for ourselves when we had skin infections. I just felt like I was supposed to use it," Elam smiled. "Stinks, but it works."

"I guess it sure does." The doctor was amazed. He'd never seen such a fast recovery from burns before in his entire career.

· · · · ·

A month later, Elam, Barbara, and baby Lisa sat alone on the deck of the completely rebuilt houseboat and enjoyed the stillness of the jungle around them after a long day. God was so good. Not too many days after the explosion, they had made contact on the ham radio with a good friend in McAllen, Texas. Bill Leys had just bought a new airplane, so he and two of his buddies, Paul Johnson and Bruce Wilkins, hopped onto that plane and headed for Guatemala. They had stayed for two weeks and very joyfully fixed up the damaged boat. They made it good as new. It was incredible.

As Elam considered all that had happened in these first years in Guatemala, all the people they had already helped, all the friends they had made, and all the times they had seen God do really cool things, he knew that definitely the safest and most fun place in the whole world to be was in the center of God's will.

Chapter 16

Like a Christmas Tree

Trust in the Lord with all your heart and do not lean
on your own understanding. *Proverbs 3:5*

The boat driver thought he sensed some rustling in the bushes ahead. Maybe it was an animal? Maybe it was a guerrilla? He kept an eye on it and tried to steer clear of whatever it was. The river was low, and the deepest part of the river took him about twenty feet away from the river's edge just at the spot where he'd seen the weeds moving. He steered the boat where he needed to go and waited to see what might pop out.

Even then, even though he was prepared for *something* to appear, when the creatures suddenly appeared and ran toward the boat, he still jumped! One older lady and her sister who were seated toward the front of the boat nearly fell over backwards, and the rest of the passengers had a moment where their eyes popped out of their heads and their hearts skipped a beat. One lady who was about eight months pregnant even felt a contraction when she saw them. Then, when they all had a chance to really see what the creatures were, they almost died—from laughter.

There, on the shore of the river, hollering and jumping around like crazy people, were three little white boys totally coated head to toe in mud. They had made white streaks on their chests and faces and were jumping around and making all kinds of noise.

"We scared them!" Virgil giggled as they all dove back to their hiding place in the mud hole.

Miguel was laughing hysterically.

"That one lady looked like she was going to fall out of the boat!" Andy Petersheim Jr. rolled on the ground.

"Did they see my tail?" Virgil asked, twisting around to show the vine he had stuck in the back of his pants.

"I don't know, but they sure were scared, weren't they?" Andy agreed.

"They don't even want to come past here again!" Miguel snarled again like he had when the boat had passed, and the boys cracked up again.

The boys were wild cats, you see, and felt sure that their disguises were perfect. Surely, no one could tell that it was the three ornery gringos that lived at La Anchura playing in the mud hole. No, the people in the boat all thought that they were some strange wild cats from who knows where. Boys.

• • • • •

Barbara pulled up another bucket of water from the river and dumped it into her little washing machine on the deck of the boat. "Do I ever worry about the children? Well, honestly I don't worry about them anymore. I started to, but I finally had to just put them in God's hands!" It was funny that she and Betty Petersheim had gotten into this conversation while she was doing laundry.

She continued, "One day, not too long after we'd been living on the boat, Miguel had casually snuck over and gotten a cup of soap out my bucket of laundry soap and then sprinkled it all over the deck of the boat. The kids had a good time for a while, playing on the slippery deck, sliding to the end, and grabbing the rail at the last minute. But, see, then Miguel decided to take it a step further, and when he reached the end of the deck, he "accidentally on purpose" slipped and *splash* went right into the river."

Betty Petersheim's eyebrows went up. She and her husband Andy Petersheim Sr., and their two children, also from Pennsylvania, had come to Guatemala to serve as missionaries along with Elam and Barbara. Their house would be the first house completed on the property at La Anchura. In the meantime, they had been living with the family on the houseboat, and she understood all about worrying that the children might fall in the water and drown somehow.

"I see the boys playing for hours and hours in the water, and I can see that they're good swimmers, and it seems like Andy Jr. and Rosa have gotten the hang of it, too, so in some ways I don't worry about them that way. Still, it seems like whenever you hear of people drowning, it's usually people who *do* know how to swim, not people who don't!" Betty had done a pretty good job of adapting to life on the houseboat, but it had taken a little getting used to.

Barbara continued, "I know what you mean, and like I said in the beginning I did worry a little, but I knew that I couldn't watch the children all the time. I believe the Lord is the one who brought us here, and He *is* able to watch them all the time, so that day I gathered the children together and just prayed, 'Lord, you brought us here to Guatemala. I can't watch them every second and keep them safe, so I place them into hands that can: Yours. Please, keep my children safe!'"

"And, ever since then, how have you felt?" Betty asked, noticing three muddy boys hopping around near a boat off in the distance by the river's edge.

"After that, I never worried even a little bit." She smiled broadly, and then also took notice of the boys ducking into the weeds. As the passing boat neared the houseboat, they could hear the roaring of laughter.

· · · · ·

A small generator made a noisy rumble as it produced the electricity needed to operate the new radial saw that had been donated to the mission. Elam looked at the pile of 2x4s and 4x8s they'd managed to cut with it. "This is awesome. We'll have your house done in no time with this!"

"Can't we just call the lumber yard and have some delivered this afternoon instead of doing all this work?" Andy Petersheim Sr. teased.

"Yeah, right! We could send for a pizza while we're at it, too."

"Ooh, pizza. Haven't had that for a while, have we?" Andy said.

They joked, but they were very thankful for the newly donated piece of machinery that had made life a lot easier. Making a 2x4 yourself started with going out into the jungle, walking around while a fog of mosquitoes shadowed your every move, and finding a suitable tree. Once the tree was chosen, then it needed to be cut down, and then into more manageable pieces. Then the pieces needed to be sawn into the sizes of lumber that you needed. Before the days of the radial saw that meant spending hour after hour cutting and cutting while thousands of mosquitoes swarmed around and the merciless sun pumped out its intense heat. Then all the lumber would need to be hauled out of the jungle and to your home. It was a long, hard process.

The machines and equipment people from the States donated to the mission made life so much easier that it was hardly possible to express in a thank you letter. Machinery to clear the property would be a little harder to come by, as what they really needed was a bulldozer. It would be many years until one of those would ever find its way to the property. Until then, even with Elam and the boys working six days a week clearing the jungle away, they had so much yet to do.

Elam decided that it was within their budget to hire some local guys to help. Hiring some local help would get the land cleared faster and also give them a practical way of getting involved with the local community. They could provide some men with jobs and get a chance to work alongside their neighbors and get to know them better.

It wasn't hard to find men eager to work. Elam and the boys would take their boat to Mario Mendez early Monday morning, and as many as thirteen men would come to work all week, chopping the jungle with their machetes to clear the land for buildings and a future airstrip.

Elam was always working either with Andy on their house, or with the men who were clearing the land. He thought he was just enjoying life and having fun building his ministry, but he didn't realize exactly what he was building until later. The local people were poor Guatemalan people, but they were people just like any people anywhere. They were full of preconceived notions and all had their own ideas about gringos and what they were like. In their culture, all Americans were considered rich, and rich guys didn't work hard; they paid their workers to do it. Just the fact that Elam was out there working as hard as and sometimes harder than they were spoke more to them than he would realize for many years. It eventually made everything he had to say to them about God that much more believable, because they knew that he was not so different from them.

· · · · ·

By June of 1975, Elam and Barbara's ministry had really taken root. They now had many acres of land cleared on their property, and the first building on the property, the Petersheims' home, was complete. Relations with the villages were going great, and there were many churches already planted and growing. There were new believers baptized almost every week and couples having their marriages legalized every week as well. They also had many people from the States standing behind them in prayer, with finances or equipment, and in service, coming to help on short-term missions trips. They had several missionary couples and other people committed to coming and staying for years.

All of the children were happy and healthy. Little Lisa was holding her head up and smiling and cooing at people. Barbara was feeling back to normal, and Elam's burns were completely healed. Groups were scheduled to come work on a guesthouse so that as the work progressed the workers and visiting missionary groups could be better cared for. As it was now, everyone slept in tents on the ground, so a guesthouse was definitely needed even before they would build a house for themselves.

It was the end of the dry season, which lasts from about February to June. During that time it is not unusual for it to rain only once a month, so everything was brutally dry. The local farming technique for clearing a field was to chop all the weeds by hand with a machete. Hack after hack in the hot sun, acre after acre. Then, taking advantage of the dryness of the dry season, the hacked-down weeds were then burned. It worked nicely, and the burning actually gave nutrients to the soil.

Andy was excited to start working with the recently donated roto-tiller, as he was getting a field cleared to plant their own garden. Then, like the locals did, he burned it off. He watched it for a few days, and once he felt the fires were all out he and Betty and the kids piled into their boat and headed to Sayaxché on a two-week trip to pick up cement and other supplies for the next building team that was coming.

Elam went out with another visiting missionary, Dwayne, to check on the field while Barbara and Dwayne's wife Nancy took a walk. It was a hot day, but there was a bit of a breeze. Normally a breeze is a blessing on a hot day, but not when there are hot embers still lingering in a burnt-off field!

"Looks like the fire spread under the grass over here," Dwayne said, noticing a telltale trail of black in the underbrush.

"Yeah, that's what it looks like." Elam followed the trail as it went over a fallen tree and out into another large open area of tall grasses.

"Maybe we should keep an eye on this for a while?" Dwayne suggested.

Elam nodded in agreement. "I'll go check to see how close that fire is to the pig corral." He started off to go see.

Just then, the alarm went off. It was Barbara. "Fire! Fire!" she was screaming. The men both turned toward the sound, and there in the distance they could see the tip of the Petersheims' thatched roof smoldering.

Everyone ran toward the house as fast as they could. If you have ever burnt a Christmas tree after Christmas was over, you'll know what it looks like when flame hits a thatched roof. It just burns, and fast. So, although there was just the slightest flame on the roof and they responded immediately, it was futile. Barbara and Nancy moved as fast as they could to get things out of the house. Part of the house also served as a storage area for Elam and Barbara as there was such limited space on the houseboat. All of the things they had accumulated since getting married were in that house, as well as tape players and cassettes and other ministry items. Rather than saying that nothing happens fast in Guatemala, it should be said that the only thing that happens fast in Guatemala is the burning of a thatched roof. Within five minutes, the house was gone.

Once this house had been finished not too long before, the Petersheims had brought everything they owned to Guatemala. Now in the grass in front of what had been their house were their clothes, some papers, the washer, a power saw, and one of their beds.

The four of them stood there as the children all came running out to see what had just happened. They all just stood there silently taking it in for a minute. While the locals were living in little stick huts with dirt floors, the Petersheims had been living in luxury! Their little thatched-roof house had had wood-sided walls, a few partitions in it, a nice plywood floor, and screens in the windows. They had even had their own outhouse with a door on it and everything! Now, that fast it was just gone. Only the foundation remained.

"Well, now what?" Dwayne said.

Elam knew that, though this was a setback and a sad thing, what really mattered had not been touched by the flames. "Well, we press forward toward the mark for the prize of the high calling of God in Christ Jesus!"

Barbara smiled in agreement. "We build another house!"

Already Elam's mind was working on how to fix this problem and how they would build a new house for the Petersheims. This was just a little bump in the road, not a roadblock. Their hope and their reason for being in Guatemala would not be affected by bad times.

If satan dared to challenge God about Elam and Barbara as he had done with Job, he would soon see that the positive attitude they had didn't only apply when it was someone else's home that was burning here at La Anchura: it would be their attitude no matter what they lost or how.

Chapter 17

Mapache's Earthquake

The sound of Your thunder was in the whirlwind;
the lightnings lit up the world;
the earth trembled and shook. *Psalm 77:18*

Mapache was a big male cebu—a cebu bull with sometimes nothing better to do in the middle of the night than to come and rub his head up against the side of the house. When he would do this it would seem like the whole house was shaking! And, right now, the whole house was shaking. Andy jumped up out of bed and headed for the front door of their new house, grabbing the broom on his way out the door and mumbling at the bull the whole way. He exited the house and looked for the source of the shaking to shoo it away with his broom, but Mapache was nowhere to be seen.

· · · · ·

The houseboat started banging up against the shore where it was tied in Sayaxché at its usual location on the riverside lot Elam had recently completed purchasing. It wasn't the normal rocking it would do when a boat would pass by, but an actual bumping. Elam peeked his head up and looked out the window, wondering if it had been a boat. Seeing no boat, he lay back down in bed and went back to sleep. Barbara also looked out the windows and saw Bill Leys, who was visiting the family again with a missions team, come out of the mobile home they had by the shore on the property.

"What was that?" Bill asked quietly across the yard through sleepy eyes.

Barbara just smiled and shrugged her shoulders and quietly said, "I don't know?"

Bill thought for a second, also seeing that there were no boats that had just gone by. "Must have been some mild tremor or something?"

"The whole trailer was shaking!" another of the missionaries said as he exited the trailer and stood outside on the lawn.

At first they all thought they had experienced a gentle earthquake. After the initial tremor, nothing seemed particularly out of the ordinary, so everyone went back to bed. But what they had been feeling had its epicenter over 100 miles away, and there it was far from gentle. As they settled back down peacefully into their beds that morning of February 4, 1976, the gentle rumble they had felt would enter the history books as one of the hugest natural disasters in the twentieth century. In those few minutes of rumbling, almost half of Guatemala City was gone. In the southern parts of the country, more than 23,000 people were dead. Over one million people who had gone to bed the night before just like any other night and had plans for the next day had had their lives completely turned upside down and were now homeless. Over 100 towns and villages were totally destroyed.

In the morning in Sayaxché, the news was all over town about what had happened in Guatemala City. So a few days after the quake, Elam headed into Guatemala City with Bill Leys and one of the other missionaries, Harley Fiddler. Plans for work at La Anchura would just have to go on hold. They went in to see just how bad it was and to see if the team of over twenty people would be able to get their flight back out to the U.S. on schedule. What they found was more shocking than they'd expected.

It wasn't just that there were cracks in the buildings or the occasional building crumbled; it was everywhere. Entire city blocks were just flattened! Everywhere they went they saw destruction. The worst part of all was the death that those collapsed buildings had caused. Maybe had this happened in the daytime while people were awake, they would have gotten to safety, but this happened at night while people were vulnerable. The missionaries met people who had lost all their children as they'd slept in their beds. Some children had lost their parents, and some families had perished entirely. Graveyards had been unearthed, and stray dogs were scavenging in the graves. Even more gruesome were the thousands of people buried and missing who were found not by rescue crews but by wild animals. It was so gruesome that the police began shooting any stray animal on sight.

Elam, Bill, and Harley arrived and met up with Tim Rovenstine, a missionary working through an organization called World MAP. "Welcome to my home," he smiled as he gestured toward what was left of the mission house. Half of it was completely collapsed, and a large concrete beam was lying in a bed.

"Who was sleeping there?" Bill asked with a terrible feeling in his gut.

"Howard and his wife were sleeping in that bed, but fortunately all the rumbling woke them up and they got out before it fell," Tim said.

Behind them in the street was a small tent-trailer. Every day Tim and his wife had been giving food out to whoever came and needed it. People would come running with a little cup just to get a small portion of food that day. Even sadder were the people who had to be turned away when the food ran out. One of the saddest things was the children who were alone in this. Their parents and families were gone, and now they were left to fend for themselves in the streets.

Elam had seen suffering since coming to Guatemala, but there was no comparison to what he saw around him. He ended up staying in Guatemala City for several weeks, helping to rescue people, clean up, and feed people.

Back at home the family waited, not knowing exactly when Elam would return. Virgil looked over at the calendar on the wall before he went to sleep and tried to think of how many days his dad had been gone by now. He thought about what he and Miguel had played today and then remembered watching Miguel as he had sat at breakfast this morning, uncomplainingly digging into his bowl of cold banana soup as though it weren't the grossest thing in the world. He shuddered thinking about Mom's trusty standby. It stretched far, was nutritious, and it was easy to get. Bananas, after all, grew like weeds everywhere in Guatemala. Virgil was certain that it wasn't an apple Eve had eaten, but a banana. He fell asleep with images of his siblings also digging into breakfast. "Just what is wrong with them all?" Virgil wondered and soon was asleep.

He awoke sometime in the middle of the night, his pre-sleep nightmare forgotten. Maybe it was his silent and sacrificial suffering at the breakfast table that had earned him this vision. As his eyes began to focus in the dark room, he could see that outside his window was an angel.

He sat straight up in bed with his heart racing. Looking out of the second-story window in his bedroom on the houseboat, he could see a tall white flowing robe of an angel just hovering there over the water. It was definitely too high up off the water for it to be anything else. He sprang from his bed and bolted down the ladder to his mom's bedroom and burst in. "Mom! There's an…" he stopped.

His mom was not alone in bed. Sleeping beside her was Dad. Dad had come home. Wow. Yeah! Then Virgil got a sneaking suspicion and quietly went to another window. He looked outside. There was the boat that his dad had used to get to the houseboat. For some reason, he'd tied a white sheet to the mast, maybe to be more visible in the darkness. There hanging from the mast of the little boat was the angel. Oops. Silently and extremely embarrassed, Virgil then tip-toed back to his room and to bed and never said a word to anyone.

• • • • •

It wasn't long until another trip to Guatemala City became necessary for Elam. The dreaded Paperwork Monster was calling his name, and whether he liked it or not he needed to make a trip to the city to take care of some things. He hated leaving his family and the ministry behind to go do paperwork, but nothing could be done by mail as in the States. The government didn't send you your car registration form to fill out, and you couldn't just write a check and mail it back and in a week, *viola!*, have your sticker to put on your plate for the year. No, everything back in those days was a hassle that had to be done in person in the correct office, and that could take days or even weeks for just one thing!

So when the calendar opened up and there were no groups of missionaries coming for at least a month, Elam left his family with the Petersheims and headed out on the long 200-mile, twenty-four-hour journey to Guatemala City.

He ran around from office to office doing paperwork on all sorts of things, and even visited the dreaded Finanzas building. (The author of this book dreams of being there someday when they have to demolish it, but that is another story entirely.) He visited with a few missionary friends, did a little shopping for their construction projects, bought some tractor parts from three different places, managed to actually find a small jar of peanut butter to surprise the kids with, and got a part for the houseboat's motor. All the while his mind was focused on getting back to the mission in Petén.

He ran into a lawyer friend of his who worked at the Presidential Palace and ended up getting together with him to do some translation work for him.

"I am so impressed that you would leave the comforts of your home in the United States to come to our country and help the people in the villages this way, especially out there in the Petén," his friend said as they finished up what they were doing.

Elam heard comments like that a lot from people in Guatemala City. The people in the Petén sometimes had reason to come to Guatemala City to do legal work and to shop for certain things, but not many people had any reason to go out to the Petén. Unless one had relatives out there to visit, the only other attractions were mosquitoes, heat, and civil war. Most everyone in Guatemala was afraid of the Petén. Not too many Guatemalan Christians would even consider going out there to help people, so for Elam to have come all the way from the United States was usually something that really impressed them.

"What do your children think about living in Guatemala instead of in the United States?" Elam's friend asked.

"Oh, the kids just have a blast out there," Elam smiled.

"Really?" His friend heard the word "blast" and thought of all the blasts he saw on the news that went on out there between the army and the guerrillas.

"My boys are always into something," Elam went on, and told him stories about the boys chopping the jungle with him, hunting with him, and swimming in the river. "One time," he told him, "Miguel got it into his head that he wanted to eat an orange, but of course the one he wanted was still way up high on the tree, so up he went. When he came back down, he came down faster than expected and instead of an orange he got a broken arm."

His friend laughed.

Elam thought he should stop with the stories about his kids, because all parents can be so proud of their own, but he also remembered the time that Miguel had gotten a hernia. "So there he was in the hospital overnight after having surgery, but instead of being sad about it he spent the night with the other hospitalized children shooting cockroaches off the walls with IV tubing."

"Cockroaches on the walls?" His friend had never been to a government hospital, but he had heard stories.

Elam laughed. "Sure, the cockroaches around here get sick, too, you know!"

His friend's brow furrowed for a minute. He thought maybe Elam didn't know what he'd said and had chosen the wrong Spanish words, but looking at his face he saw that he was kidding, and then he laughed.

"Yeah, Miguel is somethin' else. That boy has got such a curious mind! He's always taking his toys apart and trying to fix things that aren't even broken yet!" Elam thought he'd probably gone on about the children enough by now.

Elam's lawyer friend found him intriguing. As he listened to Elam talk, he realized that Elam actually seemed to be having fun living in the Petén, as though he liked it there—as though serving as a missionary was actually fun. That was something that had never occurred to him, and it stirred something inside him that had been gnawing at him for a long time.

He had always really liked Elam from the first time he'd met him, and it occurred to him that if anyone would be safe to talk to, it would be him. He had been a lawyer for years now, and he had learned by experience how important it was to be prepared before going in to court before the judge. He had a case that he was working on, basically his whole life, and he knew that someday he'd have to go before a very high court—the highest court—and he knew he wasn't prepared to go there.

"Elam," he began to speak and braced himself to hear a lot of religious stuff that he wouldn't understand, "I have some questions about God."

A lot of the Christians he'd encountered in his lifetime had been harsh and judgmental and had spoken in senseless riddles, using clichés that didn't mean anything to him. But there had been something so free in Elam's manner he felt he could trust him, and it turned out his instinct was right. Elam had been helping him with some translating work earlier, and now he was doing the same thing again as he explained to him things from God's Word that he'd never understood before. Something about Elam's explanation made God seem like a person, and not a Church or a set of rules or religion. Something about this conversation was making this lawyer finally feel safe to approach the bench and speak to the Judge himself.

"Let's pray!" Elam said. He put his hand on his friend's hand and began praying. At first the man braced himself for the usual yelling and crying that was so common in religious people's prayers, but instead Elam was talking to God using normal words in a normal tone of voice, as though God was a friend of his. Tears flowed from the lawyer's eyes as his heart was filled with hope, and at last filled with the love of Jesus. He knew now that when it was time to go before the final judgment seat of Christ, he was prepared!

Everyone, including missionaries, have their own idea of what a missionary is. Elam thought he was a missionary to the Petén, to the people in the villages, and that he'd left the ministry behind while he was here doing paperwork. But here he was ministering to an educated lawyer in the Presidential Palace in Guatemala City. His mission definitely wasn't a place, but a person, Jesus, and Jesus followed with him wherever he went.

Chapter 18

Jungle Doctor

And He called the twelve together, and gave them power
and authority over all the demons and to heal diseases. *Luke 9:1*

"How's that going?" Barbara asked as she walked in to where Elam was working. He was busy tonight typing up a newsletter.

When Elam would sit down to write his newsletters to his U.S. supporters, he felt frustrated by the restraint of space. There was always ten times more to write about than there was space, and there were so many little things that were hard to find a place for.

"It's coming along well, but, you know, I would love to be able to find a way to describe the look that that lady in La Bella had on her face after we asked her if we could help her somehow," Elam said.

Barbara knew what he was talking about. So often they had experiences with people that were deeply significant. They saw transformations in people's lives as they were touched by just the fact that Elam and Barbara would reach out and love them somehow, and it would change their lives forever, yet those incidents were so "without incident," you could say. So hard to describe in a newsletter.

"And I wish there were some way to make a verbal photo of our children's lives, so people could see how incredible their lives are." Elam sighed.

Many missionaries he had come in contact with over the years had urged him to send his children to school away from home in Guatemala City. Neither Elam nor Barbara felt that learning things from books away from their parents could even compare to all that they'd learned so far working alongside them.

In the beginning, Elam had been the obvious pastor of the twelve newly planted churches, so his family had been the obvious church ushers, choir, and everything else. Before the churches had buildings, Elam would preach from the deck of the houseboat, and the children would sing. The boys especially were a part of every step of the process of building a church from the first "Hi, how are ya?" in the village, to the finding and making of building materials, to the completion of a church building and the installation of the new church's own pastor. It was awesome.

"And, I feel like there is no way for me to describe the joy I have in baptizing so many new converts and performing marriage ceremonies. When I write about it, it seems so dry, you know? I mean, last month we baptized over two dozen new converts, and I performed a dozen marriage ceremonies. When I try to write about it, it just comes out as sort of a list of things, and it just isn't as passionate as I'd like it to be!"

Getting married legally was a big hassle, as the only place it could be done was at the municipal building, which for some people was a trip that took one or two days. Most people could not afford that trip or did not want to make that trip, so most people, even Christians, never actually got married. It was so common that when a couple told you they were married, you had to ask if they were legally married or not, because they did not make any distinction between a couple who were living together *as* a married couple or those who were *actually* married. Within the first year, Elam had managed to get licensed to perform marriages, and so often baptismal services for new believers were followed by wedding ceremonies for those same believers who'd now decided to legalize a relationship they were in.

When Elam had imagined what his life in Guatemala would be like, he had pictured himself with a small ministry in a small Indian village somewhere. He'd never imagined it being this big and so cool. This fun! This fruitful!

"You know, how do I describe in words what it looks like to see you getting out of bed every hour at night to feed a malnourished baby that was on death's doorstep when it arrived here, and how those babies change day after day until one day they finally look up at us and smile, and then we know they're going to be better!" he said.

So many people already had come to them with their children very close to death from malnourishment, and Barbara had committed the time round the clock to care for them. All of the children got involved with helping to care for these children, also, and sometimes they got very attached to them and even cried from joy and sadness when they went home.

Barbara smiled and sat down beside Elam, "Why don't you read me some of what you're writing?"

Pancho, their spider monkey, must have been helping with some of the newsletter layout, judging by the torn paper around Elam.

"I'm going to introduce this new phase we are entering into with the clinic," he said and began reading from his February 1978 newsletter: "We have not forgotten our main purpose of being here in the Guatemala jungle, and that of preaching Jesus Christ as the ultimate answer to every man's need. But we are overwhelmed as we see the physical needs among the people among us. We have been aware of many of the needs here in the jungle ever since we came, but until recently when we opened our hearts and doors to minister to the medical needs of these people, we have just begun to see the potential that lies within reach, by meeting the needs of the whole man."

Barbara smiled, thinking what an understatement it was to say that they had been overwhelmed by the needs they saw. "That about says it all!"

Elam took a pencil out of Pancho's hand just before it was turned into monkey chow. "And then I thought I would share a little about Julia…."

"Good idea." Barbara said.

Now, the story about Julia was definitely an incident that could be mentioned in a newsletter. Julia had arrived at La Anchura, unconscious in the bottom of a boat. She was seventeen years old and had given birth the night before to a tiny premature baby. Both mom and baby seemed to be recovering from the delivery just fine at home until later that night when Julia started having convulsions and passed out, and then her whole body began to swell. Her family was desperate; they didn't know what to do! So they put her in the boat and brought her to La Anchura, to the only people they thought might know what to do.

"What do we do?" Elam thought as he looked at the young girl lying on the bed in the house. "I've never seen anything like it!" He quickly got on the ham radio and radioed to a doctor in Guatemala City, who knew what it must be right away. "I believe she has eclampsia." Toxic shock.

"Should we send her to Sayaxché?" Elam asked. He was ready to run and get the boat ready as fast as the doctor would say go.

"No, she won't make it," was the doctor's reply.

She won't make it. Even before Elam had a chance to ask, "Then what?" the doctor told him, "I'll come to you if you can get a plane to fly me out there."

Elam put in a call on his ham radio to Don Donaldson, an American missionary pilot in Guatemala. He responded immediately.

"Now, Elam, there are some things I need you to do until I get there." The doctor then explained to him over the radio in the airplane what needed to be done to keep the girl alive the whole time he was in flight. Elam was going to have to do things he had never done before, but if he didn't at least try, the girl was going to die. One thing he had to do was insert a tube into her throat to help her breathe. It was hard, and his hands trembled a little, but he prayed the whole time and God got him through it. He got the tube into her lungs.

In what seemed like a very short time, eleven-year-old Virgil could hear the sound of the airplane approaching, and he raced to the window and then out the door to watch it come in and land. It was a beautiful sight. He knew someday he'd be flying an airplane. Someday he would be a jungle pilot, too.

In less than two hours after the girl's arrival at La Anchura, there was a doctor there taking care of her. After the doctor did some immediate emergency treatment, she was put in the airplane and flown back to Guatemala City. It was close, but she made it.

Since that time, two of the rooms in the guesthouse had been converted into a clinic. Someone had donated some suturing equipment to them in a little first-aid kit, and they had a few other things that had been donated to them. Now that the local people knew those doors were open, they had someone coming daily. Ladies came with their sick babies, and other ladies came in labor. Men came with machete cuts, and other people just came with aches and pains.

They gave out medicines and vitamins and did minor surgeries. People who had formerly been very against the family because of the gospel they were preaching, which was against their religion, started to warm up to them and then to Jesus. Later they began to show up at church.

Jesus said He hadn't come to heal the well but the sick, and often it was once He'd personally touched someone's life physically that they would turn and take time to listen to Him. Once He showed them with His actions that He cared for them, then they would listen to His words. Now, Elam was following in His footsteps, reaching out to people spiritually by helping them first physically. Not only was it productive, it was also pretty exciting most of the time! The door that had opened was obvious, and soon a foundation for a small twenty-five-by-sixty-foot clinic building was being dug.

Elam worked around La Anchura with the boys, and when someone would show up, he would put his doctor's coat over his work clothes and off he'd go. He'd pray first, and then using the knowledge he had from an EMT course he'd taken and the help of doctors in Guatemala City and the U.S., who he'd talk to over the ham radio, he would take care of them. Then the coat would come back off, and he'd be back out the door, chopping in the field or sawing planks or making concrete blocks. He was like the Energizer Bunny; he never stopped.

Elam continued reading to Barbara from the newsletter. "What a challenge and a thrill to see a dying child being nursed back to health, and then to sit down with the parents and instruct them in how to better care for their families' health, and to feel the love and appreciation that they show in return. What an open door to introduce Jesus Christ."

"I like it." Barbara always liked the newsletters that Elam wrote.

He was very good at it. They had gotten responses from lots of their readers about how much they enjoyed the newsletters they sent out, which Elam had titled, *Jungle Breezes*.

Now not only was Elam, an ex-Amish boy schooled to eighth grade, going up and down the river holding baptismal services, marriage ceremonies, and church services, but he was also a jungle doctor.

"Maybe you should also put in there about Pancho while you're telling them about the clinic work?" Barbara smiled.

Pancho heard his name and looked over at her for a second, then went back to nibbling on a pencil eraser. He was an energetic and curious spider monkey with a coatimundi for a best friend. They were a handful together and played something like tag together often.

On one occasion, Pancho and Chico were chasing after each other, and Pancho was tied to his rope. He'd been a naughty monkey that morning, so he was tied to keep him *out* of trouble. Well, one thing led to another, and Pancho went up through a hole they'd made in one of the thatched roofs on the property and then came back down through another hole and got hung up with his leash. Literally hung. By the time the kids found him, he wasn't so frisky. He was limp and not breathing. The kids panicked and ran to their hero to save their pet. Elam did the only thing that he thought he could do, gross as it could be, and he gave little Pancho CPR while the kids prayed and prayed for God to save him.

"I don't know how many people I want to tell I gave CPR to a monkey!" Elam laughed.

"But you saved him, didn't you, Daddy!" Jean had come walking into the room while they were talking and scooped up Pancho and hugged him. Her Daddy was definitely her hero.

· · · · ·

When the clinic became part of their lives, Elam and Barbara did what they could to include the kids in this part of the ministry as well. The children had always been a part of the spiritual side of the ministry in the churches, and now they would be part of this new service of New Life Missions. As they got older, often it would be the boys who would drive patients in the ambulance (speedboat) to the hospital in Sayaxché.

One night, being included in the clinic ministry meant the children had to wake up in the middle of the night to help pray for a patient.

"What time is it?" Jean asked, rubbing her eyes and shuffling into the room. Then, as her eyes adjusted to the light, she didn't really care what time it was anymore. There before the children was a very scary-looking lady.

"What's wrong with her, Dad?" Miguel asked.

None of them had ever seen anything like it, not even on TV! There on the bed in the room was a lady with wild hair. She was on her knees, swaying back and forth with a very odd look in her eyes.

Her name was Rosario. Her husband had just brought her in to the clinic around 2 a.m. because she was very sick, and he had become afraid she was going to die. When they had arrived at the clinic, she was acting very irrationally and was not easy to examine. Elam asked her husband

and the rest of her family who'd come along to leave them alone in the room, hoping she would then calm down. He and Barbara began to try to talk to her.

They had already learned that a lot of the ladies in the villages "died" when they were mad at someone. It was a game that they played for attention, and it definitely worked. Dozens of times a year, a group of people would rush a lady to the clinic, reporting how many times she'd died along the way. They would stand by anxiously as the lady would lie still with her eyes closed on the exam table. Usually sending the family away would bring the lady back to consciousness. Eventually, the use of strong smelling salts would provide the same miraculous recovery.

As childish as the behavior was, it was the only thing these ladies knew to do when they felt upset sometimes. Showing up like this at a normal hospital usually earned the ladies a stern scolding by the doctor, who did not have time for such nonsense. But for Elam and Barbara, although ladies performing like this in the middle of the night could be a bit of an irritation, it was always an opportunity to talk to them, to counsel them, and lead them to the only true source of peace in the midst of their storms: Jesus.

Elam and Barbara had both sensed when Rosario arrived that she was one of those ladies. She was probably just mad at her husband or someone in the family, so they sent the family out of the room so they could talk to her. She did settle down once her family left the room, and after talking to her a little while they asked her, "Would you like to pray with us?"

She nodded that she would. Elam began and told her to repeat after him. That was when he began to see that this lady was not the usual actress mad at her family but that there was something very seriously strange going on with her.

"We thank You for Your presence in our lives, Lord Jesus," Elam began.

Rosario repeated, "We thank You for Your presence in our lives, Looooo…rrrr…Llllooorrrrr…." She looked like she was going to vomit.

Elam and Barbara looked at each other, and their eyebrows rose.

Elam began again, "Jesus, we thank You…."

Rosario again tried to repeat, "Jeeeee…J…J…Jess…."

She couldn't say the words. She couldn't say the words for Jesus or God?!

144

In English, Elam spoke to Barbara, "I think she has a demon in her. Go get the kids to come pray with us."

Once Virgil's eyes were fully rubbed awake, they focused on the lady. From Virgil's small stature, this lady with the uncombed hair up on the bed seemed huge and really far out. All the children held out their hands toward her and started to pray as their dad went to work telling the demon to go away.

Then they all received a surprise, when, even before Elam could pray, the wild-looking woman began to speak. Rosario lived in a village that had no electricity. She had never watched TV or gone to the movies, so she had never seen anything like this on TV, yet she opened her mouth, and a very rough man's voice said, "I'm not coming out. I'm going to kill her!"

Then it was Elam's turn to speak. It wasn't anything wild or crazy like the movies portray, just a simple sentence spoken in a normal tone of voice without an echo or dramatic music in the background. "No, you're not going to kill her. In the name of the Lord Jesus, I command you to come out of her."

At that, Rosario flopped down onto the bed, exhausted, and she was free.

The kids went back to bed, excited that they'd actually helped their dad cast out a real live demon.

"*That* was cool!" Miguel said to his little brother.

Virgil smiled. "She was kind of like Jean in the morning, wasn't she?"

"Yeah, except that her voice is not that deep, usually," Miguel agreed.

Jean swatted at her little brothers, who scooted off out of her reach and ran back to their beds.

After the children headed off to bed, Barbara and Elam talked to Rosario some more and prayed with her, and she asked Jesus to come and fill the void inside her that that demon had hijacked. She gave her heart to Him.

Something struck Elam. "You have something to do with witchcraft in your house, don't you?" he said to her. Her village, Buena Fe (Good Faith) of all names, was saturated in witchcraft. Their greatest spiritual leader for many years had been their witchdoctor. He wasn't a witchdoctor like you see on TV, with the big wooden mask and the feathers around his ankles, jumping around a fire with a stick. He was just a regular-looking guy who happened to be very evil at heart. The people in the village, having no doctor or church or any other type of spiritual leader, went to him for everything. Often, things like this were the result.

Rosario looked at him surprised, put her head down, and didn't reply.

Something inside of Elam just told him this was true, and so he persisted, "Do you have something in your house that has to do with witchcraft?"

Three more times he asked her, and finally she raised her eyes to his and quietly said, "Yes."

Even this was not what one might imagine. It wasn't a hacked-off chicken's foot or a shrunken head or a vile of bat's blood. It was a ball of hair. A simple ball of hair. It wasn't what it actually was so much as what it was "spiritually." She had been told by the witchdoctor that every time she brushed her hair she was to take the hair out of the brush and keep it in a ball and never throw it away. She had been obedient to the witchdoctor and had kept this ball of hair in a box under her bed for years now. It was likely that someone had put a curse on her, and that was how she was unwittingly cooperating with them. When she went home, she got that box out from under her bed and burned it.

But there was still something else that had dug its claws into her through the ministering of the local witchdoctor. A year or so after her first late-night visit to the clinic, she returned in labor with a child. The cord prolapsed, or came out first. So, when the baby's head pressed tightly against the mother's pelvic bones to come out, the oxygen supply going through the cord was cut off and the baby was born dead. Rosario's response was one of sadness, but not surprise. This was the first baby she had ever gotten to full term after having three miscarriages, but she still hadn't expected this one to live.

The local witchdoctor had told Rosario that she would never have a live baby. The reason why was never told, but she had accepted this as her future. Elam and Barbara would not accept this, however, and told her that her next baby would indeed be born alive. The next time she got pregnant, she was to come to the clinic every month for checkups and stay as far away as possible from the witchdoctor, who also gave "prenatal exams."

In a few months she did get pregnant again. She did as she had been instructed and came monthly to the clinic. Elam and Barbara, the visiting nurse Janie, and whoever else was handy would pray with her and prayed *life* for that baby.

Nine months later, Barbara had that baby in her hands, crying up a beautiful storm, and was handing her to her mother, who could hardly believe it was true. Her baby had lived. Through love and prayer that baby had lived. The curse over that family was finally completely broken, and soon the whole family became Christians. (And about six more babies followed that first one!)

New Life Missions started out as a ministry to build churches. Now, it had new life of its own: New Life Clinic.

Chapter 19

Maria

"Whoever receives one child like this in My name receives Me;
and whoever receives Me does not receive Me,
but Him who sent Me." *Mark 9:37*

Back when they had lived in Salinas, they had always just taken her and left her out in the jungle for a few hours at times like this when she cried too much. Now that they were living in Pipiles, they just didn't know what else to do with her, so they would put her out behind the hut. They worried what the neighbors were thinking.

Her grandmother tossed her a tortilla, and Maria stretched out her arm to reach it. It had landed just on the edge of her little plastic mat she always sat on, and the chickens had seen it too and were running for it. She got it just in time and clutched the dry tidbit close to her chest as she ate it. A couple chickens came over and pecked around her foot, so she quickly covered up her legs with her skirt and tried to shoo them away.

· · · · ·

"I don't think he's going to like you butting in," the man said to his wife as he grabbed a fresh corn tortilla off the pile at the lunch table and rolled it up with a little pinch of salt and dipped it in his soup.

"Well, I have to do something!" the wife replied.

It had been only a few months now since the elderly couple and the little girl had moved into their village. Right away everyone saw that something was wrong with the little girl, but what they had come to realize was that it was probably the grandparents' fault. It was driving most of the ladies in the village just crazy seeing the little girl out there, day after day, beside the hut on that little mat of plastic crying for food. She had to be at least five or six years old, and couldn't even walk.

The wife worked up her courage and headed over to the neighbors' hut to ask them if she could take the little girl and take care of her.

· · · · ·

"It is our understanding that you were offered help by your neighbor and rejected it. Is that true?" the village leader asked the old man.

He put his head down. "Yes, that's true. But it is really none of her business."

"Well, it is now the business of the whole village, and that's why we've called this meeting," the village leader said sternly. He had been receiving complaints from everyone in the village for weeks now and had finally called a village meeting to take care of this problem once and for all. "We have an ultimatum for you," he continued. "You must either take the little girl to a clinic for help now, or we will take you to jail. It is your decision."

The old man thought for a second. "But I have no money to take her to a clinic."

While that was no good excuse, it was the truth. He didn't have any money. The whole village was very poor. During wartime, none of the villagers were prospering. Part of the guerrillas' strategy was to cripple the country financially to try to bring the government to its knees, but it was the poor people who were suffering the most.

If this was what was stopping him, they would get him some money. Everyone at the meeting took up a collection and came up with seven quetzales, the equivalent at that time to about seven dollars, and gave it to the old man. His excuse for not taking little Maria to a clinic was now gone, so he had no other choice but to take her to the nearest clinic, which was a three-and-a-half-hour paddle upriver away.

· · · · ·

A little dugout canoe being paddled by two men, one a very old man, came slowly upstream toward the clinic. Barbara was outside when they approached, and she met them at the river's edge.

"Buenas tardes!" (Good afternoon!) she greeted them with a smile, and then looked into the canoe. There between the two men a pitiful-looking little girl was lying, her legs covered in a blanket. "She's nothing but skin and bone," Barbara thought to herself.

She gently reached down into the boat and lifted the little girl out. As she carried her, something oozed onto her arm. "Ooh. I wonder what that is?" she thought as she headed to the exam table they had set up just outside the guesthouse.

Elam approached and put on his "doctor's coat."

"Buenas tardes," he said, holding out his hand as he greeted the two men and shook their hands. Then he turned to Barbara. "What do we have here?"

He looked over the sad little girl on the exam table. She looked to be about five years old, but when they weighed her she weighed only around thirteen pounds, the weight of a normal two- or three-month-old. They started working on her and could see that she was dehydrated and needed fluids, but because she was so dehydrated and thin, they couldn't even get an IV into her. So they did what they could to clean her up and found themselves wiping tears from their eyes as they worked.

"She is literally just flesh and bone—like a living skeleton." Elam was blown away by this.

Both of her legs and one of her feet had huge open sores on them that were just filled with infection. They stank very badly. The sore on her foot was so deep that her bone was practically exposed.

"Oh my goodness!" Barbara said and looked away. As Elam had been cleaning the sores on Maria's knee, the pressure had caused the sore on her foot to start to ooze.

Another lady was there watching while they worked on her. Horrified, she said, "We wouldn't even let this happen to a dog in our village." She finally had to walk away and cry.

It was clear that Maria would not be leaving anytime soon, so the two men in the dugout canoe left. The grandfather, instead of heading back to Pipiles, went to Las Cruces, found Maria's father, and told him what had happened. Maria's mom had died when she was still a baby, and her father just didn't feel like he could take care of her and all the other children by himself. He gave her to his parents to care for. For some reason, they either didn't know how or didn't want to take care of her, and here she was now, at age five, still unable to walk because of malnutrition and neglect.

The two men then headed to Sayaxché, where they found an attorney to write up an official letter giving Elam and Barbara total rights to do anything with Maria. The father went back home, and the grandfather returned the next day at La Anchura with the letter.

"It looks to me like the father is willing to totally relinquish all rights to Maria to us. That's strange!" Barbara said. "Well, what should we do?"

Elam and Barbara had already decided that there was no way they would give Maria back to the grandparents. But if the father didn't want her either, then what?

Elam looked at his wife and said in English, "Ignorance is bliss, is it? I would say this little girl would have something else to say about it." Elam had felt ever since coming to Guatemala that that colloquialism, "Ignorance is bliss" was straight from hell. Ignorance was not bliss, and when people lived in ignorance, innocent people suffered. God said that His people were destroyed for lack of knowledge. Destruction and bliss weren't two words that went together.

All around them every day the people in these villages suffered because of lack of knowledge. Because of ignorance, ladies fed their babies watered down soda or coffee in their bottles and then wondered why their children's hair was falling out and they were not growing and they were sick. Because of ignorance, so many families had had to bury children simply because they didn't know how to feed them or themselves.

Elam felt an anger building up inside of him, knowing that the devil came to kill, steal, and destroy and had been doing so too effectively here in this country. This had to stop! While Elam still felt his greatest mission here was building and supporting churches, this new branch of his ministry could not be ignored. Even their limited medical knowledge was enough already to begin saving lives. As the clinic was built, Elam began studying not only the Words of the Great Physician Himself to heal hearts and lives, but medical books upon medical books.

・・・・・

Over the years, some pretty amazing things would happen in the clinic. One of the most amazing things Elam did, he didn't even do. God did. A man named Uriah had come to him after having nearly cut his hand in half. His fingers seemed to be dangling by threads! Elam called for help on the ham radio, and the first doctor to respond told him that he could do nothing for the man because of the intricacies of working with the human hand. "Only a specialist can handle what you've got before you there! I wouldn't touch that with a ten-foot pole!" he'd said.

But another doctor was listening in who knew more about Elam's situation, and that Elam was likely this man's only hope. "I'll help you through this, but you have to do exactly as I tell you!" he said.

Elam had done exactly as the doctor had told him, and weeks later that man's hand and all the fingers were actually working. Elam didn't think a whole lot of it until he was told by many doctors how really remarkable it was that he had had success with this. Elam knew he hadn't done it. Where he had been weak, God had been strong.

It so happened then that the same man, Uriah, who seemed almost as unlucky as the one in the Bible who'd been married to Bathsheba, came to the clinic again almost a year later. This time, perhaps because he'd missed the class on machete safety in school, he'd whacked his big toe right off—almost. Just a little bit of skin was still holding the toe on.

"Just take it the rest of the way off!" Uriah had told him.

But Elam knew that walking without the big toe could be difficult and thought it was worth it to try to save the toe, even if it didn't work properly. He tried convincing Uriah to go out to the hospital, but Uriah would much prefer to hack it the rest of the way off than take that trip. The hospital in Sayaxché was at that time actually only a "puesto de salud" or a "medical center." While it did have access to doctors and nurses and had some medical equipment, it was really only a first-aid clinic. Something like this could only be handled way out in San Benito, which was a full two-day trip, or even as far as Guatemala City. Uriah was not willing to go to the hospital.

"No way! Just hack it off!" he'd said again after Elam tried to persuade him.

Seeing that there was no way that Uriah was going to go out to the hospital, Elam decided to clean the toe up really well, sew all the skin back on, and just see what would happen. He did that, prayed, and sent Uriah on his way. What happened was quite the surprise. The next time Elam saw Uriah, his toe was still attached, completely healed, and it worked. It wiggled and bent. The bone had even healed.

Elam and Barbara had also had many experiences already with women bringing their malnourished babies and children to them. Even without a medical degree, after giving the children some homemade rehydration drinks and some ultranutritious foods to get them out of danger, Barbara would just give her time around the clock. Usually within just a few weeks, they'd be plump and healthy, ready to go home.

In the case of the little girl from Pipiles who had just arrived, Maria was not only malnourished, she was very sick. To nurse a child in this drastic condition back to health would require some serious antibiotics for her infections. So they contacted a children's hospital in Guatemala City operated by a friend of theirs, Dr. Carl Heinlein and his family, and sent Maria to Guatemala City as soon as possible.

It took ten weeks of medicines, love, and food for Maria to make a full recovery, but she had recovered and was now healthy and plump, ready to return home. Where was "home" going to be?

Elam and Barbara felt good about the idea of adopting Maria. They held a family meeting and asked everyone else what they thought. They were all excited about it, especially the girls, so it was decided. They made contact with the father and the grandfather and asked permission to adopt her.

A few months after her arrival at New Life Missions at La Anchura, Maria legally became a Stoltzfus. Maria had received new life in her body and now a new life and family. Elam and Barbara went on the four-hour journey by car into Flores to handle all the adoption paperwork, which at that time was a breeze. In a short time the paperwork was complete, and they were ready to head home with their new daughter. The children were excited and were at home eagerly waiting to welcome their new sister home.

"She's our sister now?" seven-year-old Anita smiled.

"Yeah!" Five-year-old Lisa checked out her new sister, who was her same age, and said, "I love you!" and gave her new sister a hug.

Jean followed with another hug and a huge smile, "Welcome home, Maria!"

The boys each gave her a welcome home hug as well.

But then Miguel gave Virgil a look, and Virgil seemed to agree to his unspoken thoughts.

"What are you guys thinking?" Barbara asked, noticing the silent conversation.

"Well," Miguel began, "I just noticed there's an unbalance in the family now."

Barbara's brow furrowed. "What?"

"Yeah," Virgil agreed.

Barbara looked back at Miguel, waiting for the rest of his story.

"Now there's four girls and only two of us, so we need to adopt a boy now," Miguel said.

"Yeah," Virgil agreed.

"Oh, I think you two are more than enough boys than we need!" Jean laughed.

So, now the Stoltzfus family was complete. A little out of balance, maybe, but definitely complete!

Chapter 20

Te Quiero

Sarah said, "God has made laughter for me;
everyone who hears will laugh with me."
Genesis 21:6

The family all gathered at the airstrip and waved good-bye to the planeload of visiting missionaries. It was a group of people who had spent the whole month touring Guatemala looking for somewhere to serve, and this was their last stop: the hot, mosquito-filled Petén. Richard liked it here, and Elam felt good about Richard. He was for real, smart, willing, and strong, and he was excited to serve God—all the things Elam needed to help build the churches and the mission compound.

It hadn't been too long after Richard Hood had told God that he would go wherever He wanted that he ended up in Guatemala. And now, visiting La Anchura and meeting Elam, he knew he had found his calling. He was excited as he sat in the front seat of the small airplane heading out of the Petén and back to Guatemala City. He looked out over the great expanse of jungle and the winding rivers. He was amazed to see all the scattered villages out in the middle of nowhere, far from any roads. Then when they got up into the clouds, it all looked like a vast white ocean. It was just beautiful up here.

Then something else caught his eye. He was no pilot, but something seemed to be wrong with the right tire. He watched it for a long time. As they were flying through the heavy rain clouds, he could see that air was escaping the tire. The tire, one of only two this tail-dragger airplane used for landing, was going flat. He leaned over to the pilot, "Don, there seems to be something wrong with the tire over here".

Don Donaldson leaned forward and stretched across in front of Richard to look out the window. "Yup. Sure is," he concluded.

As they approached the airstrip in Guatemala City, Don called in and told the control tower that they had a possible emergency landing. Ambulances would be standing by. Then he *called in* and asked God for help landing.

The emergency vehicles were there waiting, but all they did was watch a plane land normally. As it had turned out, the little sign that Don had on the dash of the airplane proved true: "The engine (or in this case tires) in this plane may fail, but Jesus never does."

Richard's decision to return to Guatemala, and specifically La Anchura, didn't change. A few months later, he met up with Elam and Barbara at the 1978 Missions Conference at Lakewood Church in Houston, in order to return to Guatemala with them.

After the conference, the short little ex-Amish man, his wife, their newly adopted Guatemalan daughter, and the tall, bearded ex-biker dude who spoke no Spanish whatsoever hopped into the large ten-ton box truck and headed for Guatemala. What a motley crew! For Elam and Barbara this was just another one of many trips between the U.S. and Guatemala, but for Richard this was a major step in his life. He was leaving home and heading off on his own adventure.

The trip from Houston to the border of Mexico took about eight hours, but the border crossing itself could take longer than that. The Mexican laws concerning people traveling through their country for destinations other than Mexico changed so frequently, and there was such corruption among the border agents, that sometimes the border crossing, for people with integrity like Elam who didn't pay bribes, could take days.

"Always better to lose a little time than your relationship with God," Elam would always say when people asked him why he wouldn't just pay a small bribe rather than pay ten times that much to stay at the border for days and days.

Today was not one of those days; the border guys were cooperative, and they made it through right away with no hassle. Elam and Barbara were excited to get home. They'd been away for six weeks now and had very little contact with the family down in the jungle. Ham radio was the only communication, and it was scratchy and odd having to take turns speaking like on a walkie-talkie. Sometimes the signal wasn't so clear, either, and they had to practically yell for the other person to hear them.

About halfway through Mexico, into their second day of driving, they arrived at a ferry crossing at Tampico and had to wait for four hours for the ferry. To make up for lost time, they decided to drive through the night. The only other inconvenience to take note of at this point were the dash lights. They didn't work. But it wasn't like they had to worry about the speed limits where they were, so not being able to see the dash didn't seem like too much of a problem. The trip was going great!

"Drip" was the sound of the drop of oil that escaped the engine and landed on the road beneath them in the dark. "Drip, drip, drip!"

· · · · ·

Richard popped the hood on the truck and was pulling out the dipstick to check the oil while Elam talked to some guy about something in his trunk.

"Oh, sure, I have three sets of American tools here," the friendly Mexican guy had said when he found the two gringos stranded alongside the road. "I can give you a discount. I will sell them to you for half price."

It was morning. The night before, after a few hours of driving, the engine had started to act up, so they had pulled over and decided to wait till morning to see what the problem was.

"You're out of oil, Elam," Richard said.

"Out of oil?" Elam exclaimed and motioned with his hands something that was along the lines of, "Oh, darn!" It had been more of a problem than they'd expected to not have the instrument lights working.

"OK, so where do we find a diesel mechanic out here in the middle of nowhere on New Year's weekend?" Richard asked.

Good question.

Elam prayed, and then he hitched a ride into the nearest town to look for a mechanic. Richard stayed with Barbara, Maria, and the truck, which was loaded full of supplies for the clinic building.

Elam's search came up empty. No mechanic. He returned to the truck to find a disabled car parked right across the highway. Who would happen to be in that car but a diesel mechanic! His shop was about 125 miles south of there. So, with the tools Elam had just bought that morning, the mechanic completely took the engine apart there by the side of the road.

"Whoa, this engine is hurting," the mechanic said.

"How hurting?" Elam asked.

"Well, it needs to be completely rebuilt. Running it without oil totally ruined it. We're going to need to take the engine out and take it to our shop to fix it."

Richard read the look on Elam's face. "What did he say?"

"Well, how fast can you do that?" Elam asked the mechanic. How fast can you completely rebuild an American diesel engine deep into Mexico in the late Seventies out in the middle of nowhere? Another good question.

Barbara wasn't about to wait around to find out, so she and Maria took off. She had a few pesos in her pocket and dug a few more out of Elam's. That would get her far enough, and she'd figure out the rest when the time came. With a kiss and a prayer said with Elam, she left on a bus headed toward Guatemala.

Then Richard watched the engine be packed into the back of the pickup and driven away.

"We'll never see that engine again," he thought to himself.

With that taken care of, it was time to settle in for a little while. There were no motels or restaurants around these parts; just a few little stores that sold sodas and snacks. Elam didn't think that the two of them would survive too long on that, so he talked to a family in a nearby hut and made arrangements for meals.

"The family in this hut has invited us for dinner tonight," Elam was explaining to Richard as they approached the front door.

"OK." He was wondering what they might feed him.

"I talked to them earlier today, and they offered that if we buy the food, they will prepare it for us. Sounds like a good deal to me," Elam said.

Richard only nodded and followed Elam to the hut.

Elam reached the front door and began speaking in Spanish. "Buenos!"

Richard smiled at the short little Mexican family, who looked up at his more than six feet of height and smiled back at him shyly. They entered the dirt-floor hut and sat down on two little homemade wooden chairs at a rustic little table.

A young woman came over to the table and said, "Blah blah blah blah blah," and walked off.

Elam interpreted, "She says they're bringing us coffee."

"Oh, I can't drink coffee," Richard said.

"Well, you have to."

"But I can't. I don't drink coffee," Richard insisted.

"Look, don't ruin this for us. If you don't drink what they serve us, you might offend them!" Elam said.

Richard looked frustrated.

Elam got an idea. "Alright, I know. How about tea? Will you drink tea?"

"Yes, I will drink tea." Richard felt relieved.

"OK, well when she comes back out here you need to ask for tea instead," Elam said.

"I can't speak any Spanish. Can't you ask?"

"No, really, it's easy. You're going to have to learn sometime, right? Here's your first Spanish lesson." Elam was smiling inside.

"OK." Richard was ready. He knew he had to learn, so he might as well start then.

"Tea in Spanish is 'teh.'"

"Tay. OK, that's how I say tea, got it," Richard said.

"Now to say 'I want' you say, 'kee yeh roh.'"

"Kee-yeah-rroah." Richard got it out.

"Good. Now say it together, 'te quiero.'" Elam prounounced very clearly for him.

Richard repeated it a few times until he felt he had it, "Te quiero. Te quiero."

Elam smiled. "Good, you got it."

The señorita was returning with two metal coffee cups in her hands full of hot water. She set them down on the table and was about to turn to go back and get the jar of instant coffee and the sugar when Elam asked her to wait.

"Go ahead," Elam prodded.

He motioned to the girl that Richard had something to say. The whole household was there, as having gringos in the house was a very special occasion. Everyone wanted to watch and see how and what they ate. All eyes in the house were on Richard. It was just two words. How hard could this be?

He said to her as clearly as he could, "Te quiero."

Everyone's eyes got wider. They all looked a little uncomfortable and then burst out laughing.

Richard looked back to Elam, who sat straight-faced looking at him. "What? Didn't I say it right?" It was just two words! How could he have gotten them wrong?

"I don't know, Richard. Maybe you need to try again. Say it a little louder, maybe. A little clearer," Elam urged seriously, while laughter was building up inside him.

Richard turned toward the girl again and said with a little more force, "Te quiero."

The whole room roared in laughter.

Richard wondered if this was the normal reaction when English people started speaking Spanish to Spanish people. Were they were all happy that here was this American guy learning his first words in Spanish? Were they just proud of him or something, and it came out in giggles? Maybe he hadn't pronounced it well or had a really weird accent? Finally, he noticed that Elam was also laughing himself right off his chair. His false teeth even seemed to be about to fly out, he was laughing so hard.

While "té" is the Spanish word for tea, it's also the Spanish word for "you." I want tea is said, "Quiero té". If you reverse the word order, you're saying, "I love you." Richard had just been introduced to Elam's ornery sense of humor.

· · · · ·

In a couple days, the guys who'd driven away with the engine of their truck actually returned. They said there was no way they could find parts for it in Mexico. If Elam and Richard wanted to get that truck moving ever again, one of them would have to go back up through Mexico to Texas to get the parts themselves. Since the only Spanish Richard knew was "I love you," Elam was the one who would have to go. That meant that Richard would have to stay with the truck by himself.

Elam was gone for almost a week. Every morning, Richard awoke to see curious faces of half the town pressed up against the windows of the truck, looking at him. People this far south of the border didn't see white people too often. They didn't have televisions to watch. So, they watched Richard. They watched him eat. They watched him brush his teeth. They watched him when he went down to the river to take a bath.

Although Elam had already made a deal with the family to prepare their meals, Richard stayed as far away from that hut as he could. He didn't know what kinds of traditions they might have here, and he'd already told the young woman in that house he loved her! Who knew if that meant, "shotgun wedding ahead" in this culture or not?

Instead, he tried his luck and his Spanish at the local store. He found another easy phrase, "I want to buy crackers." He looked down at the traveler's hand guide to Spanish in his hand and read over and over, "Quiero comprar galletas." Then he walked up to the counter and put the book down to say it from memory: "Quiero comprar *gatos*." Cats. I want to buy cats. The store operator, of course, laughed and went off a hundred miles an hour that they didn't eat cats in Mexico, "Blah blah blah blah." Fortunately, pointing always works!

Elam returned, and the mechanics needed yet more parts. They weren't heading off to Guatemala anytime too soon, so they had the truck pulled to a nearby village where they could find a better place to stay. They were there for five more weeks. Elam ended up taking another trip back to Texas to get parts for the truck, while Richard remained behind by himself, trying not to fall in love with any other young women and trying to keep from eating cats.

By this time, it had been over two months since Elam had seen Jean, Miguel, Virgil, Anita, and Lisa. He was missing them! On that second trip, the IMRA Ham Radio Net gave Elam a portable ham radio. That was awesome! Now he could keep in contact with the family back in the jungle from wherever he was! The kids were so glad to hear his voice every night and to know what was going on!

Elam trusted God to help him through any situation, but as much as he was praying, they were still stuck in the little village. He was doing everything that was in his control to do, and he knew the rest was up to God, so why was this still taking so long when there was work to be done with the mission at home? Why the delay?

One day, Elam got his answer to that question when a timid man approached him. "We used to have a church here in town, and it was very strong, but then," he began to tear up, "but then another group came into town, and they caused us a lot of problems. Finally our church just fell apart."

The light went on. These people needed encouragement. "Listen, I want you to invite everyone who ever went to your church to come to a little service I'll hold in your old building on Wednesday night!" Elam said.

The man did just as Elam had told him, and the church packed out. After Elam preached, he offered to pray for people. Ten people came forward and fell on their knees in tears and accepted Christ. Four more who had walked away from God because of all the conflict returned. The church was revived. They then held church services almost every night. Richard even preached in English with Elam interpreting.

They had arrived in a town that was spiritually dead, but there were people praying in that town for God to do something, and He did. When all of the oil leaked out of that engine and left Elam high and dry there in Mexico, God "worked all things together for good for them who love the Lord." At first Elam wondered why God was allowing all of that time he could have been working in Guatemala to be wasted, but the time was not wasted by God. This delay resulted in the revival of a whole town, and what an exciting beginning in Central America for Richard! (The next most exciting thing on the list for Richard would be the young lady, Mirna, whom Elam had promised to bring a husband someday. Elam thought Richard might just fit the bill.)

Elam had told God he wanted to serve Him in everything and in every way, and God took that seriously. He had work He needed done, and He sent Elam in to do it. Had Elam been too frustrated with the whole physical situation and how it was keeping him from *his* mission, he might have missed out on the spiritual situation that was actually *His* mission. Most of all, had the inconvenience of the situation broken Elam's spirit, God might have missed out on all those people in that village coming to know Him.

Chapter 21

Tastes Like Beef

"He will eat curds and honey at the time He knows enough
to refuse evil and choose good." *Isaiah 7:15*

"What I don't understand is how they get the gorillas to hold the guns!" one wide-eyed lady said to Elam.

Elam looked at her and held back a laugh. "Oh, they just give them bananas."

"Elam!" Barbara laughed and then said to the lady, "They're not that kind of gorilla."

"Oh?" the lady said, a little confused.

"Bananas were the forbidden fruit, you know!" Virgil said seriously.

The lady looked even more puzzled now.

"Hey, Virgil!" Miguel came bursting into the house. "I think I saw another swarm of bees out by that big patch of strangle-vine trees. Want to come help me get it?"

"Strangle-vine trees? What are those?" another one of the visiting missionaries asked. A group of sixteen missionaries were helping to minister in the villages for a few weeks. They'd just returned from an awesome time in La Flor de la Esperanza (The Flower of Hope). Three churches had come together and had church together the first night. Then, the next morning, they performed nine wedding ceremonies including a couple who were already in their sixties! In the afternoon Elam baptized fifteen believers and saw three new converts.

"A strangle-vine tree is one of those over there." Elam pointed out the window.

A couple of the missionaries who'd heard Miguel's announcement looked out.

"It's basically just a tree which has been so overtaken by vines that the vine becomes the tree. You see?" He pointed again. "That one there is half and half. You can see the palm tree is still sticking up in the middle, and all around it is another tree. That was the vine."

One of the guys' eyes lit up, "Oh, wow. That's neat!" He whipped out his camera and headed out the door Miguel had just come through to go snap a picture of it.

Elam went back to explaining the difference between a "guerrilla" and a "gorilla" to a couple of the ladies, and a few others sat back down and started comparing how many mosquito bites each had so far. In the meantime, Virgil had headed out the door to follow his older brother. This was always fun.

In 1977, Elam had become the representative in Guatemala for the Heifer Project out of Arkansas. They had had fifty honeybee hives shipped into the jungle along with cattle, goats, and chickens. The goal had been to get the animals breeding and get the local people involved in having their own, following the concept of teaching them to fish rather than giving them fish. It wasn't too long until Miguel had learned how to handle the bees and really had a lot of fun with it.

Just like the better orange that was on the top of the tree while 300 sat in baskets on the ground, what fun is a few hives on your property when there are wild swarms to be found! Finding a new swarm and capturing them was a great adventure Miguel was always on the lookout for. This morning while Miguel had been out milking the cow, the wind must have been just right, because he had been able to hear the low buzz coming from the swarm quite a distance away.

The boys arrived at the foot of the tree. "They're up pretty high," Virgil commented.

"Not a problem!" Miguel smiled. He quickly got into position around the tree and started to climb. As he reached the mass of bees, he moved purposefully and fluidly so he wouldn't alarm them. He slowly reached into his pocket and pulled out the matchbox that had little air holes punched in it. Then, he slowly put his hand right into the swarm and searched until he found the queen. He gently cupped her in his hand and put her in the matchbox. Then he closed his hand around the box gently and waited. Quickly, the bees, who were all attracted to her scent, swarmed all over Miguel's hand and forearm. He then began his descent of the tree. This was the tricky part. He had to climb back down the tree using only one hand. The other hand, of course, was now full of little creatures with stingers.

Virgil was waiting at the bottom of the tree with the bees' new home. Everything was going smoothly until, "Ai!" Miguel said.

"What?" Virgil looked up.

Miguel's pant leg was pushed halfway up his calf with a thick, broken branch stuck inside.

"Careful. Don't fall on me!" Virgil said compassionately.

"Sure! I've got it all under control!" Miguel said, struggling with his pant leg. He gave his leg one final kick. His pant leg came free, but he lost his balance. Not a problem. All he had to do was grab the tree with his free hand!

"Oww." Virgil winced when he saw what Miguel had just done.

Miguel looked down at Virgil and just smiled and then winced also.

· · · · ·

"Wow," Barbara commented looking at Miguel's arm, "the stings aren't even swelling."

"I'm a real man, Mom!" Miguel had been stung so many times since they had started having bees that his body had become immune to it.

Jean walked past, had a look, and laughed at her crazy brother.

"So, you guys just went out and got a swarm of bees out of a tree, just like that?" another of the visiting missionaries asked.

"Yup." Miguel smiled, showing off his arm to Anita, Lisa, and Maria, who'd come in to see what he had done to his arm.

"It's pretty dangerous," Virgil said seriously.

"Well, yes, I agree, it must be to put your hand right in the middle of a swarm of bees like that!" said one of the missionaries.

"No, I mean dangerous for me. What if he would have fallen on me?" Virgil said.

"You're right," Miguel agreed, also looking serious.

"Actually," Elam began, "we've started having a problem in the area here with the killer bees that have migrated up from South America."

"Killer bees? What kind of trouble?" asked another man. He had heard the stories about killer bees that were headed to the United States and possibly going to wreak worldwide havoc. He'd even seen previews for a movie about it once.

"The killer bees look almost just like regular honeybees, but they're more aggressive. When you disturb them, they don't just give you a few stings and then forget about you. They will pursue a person for miles, and keep stinging them and keep stinging them. There have already been a few deaths in the area because of them," Elam said.

Both of the boys had had several experiences finding swarms of those. One swarm had chased Virgil the entire length of the airstrip, through a bush that he'd gone through to try to confuse them, and then had waited for him above the water in the river after he dove in to escape them! A few local drunks had not made out so well in their run-ins with swarms of them, though, and had ended up dead as they were too drunk to try to get away from them. It was because of this problem that eventually they got rid of the hives altogether.

• • • • •

After all the excitement of the morning bee hunt, one of the missionaries got to thinking about these boys being so isolated here in the jungle.

"So, Virgil, Miguel, you guys ever feel like you're missing out on life because you don't live in the States?" he asked.

Miguel and Virgil looked at each other, both with a thousand memories rushing through their heads at once. With smiles on their faces they replied, "No. We feel like it's kids in the States who are missing out!"

That was actually one of the most common questions the boys got whenever they went to the States with their parents, and the boys just couldn't fathom how kids in the U.S. could possibly really have any fun. Where was the river for swimming and the crocodiles for catching in the States? In the States, if the neighbors were to look out their windows and see the neighbor boy practicing throwing knives at trees that his brother was hiding behind for the sake of making knife retrieval faster and more convenient, well, the police might come by and ruin the fun. Or, if you were trying to fly your new ultralight airplane around the property with your brother dangling by a rope from the bottom, again, the police might stop by and ruin your fun. Maybe even take your toy and your rope. In the U.S., you weren't even allowed to ride in the back of a pickup truck. Now what was up with that? In the U.S., if they went to "fun parks," they would have had to be a certain height to ride certain rides for safety! Safety! What fun was that? And they called them fun parks? And, in the U.S., you didn't have too many opportunities to feed your friends monkeys for dinner.

One important thing about their lives in Guatemala was that they felt like their lives had meaning and purpose. All the work that Miguel and Virgil did each day was necessary for the family to survive out there in the middle of nowhere. It wasn't just Elam going to work and "bringing home the bacon." No, sometimes the boys did this, and it didn't come in the form of a paycheck or packaged in cellophane. Rather, it came in the form of a heavy, smelly, dead wild boar slung over very tired shoulders that had just carried it through miles of jungle. Because of the ministries that Elam had with the churches and the clinic, there were many times that their lives could have fun, adventure, danger, and purpose all wrapped up in one night of being threatened by guerrilla groups or rushing dying people to the hospital in the rain in an aluminum speedboat hours up the dark river where crocodiles swam and logs floated just below the surface of the water out of sight; in the jungle where jaguars and poisonous snakes and guerrillas (but not gorillas) lurked. They didn't even have to be a certain height to get on this ride. Really, could it get any better?

· · · · ·

Ever since coming to Guatemala, Elam had always taken the boys out with him when he went hunting. He felt that it was important to show the boys, who were living in a household where there were guns and ammunition, the proper use of a gun as soon as they were big enough to hold one. So, from a very young age, each boy had had his own gun and had been using it to help feed the family.

With as much time as they spent in the jungle, no too many years went by before Elam felt confident allowing the two boys to go out hunting on their own. They knew how to handle their guns, and they knew the jungle.

One time Elam and Barbara were preparing for a huge pastors' conference that would be held on the property. If they were going to be able to feed everyone, someone needed to "go to the grocery store." The boys headed out a few days ahead of the scheduled conference to get the "groceries." They piled into their boat with four of their neighbors and their hunting rifles and headed downriver, hoping they would find some wild boar or some deer.

They really couldn't be too picky; it wasn't as though the animals sat on a shelf with shiny packaging just ready for the choosing. And, in spite of what some people might want to think, the local people did not live in harmony with nature. Most of the animals were already hunted to oblivion, which limited the selection. Because of that fact, Barbara and Elam's family had to get adventurous with their food choices. Sometimes, the locals made fun of what Elam's family ate, because the gringos seemed to eat anything! It didn't matter if it was cute and cuddly or big and ugly; they ate it. The family had eaten crocodile, iguana, boa constrictor, tepesquintle (which in English is called an agouti and is somewhat like a guinea pig with the coloration of a fawn), deer, macaw, monkey, wild pig, coatimundi, kinkajou, armadillo, raccoon, tapir, cotuza (which is like a tiny guinea pig), eel, and more. In fact, the first time Elam and Barbara took the kids to a zoo, they thought it was a grocery store. OK, just kidding!

· · · · ·

Many years before, Elam had gotten lost in the jungle less than a mile from home. Back then, in the days when they'd first arrived, they'd had a lot of things to learn about the jungle—like the sounds of it, for one thing. The jungle in Guatemala can make some very unusual noises. Once, during their first year in Guatemala, Elam had been out hunting with Miguel and Jean and heard what sounded like some wildly scary wild pig. Elam told the kids to be quiet and listened. They continued creeping slowly and quietly through the jungle. The sound seemed to be getting closer, so they all made for the nearest tree and headed up to safety to wait until the pigs passed. But, as they climbed the trees, the noises were getting louder, and they saw nothing in the brush below. Finally, they looked up, and there above them was the source of the noise. Howler monkeys.

Howler monkeys make a noise that is kind of like a cross between a lawn tractor, a rabid lion, and a sick donkey. Sure, just try to imagine it, and yet it's worse than that! Very scary! The three of them laughed at themselves once they realized what they'd done and then did what any red-blooded, hungry American family would do. Pulled out their camera and took pictures? No. They pulled out their guns and shot one of the monkeys to take home for dinner.

"Tastes like beef!" Elam would always tell the visiting missionaries, who would just gag at the idea of eating a monkey.

· · · · ·

Elam said good-bye to his boys and sent them off to hunt. His mind immediately went to work preparing for the weekend ahead with all the pastors arriving. He was thankful for the two boys he had and the men they were growing up to become. He prayed that they would have a safe and successful hunt.

The hunting party traveled six hours down the river toward Mexico and pulled their boat into shore. One of the men waited with the boat, and the other five headed off into the brush. They went up over a bank, and their trip was over. They, the hunters, found themselves looking into the wrong ends of guns as they stumbled onto a guerrilla camp, and these guerrillas were holding machine guns, not bananas. They were ordered to leave immediately, which they did.

They returned to their boat and set off again for another of their favorite hunting areas that was a long way around a big loop in the river. By the time they finally arrived at their new happy hunting grounds, it was basically bedtime and they hadn't even gotten started hunting yet. They hadn't brought any food along with them as they figured when they had set out on their trip they'd be eating something they had shot. Fortunately, one of the guys had some soggy tortillas tucked into his knapsack, so that was dinner.

They got close to their destination and made camp. Now, you can get those pictures of them putting up tents out of your minds right away. With their machetes they each cut down two large palm branches, split them down the middle, and laid them on the ground so that the leaves were facing toward the middle and the halves of the hard centers were on either side on the outside. That was their bed. No tents. No warm shower. No mosquito netting.

The next morning, they awoke with a little less blood than they'd gone to bed with to the familiar sound of thousands of buzzing mosquitoes out looking for breakfast. They got up and headed into the jungle again to hunt. This time no one wanted to be stuck sitting around with the boat waiting, so they all went. Not too long after that they were chased out by other hunters. They turned around and headed back to their boat, but now they had another problem.

"This is getting a little ridiculous," Miguel said.

"You have got to be kidding!" Virgil laughed.

Their boat was gone.

One of the men went downriver, found the boat, and brought it back. Then the six mighty hunters set off on their quest once again.

Day two of their hunting trip was coming to a close, and they had not found a thing yet. They found a place to camp for the night again. Fortunately, some dinner came flying in and landed in a nearby tree.

"I got it!" one of the neighbors called out to the others. He raised his gun, and two of the night's dinner entrees fell from their roost.

Neither the Guatemalan men nor the two American missionary's kids knew that their dinner was considered an exotic pet in the United States worth thousands of dollars. All they knew was that there were gobs of these big red macaws everywhere. In the tree there had been at least 150 of them roosting, so nature wouldn't miss a couple of them. Besides, they were free, the guys were starving, and they tasted like chicken!

In the morning, the guys decided to just head back. It was a long boat ride back up to La Anchura. Although last night's dinner had been satisfying, it was digested and gone, and the guys were hungry again. One of them spied a banana tree with a big stalk of ripe bananas, and the one driving the boat happily drove straight for it. Once the branch was hacked down and in the boat, all the guys dove in and started eating bananas.

"Don't think about it, little brother!" Miguel teased.

Virgil was peeling a banana slowly. "You know this is against my religion to eat this," he said glumly.

Miguel just laughed. "It's OK to do things against your religion just as long as they're not against God."

Virgil didn't look convinced.

A few hours up the river they passed Buena Fe and thought they were soon to be back at La Anchura with the bad news that no food had been found. Then they heard them: howler monkeys. They turned the boat back around and found their jackpot.

The same man who'd brought down dinner the night before started shooting again, and the monkeys started falling out of the trees like rain. They butchered the meat right there and filled several burlap bags.

When they returned home, they were greeted by hundreds of smiling faces as they heard, "Dios le bendiga," said to them over and over by everyone they ran into. "Dios le bengida" is the standard, "Hi, how are ya?" greeting for Guatemalan Christians. It's sort of like a secret handshake, except that it's not a secret. It means "God bless you," and they say it to you whether you have sneezed or not. The pastors' convention was already underway, and the guys had returned just in time. The meat was quickly plopped into fifty-five-gallon drums full of vegetable soup that were already simmering over fires.

Their 400 or so dinner guests ate that night, and as they finished up their soup they all thanked, God-blessed, and complimented "sister Barbara" countless times for her awesome beef stew.

Chapter 22

Crocodile Creek

For the wisdom of this world is foolishness before God.
1 Corinthians 3:19

Though it got to the point at times that La Anchura was like Grand Central Station, there were also times that were more peaceful when there were no groups of visiting missionaries or pastors' conventions going on. Now was one of those times.

Elam and Barbara were away in the States visiting with churches, and Jean, who was now fourteen years old, was left in charge. As the sun came up, Jean lay awake on her bed looking out her window. She was daydreaming about growing up and getting married someday, like girls like to do. She smiled to herself just dreaming of how they would meet and what he would be like, and where they would get married.

"I want him to be able to play the guitar," she thought.

The sun was rising, and it was soon time to start her day, so Jean began to pray. "Thank you, Lord, for all You did for us yesterday, for taking care of us here while Mom and Dad are away, and…." Just then she heard some scuffling and then heard a loud splash as her two younger brothers left the deck of the houseboat. "…and for helping me deal with Miguel and Virgil!"

· · · · ·

"Quit it! You're going to scare the fish!" Miguel scolded his little brother.

"What fish? You mean the ones that are already caught on the line?" Virgil replied as he soaped up.

The fish in question were ones caught on the line the family baited every night. During a certain time of the year they'd catch one or two big catfish on it—enough food for a whole day, anyway.

"Right. If we scare them right before we eat them, they will give us heartburn," Miguel confidently stated.

"Oh, is that all?" Virgil dunked his head under, rinsing his hair.

"Yes, I read about it just this week in, oh, um, *The Jungle Journal of Highly Technical Medical Stuff Magazine*," Miguel said very seriously.

"Well, I heard that if you scare 'em real good just before you eat them, it will make, like, lots of hair grow on your chest, or something," Virgil added.

"Looks to me like we need to scare them a bit more then, for your sake," Miguel said, motioning toward Virgil's hairless chest.

Miguel thought for a moment and then began thrashing wildly and making all sorts of noise for about ten seconds. Then he stopped, as though nothing had happened, and he soaped himself up, too. "You have that wrong, anyway," Miguel said, soaping up his own hair.

"What?"

"It's coffee that will put hair on your chest. Not scared catfish."

"Oh, yeah, right." Virgil thought it was about time he started drinking coffee.

Later that morning, as the family was busy doing their daily chores, a boat came up the river toward them and pulled in to the clinic. It was Checha, a friend of Jean's from Buena Fe.

"Good morning!" he greeted the boys, who were busy chopping weeds with machetes down by the river's edge.

"Buenos días!" they replied, stopping a moment to shake hands.

"Is your sister Jean here?" Checha jumped out of his boat, which he had made himself.

"Yeah. She's right up there in the clinic," Miguel told him.

"Gracias." Checha nodded and headed toward the clinic building. He found Jean cleaning the floor in the main exam room, her Bible lying open on the exam table.

"Buenos días, señorita!" he said as he approached the front of the building.

Jean looked up and smiled. "Good day! How are you doing today?"

Checca had one main reason for coming to the clinic that day. "My wife is about to have our first baby, and there is no midwife in Buena Fe to deliver it," he began, "so what I would like to know is if you would deliver the baby for us?"

Jean's eyes widened with surprise. "Me? But I'm not qualified to deliver babies!"

"Yes, but haven't you helped your father deliver babies?" he continued.

"Well, yes, but only two, and I didn't really get to do much more than run around and get things for him. I, I don't really know what to do!" she laughed.

"We trust you," he said.

It was amazing how much trust the whole community seemed to have in this family. "You trust me, maybe, but I don't know if I trust me!" she said. They both laughed. "Look, I'll talk to my dad on the radio tomorrow, and I'll see what he thinks I should do."

With that, Checca left and headed for his boat.

· · · · ·

"Me, deliver a baby by myself?" Jean said into the microphone.

"Sure, you can do it. Just get out the book and read up on it. Dennis and Paula are there to help you, too, if you need them," Elam encouraged her from 3,000 miles away.

Her heart beat a little faster. "He thinks I can do it!" she thought to herself.

The book Elam was referring to was one that the family relied on heavily in the clinic. It had been written by the Hesperian Foundation specifically for people too far from good medical care that often had to just do things themselves. It was appropriately titled, *Where There Is No Doctor.*

"OK, I'll send word to Checca that I'll do it, then," Jean told her father.

A week later, Checca's boat was again at the shore in front of the clinic. This time, his wife was along, and she didn't look very happy. It was time.

Jean went over to the guesthouse that was now serving as the home of another missionary couple staying with the family, and asked the wife,

Paula, to help her. Jean's heart was racing, but not from nervousness. She was excited. She prayed that God would guide her to safely deliver the baby, and He did. In no time at all, Jean had a healthy newborn baby cleaned up and wrapped in a blanket, ready to hand to the new mom, who was cleaned up and resting in a bed. "I think I could do this again!" Jean thought to herself.

And she did. One thing that is amazing is how fast word can travel even in a country where there are no cell phones or telephones—or even carrier pigeons, for that matter! The word was out that Jean was "a midwife." Jean could deliver babies.

A couple of weeks later, another lady showed up to have her baby. That delivery, too, went smoothly, and Jean really enjoyed it. Then another week or so later another lady came. This lady was in a lot of pain and would not lie down. Jean helped her as she walked around and helped support her as she made it through each contraction. It hadn't been very long at all when the lady began to push with a contraction. The baby was on its way!

"OK, señora, I need you to lie down over here on the bed now," Jean urged her toward the bed after the last contraction was over.

"No," the lady said flatly, and didn't budge.

"Please, señora, lets just go over to the bed now; it's time for your baby to come," Jean urged her some more.

This time she just shook her head and grunted. Another contraction was already upon her, and she was pushing some more.

Jean hadn't read anything about this in the book she'd been studying and was just a little nervous. The lady needed to lie down on the bed! Fourteen-year-old Jean looked pleadingly at her assistants, the two grown-ups Paula and Dennis.

"Jean, it's OK to let her have the baby standing up if she wants to," Dennis said reassuringly.

Jean looked at Paula for a moment and then simply looked disbelievingly at Dennis.

Dennis caught the look. "No, really. I'm a Houston Police Officer. We get trained in this stuff."

Jean's eyebrows rose. "Oh, OK." She believed him. She stopped focusing on getting the lady to the bed and just lifted the lady's skirt to be able to see underneath. There was the head. Jean reached under, and soon the whole baby was dropped into her hands. Just like that.

. . . . .

On this trip to the States, which would last three months altogether, Elam, Barbara, and their two littlest children Lisa and Maria had traveled around to visit with and speak in several of the churches that had been supporting them in Guatemala.

"The people there trust us and have so much confidence in us," Barbara told the congregation.

"It all started with a machete wound I sutured up a few years ago…." Elam told the story of Uriah, who had missed his machete safety classes in school. "That same man returned again to the clinic about a year later…."

Then he beamed at the congregation. "Our children are excited about the ministry and involved in so many ways." He had a great bunch of kids back home in Guatemala, who were excited about life and were learning things most kids in the States could never even imagine.

The congregations heard many stories about miracles and also about the war. People would laugh, and sometimes they would cry. Always they were moved and at the end of the service usually passed around an offering plate to help the ministry. Then, after church, Elam and Barbara were almost always invited over to someone's house for a yummy lunch.

. . . . .

"What is this stuff?" Virgil whined. He wasn't allowed to act like that when his mom and dad were at home, so he was taking advantage of this opportunity to give his sister a hard time.

"Look, quit complaining and just eat it," Jean scowled. She didn't like cooking anyway, especially not when her little brothers complained about everything she made for them.

"Check this out, Virgil," Miguel said, pointing to his plate. He had stuck his fork in his food, and it was standing straight up.

"Is it supposed to do that?" Virgil cocked his head to look at it from a different angle.

176

"Just stop it!" She grabbed the fork out of the potatoes and set it next to Miguel's plate. "Just eat it!"

The boys laughed a little and then gave each other a knowing glance.

"Hey, Jean, do you want to take a ride in the boat with us this afternoon?" Miguel offered kindly.

Jean looked at him suspiciously. "Why?" she asked.

The boys never let her go on their adventures, even when she would beg to go, much less offer to let her go.

"Well, we were just thinking that you have had a lot of work to do with Mom and Dad gone, and that you might want to have a break for a few hours." Miguel put a forkful of whatever it was that Jean had made in his mouth and wrinkled up his nose.

"Quit it," Jean said, seeing his face.

"Well, do you want to go or not?" Virgil smiled.

Even though Jean was very suspicious, she was curious. "OK."

· · · · ·

The boys were unusually quiet as they drove the small speedboat down the river.

"Where are we going?" Jean asked, glad to be away from home for a bit. Anita had stayed with Paula and Dennis, and Jean was now free to just be a kid for the afternoon!

"Crocodile Creek," Miguel said and smiled.

"Hmm." Jean wondered what in the world the guys had up their sleeves.

Crocodile Creek was a little creek that went off of the main river. The current was a lot slower there, making it a perfect breeding ground for crocodiles. The boys liked to go down there after dark with a flashlight and flash the light along the edges of the river, looking for the red dots that were the reflection of baby crocodiles' eyes. Then they could slowly float the boat right up to the edge of the river, reach into the water, and grab them by surprise right at the neck so they couldn't bite. The crocodiles would squeal and thrash for a minute until they gave up and went limp. The boys were always challenging each other to see who would catch the biggest ones.

"Weren't you guys out here this morning?" Jean asked as they pulled into Crocodile Creek.

"Yup." Miguel smiled and looked at Virgil.

Jean looked back and forth at her two mischievous brothers as they did their best to look casual. She knew better. She knew this was going to be good, whatever it was.

Depending on the amount of rainfall at different times of the year, the river rose and fell accordingly. At this time, the river was on its way back down, and you could see in the brush along the sides or the river the mud line where the river had been just the week before. Miguel slowed the boat as they went around a bend, and headed toward a fallen tree by the side of the water. There, caught in the branches within the mud line was the *something* that the boys had up their sleeves.

"Oh gross, guys!" Jean's eyes were huge. "Yuck!"

"Yeah, sick, isn't it?" Virgil agreed.

"Oh, guys!" Jean had never seen anything like it!

Jean had thought the afterbirth was gross when delivering babies. She'd thought the fact that ladies often had to empty their bowels just before the baby's head came out was gross. She had thought a lot of things she'd seen in her life were gross. But she realized that she hadn't known gross until now.

"Should I move the boat closer?" Miguel teased.

Jean took a swat at him. "No! You guys are terrible!"

The *something* that the boys had found and had now successfully grossed out their sister with was a bloated, oddly-discolored, headless body of a naked woman.

"I knew you guys were up to something!" Jean wailed, unable to take her eyes off of what she was seeing. "You guys are so bad!"

When people die in the water, it isn't like on TV. A drowned person does not do the dead-man's float and then look just like they are asleep when they are removed from their watery grave. No. As soon as the lungs fill with water, the person sinks and stays sunk for twenty-four hours until bacteria do enough work to bloat the body with gases so that it will emerge from the water again, looking horrifically different from when it went in. Apparently, this woman had been killed and dumped into the river when the river was higher, and as she traveled along the river's underwater currents she had gotten hung up in the branches of the trees alongside the river. The river had gone down, so now she was exposed.

A few moments passed, and no one said anything. The whole idea with this trip with Jean was to scare her and gross her out. That was accomplished, so now what?

"What should we do now?" Virgil asked.

"Should we get her out of the tree?" Miguel suggested.

"And then what?" Jean didn't want to sit next to *that* on the ride home! No way. "Let's go on down to the army base and tell them, and let them take care of it!" Jean decided.

Miguel turned the boat around and headed for the army base.

In the weeks to come, nearly a dozen headless bodies got hung up in the branches near the houseboat. It was apparently a wave of executions being carried out by both sides of the war. At first, when they would see a body, Miguel and Virgil would go to the army base and report it. The leader of the base would write a letter for the boys to take back to the village nearest to them, called Mario Mendez, to give to the village leader, who would then send a dozen or so men up to where the body was to get it out of the water and bury it. Eventually, the men in Mario Mendez got tired of this and told the boys to stop reporting it to the army. So, finally, Virgil and Miguel would lasso the body, pull it ashore, and spend two or three hours digging holes and burying the bodies themselves.

The war was getting more terrible every day, but they had never felt afraid. You're thinking what was their problem? Were they just naïve or something? Clueless? Tempting God? Open up any major newspaper in the U.S., though, and what are you going to find? Will you find that the populace has got joy joy joy joy down in their hearts? Or are you going to see murder, death, muggings, theft, road rage, rapes, and suicide? Violence and scary things are everywhere. Therefore, the safest place to be is wherever God wants you to be, and He'll take care of the rest. Elam and Barbara knew that.

Both of Barbara's brothers and her sister Edna's first husband had died young in traffic accidents in the *safe* United States of America. To most Americans, being a foreigner in the midst of a third-world country civil war was an especially dangerous situation, but just like Elam had said, God had kept them safe because they were where God wanted them to be. It was much like a father leading his child across a dangerous city street full of traffic: as long as the child holds his father's hand, he is safe in that otherwise dangerous situation. Elam was holding God's hand, and God was leading him and his family safely through the war.

Chapter 23

The Ninja

_____

"...I have set before you life and death, the blessing and the curse.
So choose life in order that you may live,
you and your descendants...." _Deuteronomy 30:19_

Elam had just finished up another batch of cheese he had made and had just covered it in wax. He set it up on the cheese shelf to let it age. Then he came out of the house and rounded a corner to cross the airstrip just in time to see the tall man toss Miguel over his shoulder and down onto the ground. The man stood erect again, and turned his attention toward Miguel's little brother. He walked toward him and in true ninja style grabbed him like he weighed nothing and tossed him, too, over his shoulder and onto the ground.

Jack Roach, a visiting missionary, was there just standing by, watching and not moving a muscle. Elam approached, and the man turned toward him. Both of his boys were helpless on their backs at the feet of this man dressed as an army lieutenant. He reached the man just as his boys were getting on their feet again and faced him.

"Buenas tardes, Emilio!" Elam said smiling.

"Would you like a lesson in Kung Fu, too?" he said teasingly in perfect English.

Elam laughed. "Take it easy on my girls, I mean, my boys!"

"Hey, we were just getting started!" Miguel protested.

"Yeah, all that was part of our strategy!" Virgil added.

"Sure." Elam laughed again and continued in the direction he'd been heading.

"Don't worry. I'll take care of them, Elam!" Jack said.

Elam called back to Jack, "Oh sure. I feel better now!"

Emilio was an army sub-lieutenant in his late twenties, who had recently been stationed at the army base in Pipiles. The family had been very familiar with that base ever since they'd come to Guatemala. Because of the war, anyone who wanted to hold a meeting of more than three people needed specific permission from the military. It was so serious that the villagers dared not gather in groups of three or more even just to chat in the street or anywhere in public for fear they would be in trouble. So several times a week, every time Elam wanted to hold a church service, they'd needed to first go to the base for permission. In this way they quickly got to know everyone there.

Then, once the clinic was opened, the military base often came to them. La Anchura was now the closest clinic and store, and it was a virtual paradise to the local people. Normally, people didn't mow their yards: it took too much work and equipment they didn't have. But they had to do something. Otherwise the jungle just overtook them, as things grow 365 days a year in the jungle! The easiest thing to do to maintain an area that you didn't want to grow back up into jungle again was to spray a grass and weed killer on it called Paraquat. (More commonly known as Agent Orange.) Everyone was accustomed to either seeing jungle or dirt. Most of the local people had never even dreamed of something that looked as wonderful as La Anchura. It wasn't long until it seemed that every booboo or ache or pain the soldiers got was a perfect excuse to head up the river to La Anchura. They could buy a soda, check out a pretty nurse (Jean), and just enjoy the beautiful surroundings.

The first time they had met Emilio, he had brought some soldiers to the clinic who needed attention. He was unusual for a Guatemalan. He was very tall, light-skinned, thin, and spoke English, Spanish, a bit of German, and a bit of Japanese, which he had learned from his Japanese grandfather. He was serving as a sub-lieutenant and had the specialized training equivalent to or higher than a Green Beret in the States, which gave him the title of Kaibil. On top of all that he was also was a ninja and was registered with the government as "a deadly weapon."

He seemed to just *click* with the family right away and made many trips up to the clinic to visit with Elam or hang out with the boys. The boys really had fun with Emilio. He was older than them. He was cool. He was interesting. Heck, he was "a deadly weapon!" What boy would not love to have one of those for a friend?

While the boys at home in the States were watching movies about martial arts, Miguel and Virgil got personal lessons from a real-life ninja! And while boys at home in the States were playing with bb guns and going hunting once a year with their dads, Miguel and Virgil were getting to "play with" a real live Galil (an Israeli machine gun)! No little paper targets with little tiny holes peppering it from bb fire. No. They would set up concrete blocks and obliterate them with one shot of the Galil.

Sometimes Elam, Miguel, and Virgil had reasons to take trips downriver into Mexico. There was a town just across the border where they could buy diesel, and a beach in the river where they could dig and bag sand for free for building projects. Whenever they traveled like that, it was required that they stop at the military base, show their ID, and check in and out of Guatemala. On some of those trips when they had time, the boys would do more than just stop and check in and out. They would stick around for a few hours, and Emilio would allow them to run their obstacle training course; running, crawling on their bellies under barbed-wire fences, and climbing walls, competing against one of the soldiers.

After a while, Emilio began asking Elam serious questions about spiritual matters when he would visit. He was very in tune with the spirit world. He told Elam of how he would, "cross over to the dark side," as he put it and would, "open up to the dark spirits," to guide him when he went on missions, and that they would literally take him step by step through the whole night before it would happen. With their help, he could move fluidly through the dense jungle without making a sound or bumping into anything.

"With their guidance, it's as though it's daylight in the middle of the night. I can see perfectly in total darkness," Emilio explained.

Elam knew this was dangerous spiritually and told him so, but understood also that this was the life that Emilio had been taught by his grandfather, whom he loved. Just blurting it out wasn't going to help him any. He often told Emilio stories from the Bible about spirits and whenever it was appropriate explained to him again why Jesus had had to die on the cross for mankind.

"You know, Elam, I have heard all this stuff," he would say.

Aside from his grandfather, who had taught him to be a ninja, everyone in Emilio's entire family was a Christian.

"Look, Elam, even if I wanted to, I don't think the government would allow me to become a Christian," Emilio admitted one night.

That was probably one of the strangest excuses Elam had ever heard in all his days of witnessing to people about Jesus. He just looked at him and waited for the explanation.

"Seriously. I know that sounds crazy, but I am on a special…task force, you could say," he began hesitantly.

"But you can't tell me about it, or you'll have to kill me," Elam said jokingly.

Emilio didn't laugh. Instead he continued, "I am often assigned to go out and, well, eliminate people in the middle of the night. And in order to perform my duties, I have to connect to the dark spirits."

Elam understood. "And you know that if you were to become a Christian, you would have to abandon those spirits."

"Exactly. I would no longer be able to perform my duties. And I have a contract with the government. It is my job." He looked out a window thoughtfully.

"But you need to make a choice to do the right thing, and you know this isn't it. No matter what good you think you are doing for your country by working for the government, you are only part of the problem as long as you are not doing what you do for God."

Emilio looked at Elam. He knew what this gringo was telling him was true, but how could he leave? His whole life he had worked and trained for this, and he did have a contract. How could he just set aside what he'd worked for his whole life to become a Christian?

Emilio was hungry for God and could not let this drop. He didn't like what he was hearing from Elam, even though he did. He knew these were the answers that he was looking for to have peace, but it was frightening to think of letting go of his life. He finally came to the conclusion one night that he did in fact want to become a Christian, but came to talk to Elam a half dozen more times until he actually did it. He worked it out with his job that he would be able to be released from the contract. He was going to be completely free after he completed just one more mission.

The night of that mission, there was a knock at the door. Emilio had arrived looking for Elam, although no one had even heard a boat. He had not arrived with other soldiers as he usually did and was not dressed in his military uniform, but was covered in black head to toe, leaving only his eyes exposed. A large Samurai sword was strapped to his back.

"I need your help, Elam," Emilio said seriously, pulling his mask up off his face.

Elam brought him into the house. "What can I do for you?"

"I need you to pray for me," Emilio stated.

Elam could handle that.

"I need you to pray for God's spirit to leave me for tonight, so that I can complete my mission." Emilio almost looked desperate.

Elam shook his head. "I can't do that. I wouldn't even if I could. You know that."

Emilio paced the room a bit. "But as long as the Holy Spirit is in me, I can't connect to the dark spirits, and without them I can't complete my mission tonight."

"Emilio," Elam began, "I know you have already thought about this. You know you can't serve both sides. You have to choose. You can't just flip back and forth when it's convenient."

"I know that. And it's only this one time that I need to do it," he insisted.

"Look, I will pray for you, but not that the dark spirits would guide you. I will pray that God's Spirit will," Elam said.

Emilio sighed and agreed, and they prayed together. Then, as quickly and quietly as Emilio had arrived, he left. He pulled the mask back down over his face and stepped out into the darkness. In a few seconds there was no trace of him anywhere, not even a sound.

No one heard anything about Emilio for days. Elam wondered what had happened. Soldiers from the base had even shown up looking for him. Maybe he had died?

As people started showing up over the next few days for the clinic, the story started to come out.

"What you up to here?" Virgil asked his dad as he walked into the main exam room.

"Just putting this man's guts back in," Elam said in English with a slight smile.

Virgil looked at the man on the table. "A bull gored him?" was his guess.

"Yup," Elam said and kept sewing.

The man, who would someday be a person high up in a powerful Mexican drug cartel, had been brought by his friends all the way from a town called Beni Meritos in Mexico, several hours away. He'd been gored by a bull, and his intestines were hanging out. Elam had cleaned him up, put everything carefully back where it belonged, and sewed him back up, good as new.

"Have you heard what they're saying about what happened the other night?" Virgil asked.

Elam nodded. "People have been saying that the devil attacked a guerrilla camp in El Tumbo."

"What do you think about that?" Virgil smiled.

"I guess we'll see what happened when he shows up here again," Elam said, finishing up the last stitch.

The guerrillas who had been camping in El Tumbo the night that Emilio had his final assignment had all awoken in the middle of the night in terror: each of them had deep cuts and slashes all over his body, but no one died. Neither had anyone seen anyone. They'd concluded therefore that it had to be the devil that had done it!

Emilio showed up again a few days later, smiling. He had not asked the Holy Spirit to leave him. He had decided that he couldn't serve two masters and that he was going to serve God. Instead of seeking the dark spirits' help, he'd asked God to help him on his one final mission and had killed no one.

In 1972, when Elam had first arrived in Guatemala, he had thought he was coming to Guatemala to be a missionary to the poor Indian people in the Petén. But his mission was not a place or a certain group of people. His mission was Jesus, and Jesus was with him wherever he went, whether that was in the Presidential Palace in Guatemala City, in Lancaster Pennsylvania, along the road in Mexico, or here in his own home talking to a living, breathing, deadly weapon.

The guerrillas who'd been camped that night in El Tumbo, who would someday have as their main purpose to destroy all the work that Elam had done at La Anchura and to kick Elam out of their country, would never know that Elam had saved their lives that night. They would never know that it had been because of his mission in life that he'd been there when Emilio needed him. The guerrillas had been sleeping that night while the real battle had been raging: the battle between life and death, the blessing and the cursing. Emilio had chosen life. He had won that battle in his own life with Elam's help, and in his victory many lives were spared.

Chapter 24

Thanksgiving Raid

My people are destroyed for lack of knowledge. *Hosea 4:6*

Thanksgiving day, 1984, most families in the U.S. were just getting up in the morning to the smell of a cooking turkey or the sounds of mom in the kitchen getting the turkey ready to cook. All the kids were sleeping in instead of getting ready for school. Everyone was expecting the arrival of guests for a day of, well, gorging themselves and then kicking back and letting their poor bodies try to digest it all while watching a little football on TV.

The Stoltzfus family had a bit of a different start to their day in Guatemala. While their relatives and friends in the U.S. were preparing for this nice relaxing holiday, the guests who arrived early that morning at the Stoltzfus household were far from invited, and they didn't bring any shoofly pies with them.

Just after sunrise, still lying in bed, Elam heard loud shouting outside and the sound of someone banging the butt end of a gun on the front door of their house they had been living in for the last four years. He jumped out of bed and looked outside to see there were armed men swarming the yard. He could hear Virgil out at the front door talking to someone who was ordering everyone out of the house. The guerrillas.

Everyone was woken up (with the exception of Miguel, who was in the U.S.), escorted from their bedrooms by large machine guns, and ordered out of the house. While the family sat guarded in the yard, a large group of at least twenty men with muddy boots went through everything in the (carpeted) house. They took all the food out of the little store in the clinic, all of Virgil's and Miguel's good jeans and other clothing, and even some of the girls' clothes. *There were actually some guerrillas who were women!* After they were done dirtying up and looting the house, they went over into the clinic and took all the medicine, a lot of new dental equipment, and Elam's special toolbox of medical supplies that he always took with him to the villages.

After a while, the guards lost interest in watching the family, as they were obviously no threat. So Elam got up and went into the house to see what was going on in there, and found one of the commanders seated at his desk.

"Hello," the guerrilla absentmindedly said in English as Elam entered the room. The man had not even a touch of a Spanish accent.

"What are you doing?" Elam could see that he was going through all of his files in his desk.

"We know that your family is working for the CIA. We are just looking for some proof." Again, perfect English with no trace of an accent. This man was no local. He was white, and as Elam talked to him he figured out that he not only spoke perfect English and Spanish, but he also spoke German.

"Do you have any books I could read?" He was still flipping page by page through all the papers in Elam's desk.

Elam reached over on one bookshelf and grabbed a Bible. He set it down on the desk in front of the guerrilla commander, who looked at the Bible and scowled, "Oh, give me a break."

"Whatever it is exactly that you're looking for, is in here. All the answers you need for everything in life are in here!" Elam smiled, thinking of the large bag of John Osteen's preaching tapes he'd seen one of the guerrillas taking from the house earlier.

The commander stopped his page turning for a second, grabbed the Bible, and held it up. "This is full of lies. I doubt you even believe anything that's in here! You're no missionary! You know it, and I know it. I just need something to prove it!"

The guerrillas just knew that this whole missionary thing had to be a front. Still, page after page, all the commander found was newsletters and Bible study notes. He'd seen enough of the phrase "Praise the Lord" for one day.

All of the guerrillas kept checking their watches, and after an hour and a half, they left just as rudely as they'd arrived. Like armed Santa Clauses carrying huge bundles over their shoulders, they all had soon vanished into the jungle.

Virgil was up for some adventure, so he took off after them, following their trail as best he could through the jungle. Most of the time they were close enough ahead of him that he could hear them. Periodically they would stop. Virgil figured it was to rest, since they were all carrying a *lot* of stuff!

After about a half hour they stopped for a long time. Virgil was afraid that they'd seen him and were coming back for him, so he climbed up high in a tree and hid among some palm branches and waited. After an hour or so, they finally left. He climbed back down to continue following them, and when he reached the place where they'd been he noticed a suspicious-looking spot on the ground of loosely piled palm branches.

Carefully, in case it was a buried land mine, Virgil began to move away the leaves. Underneath the ground was loose; something was buried under there. Again, moving cautiously so as not to blow himself up if it was a land mine, he gently moved away the earth until he saw a bag. He kept digging and eventually he felt safe to pull the whole bag out. It was full of the medical books that the guerrillas had just taken. He removed several bags of very heavy and expensive medical books, and then recovered the spot exactly the same as he'd found it. It was starting to drizzle, so he hoisted the bag over his shoulder and headed back down the trail toward the clinic.

· · · · ·

"Hey, what did you find?" Elam's eyes brightened seeing Virgil coming back into the house with something over his shoulder.

He plopped the heavy bag down. "Books. It's all the medical books they took." He plopped himself down in a chair, too, and let out a tired sigh. Barbara poured him a glass of water. "I also found some of the dental equipment," he said.

Elam checked the books, glad to see them returned. "Where did you find them? Was the filling equipment there?"

"About a half hour from here they had a little camp and had these buried beside their trail, and no, no filling equipment." He finished the glass of water, and Barbara took it to refill it.

"Thanks, Mom," Virgil said.

Elam looked thoughtful. What if they decided to abandon the dental equipment they'd taken, too? He didn't want to see all that very expensive, technical equipment rotting in the jungle somewhere. Among the many problems in the villages, no one had taught the people how to properly care for their teeth. Usually, the villagers would greet you with big smiles of gross, chunky, white-coated teeth, black and gray cavity-filled teeth, or no teeth at all. Often, by the time the people were adults, their teeth were so rotten their only hope for a pain-free mouth was to have all of their teeth pulled. Recently, someone had donated all this awesome filling equipment, and Elam had been excited to get started on that. Filling children's cavities and teaching them all about better dental hygiene was going to be awesome!

"I can't just sit here now if there's the possibility they're going to abandon that equipment and let it rot somewhere." Elam was over forty years old by now, sure, but he wasn't old. He was up for a little adventure, too, so he and Virgil both headed toward the door.

When they had reached the trail into the jungle, they encountered one of their neighbors, Paco.

"You guys are going to follow the guerrillas?" His eyes were wide. "No one but the army follows them. Are you guys crazy?"

Elam and Virgil smiled. "You want to come with us?"

Paco thought for a second. It was true; no one but the army dared follow the guerrillas. No one dared cross them. If they were spotted, the guerrillas would shoot first and ask questions later. Then a boyish smile crossed his face. He was a guy. Of course he wanted to come along.

They walked for almost an hour with no sign of them, and then suddenly there they were. They heard the sound of dozens of guns cocking and the rustling of feet and hushed whispers as all of the guerrillas hid and got into position to shoot. Immediately, they knew they had gotten too close. Paco and Virgil hit the dirt right away, and Virgil told his dad, "Down! Get down!"

Elam crouched down and ran over to where Virgil was, and they all hid behind a fallen tree. "Did Virgil just tell me to hide, and I did it?" Elam thought to himself. He might have laughed if it weren't such a serious moment.

"It's just us, the gringos. We want to talk to you!" Virgil called out in the chaos over and over, hoping they would hear him before someone shot them. He kept expecting a hand grenade to come flying in any second, and he was ready to catch it and throw it back!

He waited. Finally, there was silence. "It's just us! The gringos! We want to talk to your leaders! We're unarmed!"

Several minutes passed as the startled guerrillas decided what to do. Finally, one guy in a white t-shirt came crawling on his belly out of the bush, weapon aimed at Virgil. Slowly, more appeared, and then they surrounded the three and checked them for weapons.

The commander appeared. He was a big guy with a big beard who spoke like an educated Guatemalan. He was probably a college graduate from the city. "If you see anyone else out there in the jungle following them, shoot to kill," he told his men.

He then turned and motioned for Elam, Paco, and Virgil to come with him.

The leaders were all seated in a small clearing. Now recovered from their scare, they were back to the business of roasting a tepesquintle together. None of the guys looked like your average villager. They all carried themselves like they were well educated. Some didn't look or speak Spanish like Guatemalans, either.

"Buenas tardes," Elam, Virgil, and Paco all greeted the men in the circle.

"Gracias. Buenas tardes," the head commander replied in return. The Spanish language is customarily very polite, even in the rudest of situations. "Why have you guys followed us out here?" the commander began.

Elam replied, "The dental equipment you took; it's very delicate equipment that we waited and prayed for for a long time. We don't want to see it go to waste."

The commander just looked at him disinterestedly.

Elam was feeling bold so he added, "You guys claim to be for the people, for the oppressed and the poor, and yet you come and raid our clinic. If anything you should be helping us, because we really are helping the poor around here, and you guys all know that. You know the condition of the teeth of the people in the villages around here, and that equipment was going to help them. It was going to spare them from living in pain for years like they do and save their teeth before there's nothing left but to pull them out and leave them toothless."

The commander was still looking disinterested. "So what is your point?"

"My point is I don't want to see that equipment just abandoned out here somewhere in the jungle, left to rust, when there is a clinic back there ready to use it to help the people!"

"Open your mouth, and show the gringo your teeth," the commander said to one of the men.

The man rose and walked over to Elam and opened his mouth to show the fillings.

"We have people trained to use that equipment and have been filling teeth out here in the jungle for years now during this revolution. We're not taking it just to take it; we need it. We need it more than you do." The commander shifted his position and got a big, cocky smile on his face. "For us it's survival. All you have to do is cry back to the U.S. and pull on people's heartstrings a little, and all those naïve people up there will send you millions of dollars for more equipment."

He was taunting Elam, but also partly speaking from experience, as the guerrillas had made their own fund-raising trips to the U.S. and done just that even in churches. Some of the other men snickered. The commander motioned with his hand toward the direction of Mexico. "The equipment has already been taken by boat to Mexico."

Elam was a little disappointed, but at the same time relieved to hear that the equipment was at least going to go to use.

"So, is the military following you?" The commander was sure they were actually leading the military to the camp. This guy couldn't actually be risking his life to get some dental equipment back. After all, he was no missionary. This was taking the act a little far! He motioned to some of the men and sent scouts around. Anyone following was to be immediately killed.

"We're not being followed. We saw the buried books, and we just didn't want to see the equipment end up rusting in some hole out here in the jungle, too. That's all," Virgil said.

It was even a little more than that to Elam. He had just learned to do dental work and had taken it very seriously and was excited about it. He was mad. It wasn't so easy to just "send to the States and get new stuff." He'd worked and prayed and waited a long time for this equipment, and it wasn't small thing to the person who'd donated it, either. Now the hopes he'd had for all he could do with it were gone.

"That equipment was going to be a real blessing to the people around here," Elam sighed.

"A blessing, was it?" the commander rolled his eyes hearing the religious wording. "You yourself know there is no God. Why are you constantly deceiving the people, telling them to believe in God?"

Elam had heard plenty of the guerrillas' pep talks in the villages. "If that's what you believe, then why do you use Jesus to sometimes convince the people to be on your side? You tell the Indians in the churches that Jesus was the first revolutionary, and you are the followers of Christ?"

The leader simply looked at him and made no reply.

Elam had seen more than one of the churches he'd planted empty after the guerrillas had come through the village recruiting. He had also heard of some of the fund-raising that the guerrillas had done in the U.S., going around to churches, even in Elam's own Lancaster County, claiming that they were now the underground church in Guatemala and they were being persecuted.

"If Jesus was the first revolutionary and you follow Him, what about the time He taught a parable where He said that everything that had been given to the man who had little would be taken from him because of his irresponsibility and that it would be given to the man who had much who had been responsible?" Elam wondered what he'd have to say to that.

The commander chose not to comment about Jesus and changed the subject. He went off about the U.S. government and all the terrible things that President Reagan was doing. "President Reagan is our number one enemy, and you represent him. We're confident you're working for your government here, and that makes you our enemy."

"Look, I don't know where you're from exactly, but you sound like an educated person. You know you can't just take from the rich and give to the poor. You know a government can't actually function that way, and you know that's not actually what Jesus was teaching," Elam said.

The commander was getting tired of him talking and didn't want him talking in front of the men anymore. "Would you like some meat?" He was done with the conversation.

"No thank you," Elam replied.

Then, just as they had suddenly left the clinic, everyone started to get up and grab their guns like they were panicking.

"Was the army following you?" someone asked again.

The commander barked some orders to some men, sending them out in a few directions, and they ran. Then, the three of them were directed to leave. "This time if you return, you will be shot."

Without speaking, Elam, Paco, and Virgil left, knowing that this last bit of information was absolutely true.

· · · · ·

Walking home on the curvy jungle path made it seem as though this had all happened far away, yet this had happened less than half a mile from home. The guerrillas were camped on the Stoltzfus' land out by the river; land that was still uncleared and thick with jungle. They were waiting for the military to come and intervene, which they did whenever the guerrillas did a raid somewhere. That was the reason these men had stayed behind while all the others with the stolen goods had gone on. These guys were here to ambush the military.

As he walked toward home, Elam thought of the poor people's army and what they were doing to this country. People like little Hilda, a child of a poor Indian family, had been casualties of the war and would never even be in the history books.

Hilda had arrived at the clinic at nineteen months of age weighing only ten pounds. Her parents were doing the best they knew how based on what their parents had taught them and what everyone else around them knew to do.

The old wives tales and traditions that controlled women's lives after giving birth actually harmed their bodies and deprived them of the nutrients they needed to make milk to feed their babies. They believed that for the first forty days after birth they were not allowed to eat just about anything or it would harm their bodies. They were not allowed to eat eggs, or beans, or tomatoes, or onions *just for starters*.

The poor villagers lived off the food they grew, which was mainly beans. Their primary source of protein was eggs. (Chickens were too expensive to eat regularly.) Women who normally ate eggs and beans three meals a day were frightened after delivering a baby into thinking that these foods would harm them. So, having nothing else to eat, they ate practically nothing but tortillas and dried-out chicken.

The first month after delivery, when their bodies were struggling to recuperate after delivering a baby and trying to do the work of feeding another human being, these women actually ate more poorly than at any other time of their lives. Needless to say, many of the ladies were malnourished, and therefore their bodies couldn't make enough milk for their babies. They would be forced to begin feeding their babies with bottles, which would also cause their bodies to make less milk, ensuring that they would need to keep feeding with bottles.

For an educated American, resorting to bottle-feeding proves to be a hassle and an expense, but the baby gets fed, because in the United States even a young child knows you put milk or formula in a baby bottle. Most Americans even know that you give them baby formula for the first year and it is a big deal that day when you first put plain cow's milk in the baby's bottle. The people here didn't know about baby formula. Even if they had, one can would cost the equivalent to a whole week's wage. Who could afford such a thing?

Not only was formula out of their price range, but so was milk. And try getting it. Milk was not offered in liquid form in this area of the world, where it was always over eighty-five degrees and no one had a refrigerator! Sometimes they could get plain powdered milk in bags, but even that was expensive.

So, for feeding babies they would often resort to something else. Something else that was quite a bit cheaper. Easy to get. Sold everywhere. Didn't need refrigeration. Something they had seen their moms put in babies' bottles. Something their neighbors and aunts and uncles and even the local midwives put in babies' bottles. Something they all believed must be good for you because it gave you energy and therefore must be good for babies, too. Coffee.

When the traditions in the villages led a mother to need to supplement her newborn baby's diet with a bottle, the baby would be fed watered-down coffee with sugar. The sugar would give the baby just enough calories to keep going, but the coffee would leave the baby right where she was, not gaining a pound. Just as an American feeding a baby formula would feel frustrated and confused watching their baby deteriorate and get sick, the people here felt the same way. Why when they were doing all they knew to do was their baby getting sicker and sicker?

Simple elementary school health classes or even access to watching U.S. public television would have helped, but there were no schools in the villages; only in the bigger towns like Sayaxché. And when their babies seemed sick, making a trip all the way into Sayaxché to a doctor was a hardship that could take several days and more money than the family had to spare. Plump, fat, healthy babies were not the norm. Skinny, little ones were. Often, the parents didn't even realize that anything was wrong until it was almost too late…like with little Hilda.

Hilda was pitiful when she arrived. The Stoltzfus family offered to keep her at their home until she was better. Barbara had gotten very good at this by now, having done it with more than a dozen babies. She spent many a sleepless night feeding Hilda every hour, ounce by ounce to build her little body up. The whole family helped and took care of her as though she were their very own new little sister.

It didn't take long for her to respond, and in just three months she was walking. In five months, she was a happy and very healthy pudgy little two-year-old. Just like she should be. When her family returned, they could hardly believe their eyes! This was their little Hilda! They had feared that she was going to die, and now look at her! They cried tears of joy, thanked the family for saving her life, and took her home.

Although Elam and Barbara did counsel them on how to feed her once they got her home, it's hard to undo generations of tradition in a few conversations, so poor Hilda went back to the same environment that had caused her to need to come to the clinic in the first place. In just two months, little Hilda was no longer healthy and running and playing. In just two months, Hilda died.

· · · · ·

Thanksgiving evening, Elam sat on the edge of his bed thinking angrily about all the guerrilla commanders had said to him. "Lord, why? The truth is so obvious! Why can't these people see it? Why can't the guerrillas see what they're doing to their own country?" he said.

Barbara nodded in agreement. "It is a shame they can't see that the war is keeping things from getting better here."

"That is such an understatement!" Elam got up and walked around the room a little.

Because of the war, the country could not progress. While other Central American countries were welcoming foreign businesses with all their money and jobs for the people and were building roads, schools, hospitals, and cities, Guatemala was busy fighting a war.

"It is just so frustrating!" he went on. "Every time the government tries to do something, the guerrillas just come in and blow it up or burn it down, and all the villagers know is that nothing is changing and the government is not doing anything!" The people didn't necessarily know why the government was not doing anything for them, so they gave more and more support to the guerrillas who preached about the evils of the government and how much better the country would be when they were in power.

He sighed as he sat down on their bed. "You know, as long as this war is going on there will be no good hospitals in the Petén. No new schools or paved roads. No nothing. Nothing is going to change, and people are just going to keep living in ignorance and dying for no good reason!"

He thought of the medical equipment that he'd lost; how far back that had put them. And, now they would have to give the bad news to the supporters that the equipment had been stolen and hope that more could be found.

"Ignorance is not bliss," Elam said almost to himself.

Barbara reached over and put her hand on top of his. "It is frustrating, I know, but God will replace what has been lost. He always does."

Elam smiled. "I know." He put his head back against his pillow. "The Bible says that we will know the truth and the truth will make us free, and the truth is just so far from the guerrilla movement. This country is so completely not free. There is so much bondage and suffering here, all because of this anti-God preaching of the guerrillas trying in vain to make a better world for themselves. And the results are just…look around us!"

Barbara laid her head down next to his. "If only they understood that a world without God cannot be better."

All this just gave Elam a fire beneath him to want to spread the Word of God even more, and do even more for the people. "God, let this war end!" he prayed.

Chapter 25

Visiting Widows

The Light shines in the darkness, and the darkness
did not comprehend it. *John 1:5*

Elam caught sight of it on his way out the back door of the clinic, and
he still had to stop and take an extra long look at it. A dream that was
sparked by the landing of the first airplane on their airstrip was now a
reality. Virgil really was a jungle pilot now.

Mark Moyer, the pastor of the Full Gospel Church in Narvon, Pennsylvania, had decided a few years ago that he was going to do something to
get an airplane for the medical mission and had gotten several churches
to work together on it. Now here it was: a four-passenger Maule M-4-22C.
Never would Elam have dreamed growing up that one of his own children
would someday own an airplane, yet there it sat on the airstrip. The things
that God had provided their family with never ceased to amaze him.

"Well, we're off, Virgil. You can handle things while we're gone?" Elam
said as he was heading out to the river.

Virgil and Miguel were both grown-ups now, and Jean, now a licensed
practical nurse, was in her twenties. Anita, Lisa, and Maria were all in their
teens. Could they handle things?

"We'll try, Dad. You guys have a good time!" Virgil gave his mom a
quick hug.

Elam and Barbara were off to the States to visit churches. This was
probably the two-dozenth trip they'd taken to the States since they'd
been in Guatemala. It was crucial to maintain contact with the people in
churches scattered all throughout the U.S. who were making it possible
financially for them to do the work they were doing here. Elam was good

about putting together newsletters several times a year, but still it meant so much more to people to see you in person.

When they went all the way to Pennsylvania it was over 3,000 miles. Before you start imagining how far that would be in the U.S., like "driving from New Jersey to Nevada" or something, let me just remind you that it's nothing like that. In the U.S., you pack your car and pull out of your driveway and head for the interstate. You cruise as fast as you can on a nicely paved road with the radar detector humming (unless you're the type to care about your Christian witness while you're driving). If you get hungry or need to use the potty, you simply pull over at the next rest stop, or McDonalds, which is usually conveniently less than an hour away. There, you can use a bathroom that has toilets with seats and toilet paper, and when you're finished in the bathroom you can buy some fries and a shake or use some of your change in a machine to get some coffee or a candy bar. You can even whip out your cell phone, PDA, or laptop and send a few emails while you're at it, or maybe even check out junglebreezes.com.

Traveling from La Anchura to the U.S. was not anything remotely like that. They would pack their bags and walk them down to the river's edge. No car. Just sitting by the river's edge and waiting. Waiting, sweating, waiting, and sweating in the hot sun for a boat to come by that they could catch a ride with. Sometimes they could wait all day for a boat to come by that had space for travelers and luggage. From there, it was a few hours upriver to town to their vehicle.

Today's wait wasn't long, and the boat ride was even quite relaxing. No one shot at them, and nothing exploded. There were no guerrillas. No surprises. Elam even got in a little bit of a nap on the way. When they got to Sayaxché, they paid the boat driver for the ride and then headed up the hot dusty street, carrying their luggage, smiling, and greeting people as they made their way through town. Going uphill about ten blocks they got to their truck, which they paid monthly to park on someone's property, and they loaded it. Then, it was a long bouncy ride on the dirt road to the border. The only advantage to travel in Guatemala over U.S. interstate travel was that rather than one-hour intervals between rest areas, one could pull over and use the restroom just about anywhere on these roads!

Now, although they were only a few miles as the crow flies from the Mexican border, to actually cross over legally into Mexico through a border crossing they had two options. First, they could head east, and then south all the way to Guatemala City, and then west…and then north; yes, a big circle that took more than twenty-four hours just to be able to exit Guatemala! Their other option, which was a little shorter, was to bounce east on that dirt road for about sixty-five miles (for about a day) and go through Belize, which is on the eastern border of Guatemala, and then go north into Mexico on the Yucatan Peninsula. On this trip, although there was always paperwork they could find to work on in Guatemala City and errands to run, they would be taking the shorter route through Belize. There was a little town northeast of them in Mexico where they needed to make a stop to visit some "widows."

About two years ago, some of the people living in Mario Mendez had notified the military that they'd found a guerrilla base near the next village of El Tumbo (The Tomb—not a very nice name for a village, but it was named after a Mayan tomb they found nearby). A group of about seventy soldiers arrived, and there was a confrontation—shooting and lots of noise—but the guerrillas were able to escape. The army returned to base.

That night while it was pouring down rain, the guerrillas returned to El Tumbo and told the villagers that because they had not been the ones to report their location to the military, they were now considered by the military to be on the side of the guerrillas.

"The military will return tonight, and you will be treated like the enemy and all be wiped out!"

"You will all be exterminated! We must flee!"

"You know the government has done this in the past!"

"You have to run now before it's too late!"

Some of the villagers were terrified and believed the guerrillas and were ready run, but not everyone believed them or wanted to leave. Those who didn't believe them were forced to go along with the escape anyway. At gunpoint, the guerrillas led literally the entire village, old people and young, through the mosquito-infested jungle for three days.

Just before they reached the border of Mexico, they separated the men from the women, and continued toward Mexico. At the border, both groups were informed of the horrible end that the other group had met. Both groups were told that the military had caught up with the other group and totally wiped them out. They were now alone. The men then had no women and children to go to Mexico with or for, and were now filled with hatred against the military for wiping out their families. They were given uniforms and guns and became part of the revolution.

The women, now believing themselves to be widows, fled in terror to a refugee camp in Campeche, Mexico. These were the "widows" Elam and Barbara needed to visit. They had letters from their husbands at home to deliver.

· · · · ·

"I am allowed in here once or twice a week because of my bakery business. You can just come in with me," the pastor told them as he loaded his bags up with bread.

In Campeche they had met a local pastor and found out that it was part of his ministry to go into the camp as often as he was allowed. He wasn't allowed in for religious services, but he was allowed in to sell bread. So that's what he did. He made bread and went in and helped feed the people with that and with whatever portions of the Bread of Life he was able to give them individually.

They met up in town and then headed to the campsite. At the entrance there was a Mexican immigration booth, but no one was there.

"Let's just go on in then." The pastor pointed in the direction they should go toward an office where they could check in.

The office, too, although it was already 9:00 in the morning, was vacant. So they parked their car and started walking around, talking to the people there.

"Everyone looks very suspiciously at us," Barbara noted. People did. They were afraid.

"Buenos días!" Elam greeted a man who was reclining in a hammock in front of his hut.

"Buenos," the man unenthusiastically replied.

"Do you know in what part of the camp the people from the Petén are living?" Elam asked.

"Nope. Maybe he knows?" he pointed over toward the hut next door and the man collecting sticks in front of it.

"Gracias."

They headed over and talked to the man collecting the sticks, and he thought that maybe the "Peteneros" were off that direction over *that way*.

So, they headed off that direction over *that way*. As they walked, they were noticed by everyone. This was a closed community, and all outsiders were very obvious. Especially very white ones!

Finally, they ran into someone they knew. With smiles and hugs they greeted one another. They talked for a while and finally were pointed in the right direction to hopefully find the women they were seeking.

"How did you even get in here?" one man, an old friend from a church Elam had started years before, asked.

"Well, we just came in. There was no one at the gates when we got here."

Soon, they were being asked the same question by many other smiling old friends.

Once, Elam had been going downriver to visit the church in La Bella (The Beauty) and had seen a large group of people from one of his other churches in La Flor (The Flower) "fleeing" through the jungle with some guerrillas. He'd stopped to talk to them, and asked them where they were going and why they were leaving. He'd gotten a similar story from them as the group from El Tumbo had for leaving. The military was on its way to wipe out their village, and they were fleeing for their lives.

Elam knew this wasn't true, but kept his opinion to himself at the time. Going against the guerrillas in such a case would have done nothing more than end Elam's life right there on the spot, and the villagers would have continued to their destination in Mexico anyway.

The entire congregation of the church in La Flor had gone to Mexico that day, leaving the church empty. Now, here in Mexico in this refugee camp, they all gathered around Elam, greeting him. Some of them were asking questions about the war in Guatemala and had no idea what was going on back home. They had not seen any news since they had fled Guatemala over two years ago. Some of them were unaware that a new president had been elected. Some of them believed that the entire Petén had been exterminated by the military and that there were no people left there! And they were surprised to find out that Elam and Barbara were still at La Anchura, because they had been told that all the Christians in the country had been slaughtered and that all Americans had been exiled from the country.

Barbara and Elam ran into many people from some of their other churches as well, and it was for a short time a wonderful reunion. They kept asking where they would be able to find the ladies they were looking for. Most people either didn't know or didn't want to tell them, for some reason.

"How did you get in here!" the question came from behind the group of people.

They all turned. It was a small group of guerrilla leaders in charge of the camp. The villagers scattered to their huts, leaving Barbara and Elam in the middle of the street.

"Well, when we got here, we went to the office, but no one was there, so we just started to wander around to talk to people," Elam replied.

"What do you want here? You aren't allowed to be in here!" said another equally unfriendly man. Both of them were heavily armed. A few of the villagers came back out and did their timid best to stick up for their long-lost friends and said they were just visiting and that they'd like them to be able to stay a while longer.

"Absolutely not. You are not welcome here. You must leave immediately!"

"We have some messages to deliver to some ladies who used to live near us. They're from their families back home," Barbara told them.

The camp leaders became more agitated; that was not the right thing to say. It was clear they had no interest in these messages being delivered, but they finally agreed to hold a session or camp meeting to discuss this whole problem at 2 p.m., which gave Elam and Barbara just a little more time to talk to people. Although the camp leaders wanted them out of there, they managed to visit there the entire day, not leaving until almost 4 p.m. They were able to tell the people of El Tumbo that their village had not been burned, that the army had actually stationed there for a few weeks to protect it, that their families there were alive and well, and that the men had not been killed, either. The people didn't know what to say. Years they had spent here with the guerrilla commanders telling them something totally the opposite, and now, these two people who they normally trusted were telling them they had been lied to all this time? They were too afraid to reply and said nothing.

Finally, a man told them that there was another refugee camp nearby, and that was where the ladies whom they were looking for were. Barbara, Elam, and the bread-maker pastor piled back into his bread truck and left. They had gotten some idea from a few people as to the direction of the other camp and headed there, still armed with the two letters for the two widow ladies.

They found the camp, and this time the Mexican immigration booth was manned. They stopped there, showed their passports, and told the immigration officer they just wanted to visit with some old friends. They were allowed in. They started talking to people, asking about the ladies.

Again, they were met with a lot of suspicion at first, and no one seemed to want to answer them. Finally, they ran into an old man from El Tumbo.

"I know them," he said. He didn't exactly know where the ladies were at this moment, but he offered to take the letters, risking his own life if he was found with them, to get them to the ladies. (They did eventually get the letters, and years later, after the war was over, were reunited with their husbands.)

What Elam and Barbara hadn't known was that these two particular ladies had been used as spokeswomen for "the revolution" in their fundraising efforts in the U.S. An award-winning, internationally famous woman, an indigenous guerrilla leader, had personally taken these ladies to churches in the U.S. to tell their horrible story about fleeing the Guatemalan army in the middle of the night and of the slaughter of their husbands. The guerrilla leaders most definitely did not want these ladies to receive any word from home.

After only about twenty minutes had passed, cars came rushing into the camp. Men jumped out screaming and waving guns. "What are you doing in here?" said one man.

"You have no business here!" said another.

"You have to leave now!" said another.

This time, there was no meeting to discuss it later. They were escorted out of the camp right away.

One man was screaming at the immigration officer for having let them in. He was irate. He was armed. "Don't bother the immigration officer!" Elam interrupted. "He was only doing his job! We're leaving!" and he headed toward their car.

As they got into their car, the angry screaming men also got into their car and stayed right on their tail. They were followed out of the camp and through the town. The police joined the party and also followed them. Finally, once they left the town, the cars were gone.

Seeing all the people from the churches they had started living in such bondage and fear was hard, but Elam and Barbara felt good that they had been able to make a little contact with them and hopefully shed a little light. "That is so sad! Their lives have all been torn apart by lies!" Barbara sighed.

"We were able to share a lot of news with them; I think at the very least we've started a chain of thinking in their minds that will lead to them finding their own answers eventually," Elam said.

"I guess there's not much more we can do than that. Hopefully those letters will bring a little bit of truth and hope to the ladies to know their husbands are still alive and waiting for them at home."

For Elam and Barbara, their ministry was the true Hope of the world, and that is Jesus. Since coming to Guatemala they had brought Jesus to the people through churches and church-related things, through their clinic and helping people with their health, through friendships and working alongside people in their daily lives, and more and more they were being drawn into the conflict dividing Guatemalan and Guatemalan—this horrible civil war. One of their greatest hopes was to see the war and all the suffering it was causing end and to see the people begin to live in peace. As long as it was in their power to do so, they would keep trying to accomplish that goal one person at a time by introducing everyone to Jesus, the Prince of Peace. But it would all get worse before it would get better.

Chapter 26

The Ultimatum

*For our struggle is not against flesh and blood,
but against the rulers, against the powers,
against the world forces of this darkness,
against the spiritual forces of wickedness
in the heavenly places. Ephesians 6:12*

The loud explosion could be heard from all the way up at the clinic at La Anchura. Elam was in the house, and Virgil was in the barn milking Bossy. Although gunfire and explosions were a normal part of the scenery around them, both of them just knew that sound meant something bad had just happened.

As they looked up from what they were doing, they could see a huge plume of smoke rising off of the river toward El Tumbo. Before they even had a chance to wonder about what had happened, they heard a boat coming from a long way off. Boats passing by and boats coming to the clinic had a different sound. This boat was heading straight for the clinic in a hurry. They were both at the dock when the boat arrived.

"*Baleemar*, what is it?" Elam asked, looking at the boat full of frightened passengers.

Waldimar Segura was a friend of theirs from Sayaxché, who was one of the rich guys in town. He had a finca or a ranch downriver near Pipiles and had been heading there today when he came across the results of the explosion that Elam and Virgil had just heard.

"Don Elam! Virgil! Do you guys have a radio or something to call out with?" Waldimar looked panicked.

"Yeah, what's wrong?" Elam said.

"Back there," he motioned back from the way that he'd just come, "an army boat got ambushed by the guerrillas, and there are men in the water. We were just passing through there, and I saw that Cruz was in the water, but I know the guerrillas are in the jungle right there so I couldn't stop or they would have shot us!"

Elam and Virgil both knew Cruz. He was one of Waldimar's workers and a friend. He was driving the boat for the army transport down the river to the army base at Pipiles.

A look of guilt and frustration washed over Waldimar's face. "He was motioning to me, but I couldn't stop!"

Elam agreed with him, "We understand. We know why you kept going."

It was true. In this war, if you did anything to help anybody, the other side took it as a sign that you were the enemy. Stopping to help the military would mean that you were on the military's side, and that would make you the enemy of the guerrillas. If they didn't shoot you then, they might find you at your house and take your family out with you. Waldimar had several small children including three-year-old twin girls at home. He owed it to his family not to stop.

Virgil jumped up, "Look, Dad, I'll get in our boat and head down there just like I'm passing by. Maybe I can get Cruz out of the water before the guerrillas get him." He was off and running for the boat already.

"Wait!" Elam called out, running after his son. "I'll come, too."

They got in their speedboat and took off for the ambush site, adrenaline pumping. They came around a turn and could see the boat up ahead near the side of the river. It was your typical Guatemalan cargo boat, about sixty feet long and about five feet wide in the middle, made of mahogany and then painted a lovely shade of mint green with dark orange trim. Half of it was in flames. As they approached, they cut their motor and drifted right up to the boat. Elam hopped out onto the shore, while Virgil hopped right into the flaming boat. Both of them were looking for survivors.

"Hey!" came the shout from across the river. It was the guerrillas.

Virgil looked across the river and could see that there was someone there, but couldn't see their face. "Hey!" he called back.

"Bring that boat over here!"

"What?" Virgil looked at the wreck he was standing in.

"Tie that boat to yours and drag it over here, now!" the man on the riverbank commanded again.

"No way! There's live ammo on here! This thing's going to blow any minute!" Virgil argued.

"Then grab the guns and the ammo and bring it back over here." It wasn't a suggestion or a request but an order.

Virgil looked around and could see machine guns and a big box of ammunition. Grabbing these things and giving them to the men across the river only meant that more people would die, and he was tired of people dying. Tired of flying injured people out to the hospitals. Tired of burying people at the river's edge whom they found floating down the river. He thought fast and started moving around as though he were complying with their orders. He dragged a box of ammo with his foot over to the fire, as well as a few grenades.

"Dad!" he called out, "get behind a tree and don't move no matter what you hear! Some things are going to explode!" Elam did what his son said and took note again of the fact that they'd switched roles.

"Hey! What are you doing over there? Get the stuff and get over here!" came more orders from across the river.

"Yeah, come on! Hurry up!" said another voice.

"I'm trying!" Virgil replied. He grabbed some things that would actually help the guerrillas; rubber boots, clothes that had been stripped off by the soldiers before they bailed out into the river, and whatever other things were on the side of the boat that wasn't on fire, and started throwing things into his own boat.

"Pop! Pop! Pop!" Elam could hear that the ammo was starting to go and prayed that Virgil would get out of the boat.

"Don't move, Dad! There are some grenades that are going to go off, too!" Virgil called out to his dad again.

Elam wasn't planning on moving.

"Hurry up! Get over here!" the men yelled.

The popping intensified. It was time to get out of there. Virgil jumped from the burning boat into his own, started the motor, and headed toward the voices from across the river.

He hadn't gotten too far away when, "Booom!" a grenade went off and split the boat totally in half. (Yeah, just like in the movies. Too bad the camera crew was on their lunch break.) When Virgil arrived at the oppo-site shore, he was greeted by men with machine guns.

A dangerous man known as Herman approached Virgil immediately, furious. "What are you doing here? Put your hands up!"

Several men aimed their machine guns at Virgil, while others got in his boat to see what he'd gotten from the burning wreck.

"All he got was this junk," came a protest from the boat as the pair of boots came flying out across the ground.

Another man piped up. "Hey, give him a break, he did what he could. A grenade blew up over there."

Herman wasn't moved. "I asked you what you're doing here!" He shoved his gun up into Virgil's face.

"Calm down! Calm down!" Virgil said.

"What? Don't tell me to calm down!" he yelled at Virgil.

Then, to the rest of the men he yelled, "Is this one of those gringos from La Anchura?"

Several men shouted, "Si!"

Then his eyes lit up a little, "You guys have been helping the army! We know it! And for that you are going to die!" He put his gun down and pointed his finger into Virgil's face instead. "We're coming to your place soon! You've got pocos días left!"

Virgil's brow furrowed. "What do you mean 'we have few days left'?"

Herman looked at him, still enraged. "Look, you have been trying to say you're neutral all these years, but the time is over for accepting that! No more neutral! You're either with us or against us! And, if you choose to be against us then you will die! Thirty days! That's all you have! Thirty days to decide!"

Virgil was going to ask him again what exactly he meant when he heard a PC7 fighter plane coming. "Whoa! Here comes the army! I'm outta here! I don't want to be here when they start bombing you!" he said, and he started to run for his boat.

Herman's countenance changed a little, and he scoffed, "Ha! The saf-est place to be during a bomb raid is with us! The army never hits their targets!"

Virgil had seen the guerrillas scamper when they were afraid before, but they were very relaxed right now. He wasn't, however, and hopped into his boat and headed back toward where his dad was still waiting.

Elam hadn't heard too much of what was going on on the other side of the river. When Virgil arrived, he could see that he looked worried, and he, too, could hear the fighter jets approaching. Before he could get in the boat and the two of them could head for home, more orders were shouted from across the river.

"We know there are wounded soldiers over there! Find them and bring them over here, or we will shoot you!" the voice commanded.

Elam and Virgil both got on the shore and started calling out to the soldiers, who probably were there, but although they were wounded were not insane and so did not answer to be found and taken back over to the guerrillas to be finished off. After a few minutes, the sounds of the army planes were too close, so the two got in the boat and sped away.

· · · · ·

Anyone traveling down this river from Sayaxché knew the risk, especially if it was the military traveling. Even the most vigilant travelers could be ambushed anywhere along the thickly forested riverbanks. This boatload of soldiers had not even seen the attack coming. Out of the bushes a Chinese Bastion (like a homemade shoulder rocket) was fired at the cargo boat. One shot struck near the boat's motor, and the other hit pay dirt. On the boat had been two big fifty-gallon barrels of fuel they were transporting, and the rocket hit one of them.

That was the sound that was heard at La Anchura. The explosion sprayed burning gasoline all over everyone in the boat. All the men, peppered with shrapnel and burning from the gasoline, jumped into the river. The cool water immediately provided them with some relief, but the worst was waiting for them still above the surface of the water as the guerrillas started picking the men off with their machine guns as they came up for air.

Not only that, but gasoline and water don't mix, so the surface of the water everywhere was on fire. They would stay under as long as they could and surface only long enough to take a breath, hope they didn't get a bullet in the head, and go back under trying to get away from the fire.

Some of the men crawled out onto shore and ran through the jungle, barefooted and in their underpants, without a compass or even their gun. Some villagers found several of them hours later, completely disoriented and wandering around, and brought them to the clinic. Some of the men stayed in the river and clung to the shoreline, where there were a lot of bushes and overgrowth of trees to hide in. They made their way along the shore with their goal being the clinic at La Anchura. Cruz had not been so fortunate. In all the chaos, he and two soldiers had actually swum to the shore where the guerrillas were and were found the next day by villagers, hung up in the branches beside the river. All three of them had bullet holes in their foreheads.

· · · · ·

Elam knew that all the wounded would be doing their best to get to the clinic; what else would they do? They kept their eyes open for anyone needing help but actually passed right by several of the men who remained hidden, not knowing who was in the boat.

When they neared Mario Mendez, some people waved them down. "Hey, there are some men over there on the other side of the river, and they're calling for help," one man said.

"We don't know who they are!" said another man.

No one was willing to take the chance of getting involved, even when they heard a cry for help. There were so many uncertain things during wartime, but one certain thing was you didn't take sides. You didn't trust anyone, especially someone you couldn't even see. Sometimes, even when you could see who it was, you couldn't trust that either. The guerrillas had been known to dress up as the military and vice versa.

Knowing that it was probably injured soldiers, and actually not really caring who it was—just knowing someone was calling for help—Elam headed their boat that way to pick them up. A little farther up the river toward La Anchura they found a few more. They loaded them all into the boat and took them to the clinic.

When they arrived, Barbara and the girls were already working on some injured men. Another boat was already there with a few men that they had found as they had been passing by. The five most critically wounded were stabilized and then quickly loaded into the four-seater Maule, and Virgil flew them the twenty-five-minute flight out to the military hospital in Flores.

As Elam worked on the injured men, he thought about how his life had turned out so differently than he had planned. He had come here to start churches and spread the Word of God. He had never dreamed that he'd someday operate a clinic and be a jungle doctor. He certainly never dreamed he'd ever see the things he was now seeing in this war. Growing up amidst the Amish and Mennonites of Lancaster County, who take a general stand against any kind of military violence, even toy guns had never been a part of his upbringing. Never would he have dreamed that he would live to see one of his own children with a gun pressed to their face.

It was a funny thing how he'd had a plan to preach the Word of God and thought he knew how he was going to do it. (The mind of man plans his way, but the Lord directs his steps. Proverbs 16:9) Instead of standing up behind a pulpit, he was standing next to an exam table scraping burnt skin off of a man whose pleading eyes looked up at him as though he were his only hope in the world.

He wondered what these men and so many others like them would have done had their clinic not been there. Who would have helped them? Where most people didn't want to get involved, Elam just jumped in and did what he had to do to help people, whoever they were. Had it been a boatload of guerrillas blown up instead of military soldiers, they still would have taken them to the clinic and done the same thing. They still would have loaded them up and taken them to the hospital.

The local people would never dream of doing such a thing! The guerrillas would come into a village and distribute fliers of propaganda, scattering them in the streets. The people would usually leave them there. They were too afraid to pick them up and be seen reading their literature as though they were siding with the guerrillas, or be seen throwing them away as though they sided with the army. Elam just could not stand by and worry about himself and his own safety when there were people hurting. Once they were hurt, they were no longer guerrillas or soldiers; they were people who needed help, and he helped them. Neither side of the conflict was really interested in the U.S. getting involved, so because of their U.S. citizenship, Elam and Barbara got away with a lot more than the local people could. Until now.

. . . . .

The guerrillas had sent many spies into the clinic over the years to see what the Stoltzfuses were really doing in Guatemala, and had kept a pretty sharp eye on them. Even so they really couldn't believe what they were seeing. This was not a culture of people who did things for others for no personal gain. No matter what they saw the family doing, they were convinced that they had to work for either the U.S. or the Guatemalan government.

Though they never came right out and officially took sides, how could the Stoltzfus family side with communist, anti-God guerrillas, when they could see the effects of what the guerrillas preached? Every day Elam fought against the ignorance and fear that the communist rebels were encouraging.

In that sense, they were on the army's side, but working for either side or for the government was not something of interest to Elam. It was the government's job to fight its war. Elam was a soldier in another army. The real battle was not between the rebels and the government, and the real enemy was not the educated, communist guerrilla commanders or the villagers who had joined up with them, but rather it was the philosophy that drove them: the anti-God religion the guerrillas promoted that was destroying people, families, villages, and Guatemala. Every time Elam went out to the villages to preach or took a ministry team out or prayed with someone in the clinic, he was fighting the real battle he was here to fight, the only one that mattered.

Elam saw everyone as just people. The guerrillas weren't just guerrillas. They were Elam's friends, neighbors, and members of the churches he'd planted. Most of all they were people who needed Jesus, too. No matter what war was going on around the Stoltzfus family, or how wrong the guerrillas might be, all the people involved were simply people who were all in the midst of an inner spiritual war. The guerrillas preached that Jesus was the first revolutionary and they followed His command. Elam could agree that Jesus was a revolutionary, but He wasn't about changing governments; He was about changing peoples' hearts and lives. It was for Jesus that Elam and Barbara had come to this country, and it was for Him that they stayed, even while all this horrible stuff went on around them. They were the true revolutionaries, fighting for the freedom that only Christ had to offer.

"This clinic is a place for healing, and its doors are open to anyone," Elam would say.

The guerrillas had demanded that they take a stand one way or another before. They didn't want to take any official stand, because that would turn people away from the clinic and put them directly in the middle of the conflict. It would go against their reason for being there. They had seen many entire families come to know Jesus just because one person had been sick and found healing at New Life Clinic. Some of the guerrillas had been brought into the world by Barbara's hands and their mothers' lives saved because of the medical attention they received after delivery. Those families would not come near the clinic anymore if the Stoltzfuses had to say they were not on the guerrillas' side. So, in response to the demand, they decided not to make any reply at all.

Their silence was taken as an answer. The three top commanders of the revolution wrote their orders and signed them. In "pocos días" they would be at La Anchura and deal with this problem once and for all.

Chapter 27

The Response

The Lord is for me; I will not fear; what can man do to me?
Psalm 118:6

Miguel looked across the table at Luby's restaurant at his girlfriend, Dwyanna (pronounced "D'wanna"). They had just met thanks to the match-making work of a mutual friend, April Gore, at Lakewood Church.

"Tell me, really, Miguel," Dwyanna was asking. "What's it like down there in Guatemala?"

Miguel told her stories of the wild and crazy things he did growing up with Virgil and of working with the churches and of all the things that happened in the clinic.

"But, the war that's going on there. Isn't it dangerous?"

Miguel smiled. "Yes and no. It's dangerous to be there if you're a Guatemalan, but our family has never felt like we were in any danger."

Dwyanna, feeling that this was the man she wanted to marry, was relieved to hear that the place where she might someday call home was not dangerous.

"Maybe you could take me to visit there sometime?" Dwyanna suggested.

"That's a good idea," Miguel agreed.

· · · · ·

"Hey, Lisa! Isn't it your turn tonight to turn off the power plant?" Elam asked his youngest daughter.

She smiled back at him, knowing what he was thinking. "Yes, and I'm not scared."

He smiled back at her, remembering what he'd seen one night as she had returned from shutting off the generator. The mission base at La Anchura was far from any public electricity and would remain so for decades into the future, so, if they wanted to run their saw mill or have things like a refrigerator, a television, a washer and dryer, lights, you name it, they needed their own source for electricity. Years back, Stauffer Diesel in Pennsylvania had donated a huge twenty-five-kilowatt diesel generator, which was housed in a little shack about a three-minute walk away from the house. They ran the generator for much of the day and then used an inverter and some car batteries to provide them with electricity enough for lights and fans when the generator was not running.

Every night at 8:15 someone had to go out and shut the generator down, and tonight that someone was Lisa. While the shack that housed the generator was visible from the house, it was pretty far away, and the jungle was very close. In the dark, your mind can play tricks on you, and it did so often with Lisa as she walked alone out across the airstrip and over to the dark little building. Sometimes she'd get that feeling, you know the one that makes the hair on the back of your neck stand up when you just know that someone is behind you. She would spin around and frantically shine her flashlight around. Seeing no one was there didn't settle her heart from racing on those nights, so usually she would turn that three-minute walk into a thirty-second sprint back to the house.

Lying in her bed one night after one such race back to the house, she had looked up at the ceiling in the room she shared with Anita and Maria and determined that she was not going to be overcome with this senseless fear every time she walked out to the generator. She knew fear was not from God, so she started to read her Bible and to pray for courage.

"Are you sure you don't need a big, strong man to be your bodyguard and go along with you?" Elam puffed out his chest and showed some muscles to his daughter.

Lisa giggled. "No. I'm OK by myself!"

That night, August 31, 1990, she walked fearlessly out to the generator and turned it off, and slowly and calmly returned to the house. She heard no branches break and did not have the feeling anyone was watching her.

. . . . .

Although the generator was far enough away from the house so as to not be noisy, it did create a constant and gentle hum that was always in the air. When it went off, there was a sudden and total stillness that was always welcome after a long, busy day.

Virgil, who normally turned into a pumpkin as soon as the sun went down, had been lying in bed for some time just thinking and talking to God. One thing he thought about a lot was that he hated hell. He would sometimes come up with ideas for God, ways that He could not have to send people there—even ways to try to save the devil. He just hated it and hated thinking that anyone had to go there, that anyone had to spend the rest of eternity away from God.

He thought about all that he was doing for God and felt frustrated. There were just too many people he wasn't reaching. Wasn't there something more he could do? He thought of his airplane, and didn't know why exactly but he'd had this feeling now for a few months that he wanted to give it away. It seemed crazy considering how much he did do for God with that airplane, but he'd heard the testimony of another missionary in Honduras who really seemed like he needed an airplane more than he did, and he knew that if he gave his airplane way, God would give him a bigger and better one, anyway.

"Are you crazy?" Elam had reacted when Virgil ran that idea past his dad. So, he'd set that idea aside and moved forward. Still, he just felt like there was something more he could do. He asked God, "What is it that matters to You most, God? What is it? What do you want me to do with my life? Whatever it is, that's what I want to be doing with my time!"

Some howler monkeys off in the distance started making noise, and then the dogs started to bark. The dogs barking wasn't an alarming noise; it just meant that someone was coming. They lived at a clinic; someone was always coming!

Barbara had been propped up in bed next to Elam, each of them with a book in their hands. They looked at each other and smiled as she hopped out of bed, and laughed, "What is it with babies that they always want to be born in the middle of the night?"

Elam set his Bible down. "I am sure when I was being born I was more considerate than that!"

Barbara laughed at him on her way out of the bedroom. Elam got out of bed and followed behind his wife.

In the beginning of the clinic ministry, Elam had always delivered the babies, but because the local women felt a lot better about a woman delivering their babies it wasn't long until Barbara took over that job. She was very good at it and had saved many lives already. Jean also delivered babies or helped Barbara, and someday Anita would follow in their footsteps as well.

The girls got up, too, and went to their bedroom window to see who it was. "Who is it?" asked Maria.

Lisa squinted and could see some men dressed in army uniforms and holding guns. "Oh, just some army guys." Lisa was always curious and decided she wanted to go see what they needed.

Jean, who was living in the guesthouse between the house and the clinic building, also heard the dogs, so she looked outside.

"Buenas noches!" one of the men called out and then followed with what they really meant: "Get outside! This is the army!"

Jean's eyes grew wide as she knew from the tone in the guy's voice that it wasn't the army.

· · · · ·

Lisa was halfway down the steps to the first floor when she was stopped by the sound of her dad's voice. He was talking to the men and sounded angry. "This is our private home. If someone wants to talk to me, let him come and talk like a gentleman."

Lisa's heart jumped a little. Something was wrong.

"Don't you know who we are?" a man with coke-bottle glasses at the door said to Elam.

"Yes, I know who you are, and it doesn't make any difference." Why couldn't they show up at a normal time of the day for this? Elam tried to stand his ground. "This is still my house, and if your captain wants to talk to me he should come here."

With that, the men started cocking their guns. The man with the thick glasses informed Elam, "We are part of the Unidad Revolucionario Nacional Guatamalteco (Guatemalan National Revolutionary Union). Everyone out of the house, and out to the airplane on the airstrip!"

"Dad, let's go see what the captain wants," Virgil encouraged his dad as he, Elam, and Barbara headed out the door. Lisa ran quietly back up the stairs to hide.

They led the family out to a small building in front of the clinic building that served as an outdoor kitchen.

"Who is the pilot?" the man with the thick glasses asked.

Virgil motioned with his hand. "I am."

The man pointed his gun at Virgil. "You, come over here by the airplane."

Without hesitation, Virgil complied and followed the man to the airstrip and his Maule. Once they arrived at the airplane, the man with the thick glasses, who was apparently the top commander of this group, ordered four men to guard him.

"So, what do you do with this airplane?" the commander asked, pushing his glasses up.

"We use it for medical emergencies to fly people out to hospitals." He had logged over 800 hours on the Maule in just the last few years. Considering that Guatemala City was one hour away, that 800 hours represented a lot of flights and a lot of saved lives.

"Have you ever used it to transport soldiers?" he asked with a knowing tone in his voice.

Virgil realized what this must mean. They knew about the flight he'd made with the wounded soldiers a month ago after the ambush, and they were mad. "Yes, I flew some of the critically wounded soldiers who were in that transport boat you blew up last month out to the hospital in Flores."

The eyes behind the thick glasses got even bigger for a moment. He wasn't used to honest answers. He'd been prepared to have to interrogate this guy for a while. "That was your big mistake," he said, pointing a finger at Virgil. He then got into the airplane and started checking out all the instruments and radios. He asked a bunch of questions about everything and then seemed to come to a decision and began to take out the ham radio.

"Hey, what are you doing? You don't need that!" Virgil said agitatedly. The commander ignored him.

Virgil was normally not an argumentative person, especially when it came to dealing with the guerrillas, but he remembered the buried medical books that the guerrillas had stolen during their Thanksgiving raid, and he knew that the guerrillas didn't use ham radios for their communications.

"I'm serious, you don't need that. That's a ham radio; it's not the same frequency you guys use. You can't even use that. I need it! I use that every time I am in my airplane, and sometimes my dad needs to use that to talk to doctors while we're in flight to know how to keep the patients alive until we land!"

"Shut up. You don't know what frequency we use, and you don't know what I need," the commander snapped back at him. "Besides, you're not going to be needing it anymore."

Virgil made eye contact with the man. There was a look there that told him that tonight was not like any of the other times they had had run-ins with the guerrillas. Something very serious was going on here. Because of his last comment, Virgil had the feeling that maybe they were going to destroy the airplane. The look the commander had in his eyes made Virgil feel like a dead man, and the idea that maybe these men were also planning to kill him and Elam crossed his mind.

· · · · ·

Two of the guerrillas had gone into the house after Virgil, Elam, and Barbara left. They went right to Elam's bedroom, and turned on the light. They looked around and then went into the connected bathroom. They looked around a little bit and then left.

Instinctively, Lisa, who was still hiding, went and turned off the light and closed the door, so the mosquitoes would not get in. Then she went back to look for her sisters.

"Anita! Maria! Are you guys still in here?" she whispered.

When she couldn't find them, she ran outside to do some spying from behind the hedges. A couple of guys started to head back toward the house, so she ran back inside and finally found her sisters hiding in the secret part of the basement.

· · · · ·

Jean stood watching the commotion with her parents. She was frustrated and wondering what this was all about. She knew the girls were still inside the house, so she kept her attention in that direction. That was when she noticed it.

"Dad! Look! Is that gasoline?" She watched as some of the men walked over with canisters of gasoline on their shoulders. "They're going to burn our house!"

Elam looked up and at first thought Jean had to be overreacting. He could see that the men heading toward his house had canisters of gasoline, but their house was also in the same direction as the river. The gasoline was probably for the boats. He watched them, but once they got to the house, they didn't set the canisters down to use later for the boat motor. Instead, they began pouring the gasoline all over the house! It was all happening so fast. They weren't really going to burn the house down?

"Wait!" Jean yelled, running toward the men. "My little sisters are inside! Let me get them out!"

One of the guerrillas motioned at her with his hand to go ahead and get them. She ran.

"Anita! Maria!" she ran for the basement. "Lisa! Girls! Where are you? Come out! They're going to burn the house down!"

"What!" All the girls' eyes widened, and they headed toward the sound of their sister's voice.

Jean grabbed the first girl she got her hands on and headed for the door, and they went and joined the rest of the family out in the little kitchen building. Three or four men with guns watched over them silently as they all sat there, just waiting and watching. All these years living in the most intense war zone in the country, they had always felt that God kept a hedge of protection around them. The family had grown accustomed to the sounds of automatic weapons firing and bombs going off, and there had even been actual battles right there on their airstrip. Virgil had even found bullet holes in his airplane where apparently he'd been shot at while in flight. Through all of it, though, they always felt safe. What had happened tonight?

They watched as some of the guerrillas busied themselves carrying box loads of things out of all of the buildings while others spread gasoline around. Unable to do anything else the family started to sing. Then, instead of feeling frustrated, angry, or afraid, they all felt a strange kind of peace. They sang some songs in English and some in Spanish so that the men standing guard would understand the words, and they also tried to talk to them about Jesus.

One of the men guarding them said flatly, "I am a Christian."

Elam thought that was interesting. "If you are a Christian you know you shouldn't be here helping to steal the things from our clinic and house."

The guerrilla said, "We aren't stealing. You are Americans, and as far as we are concerned, you don't belong here and neither do your things."

Turning to one of the other men, Elam asked, "Well, how about you? Are you a Christian?"

He hung his head a little, and gave a more honest reply than the first guy. "No! If I were a Christian, I wouldn't be here with these men."

"Look, shut these people up, would you?" another one of them said. "They're getting on my nerves."

"What should we do with them?" replied a fifteen-year-old guerrilla.

The kitchen was nothing more than an open pavilion with a small room that served as sleeping quarters on one end. "Put them in that room," one man ordered.

So, they piled them all into the little room and closed the door. "There! That's better!"

· · · · ·

The commander couldn't get the radio out of the airplane with the tools he had with him, so he left to get some. That left Virgil out standing by the airplane by himself with four guards, and for some reason, he felt like talking. One of the guards was a short, pudgy Indian man who didn't seem like he was all there.

"You know, I don't blame you," he said to the short, pudgy man. "I believe you're innocent. I bet you don't even know what you're fighting for anymore with this war, do you? Do you even know what real communism looks like? Do you know that it doesn't work?"

The guy didn't react.

"The commanders, now they're not innocent. They know what they're fighting for…"

Just then, the commander came around the corner and flew into an instant rage. "You are *not to speak any more*!" he roared at Virgil. "You men are not to listen to him!" he ordered the men. He then pulled a grenade from his belt and pulled the pin out. With his fingers, he held in what the pin normally held in. He handed the live grenade to the nearest guard. "Take this. If he tries to run, throw this at him!"

"And, you!" he said to Virgil again. "Don't insult this man! He knows what he's fighting for!"

With that, he stormed off to the airplane and got back to the business of taking out the radio.

· · · · ·

After a while, Elam opened the door again, so they could see what was going on. Outside, the guerrillas were busy going in and out of the clinic, hauling everything they could carry as fast as they could. Only one guard had been left to watch them, so little by little they started coming out and sitting outside.

Then Elam began to question the guard. "Where are you from?"

"I don't know," he replied bluntly.

"Are you a Guatemalan?"

Again, the reply was, "I don't know."

Elam persisted, "What is your name?"

He'd had enough. "Every one of you get back into the room."

Maria whined, "But the room is too crowded."

"Yeah, it's too crowded in there!" Anita agreed.

He replied, "No one gave you permission to come out. Get back in!"

There was no use in arguing with him, because he had the gun. They went back in but didn't close the door so they could still watch.

The guards who'd been watching Virgil brought him over to the rest of the family and told him to stay. Elam noticed they were doing something with some gas tanks near the clinic. "They can't be planning to burn the clinic, too! Jesus would not allow something like that happen to us!" he thought.

His attention returned to his house, where the guerrillas looked like a team of movers. In and out they went with box after box, and carried it all down to the river. This was no short-term mission house, this was their home, and it had taken nineteen years to build it up. They hadn't built this house the way an American usually thinks of building a house. They hadn't called the contractor and paid the bills while crews of subcontractors all arrived and did their jobs until the house was complete. The family had spent the first eight years living on the houseboat, and the whole family had to some degree worked together building their house with their own hands. They had cleared the land, gone downriver with shovels and bags and gotten the sand they needed to make blocks and cement. They had made the concrete blocks for the foundation, and hauled buckets of water from the river and mixed the cement themselves with shovels. Even the girls had helped.

Virgil, Miguel, and Elam had all gone out into the jungle together and looked for tall straight trees, cut them down, cut them up and hauled them back home, planed them, sawed them, nailed them, sanded them, stained them, and turned them into their home. Because Elam was a carpenter and cabinetmaker by trade, he was a perfectionist when it came to whatever he made with wood, so the interior of the house was exquisite. The kitchen cabinets, all mahogany, were gorgeous and as custom as you got. The trim throughout the house and much of the furniture had been handmade by Elam or the boys out of mahogany, also. The house, had it been constructed in the States, would have cost more than the family could have afforded in two lifetimes because of the construction materials and the craftsmanship of it. And, because of all that went into making it, there was a value to this particular house that couldn't have a monetary value attached to it. The house was priceless.

"No!" he cried out inside. "No, Lord! Please, don't let this happen!"

"You!" one of the guards had his gun in Elam's face. "You are to come with me now. The commander wants to talk to you." Elam was then led over to where Virgil had been by the airstrip.

· · · · ·

They could hear someone trying to start their motorboat, but for a while now it hadn't been working right, so it wouldn't start. A couple of the guerrillas came to where the family was. "We need gasoline, and we need someone to start the boat."

Virgil left without hesitation and ran to get gasoline. When he got to the boat, he was the only one who could start it, so they told him he was driving. Off he went in the family's boat in the direction of Mario Mendez, after midnight, with a huge load of the family's belongings, two guerrillas, and one sub-commander on board.

The sisters watched their brother leave for the river with the guerillas and didn't like it that he'd left. Lisa looked at the guards and wondered what kind of life they had had. None of them looked much older than she was. "What a terrible life, to live hiding out in the jungle with a machine gun by your side," she thought. She sat down and prayed for the men who were destroying her father's life's work. But the real work he had done was shown by the compassion this young girl felt for these men who were hurting her, and that was something they could not steal or destroy.

· · · · ·

"Where's Virgil?" Elam asked when he returned from his talk with the commander.

"He left," Barbara said.

"Left? What do you mean? Escaped?"

"No, they left with him in our boat. They couldn't get the boat started, so they came up here and took him with them."

Elam's heart raced a little, but he had confidence that God would protect Virgil.

One of the men hopped on the yellow tractor and started driving it around in short circles on the far end of the airstrip, using the plow blade to dig ruts. Meanwhile, some of the men started pushing the ultralight out into the middle of the airstrip. After they had pushed the ultralight out pretty far, they left it there, and did the same thing to the big plane, and then they started messing around with the gas tanks that were close by.

Then in the distance there was a sound like dozens of little firecrackers going off. Someone who wasn't used to living in a war zone might even think they were firecrackers, but the family recognized the sound of automatic weapons firing. The shots were coming from the direction of the army base in Pipiles. The guerrillas stopped what they were doing for a second and started cheering. Then the flames started. Horror struck Elam's heart. They set fire to the ultralight first and then to the big plane.

So often, people experiencing trauma say the same thing: that it seemed like a dream. It's true. It's just the best way to describe it, because what Elam was seeing, those two planes on fire, went so against the reality he had grown to know and love that it was just not computing.

Elam remembered his little son, just five years old, telling him that when he was big he was going to fly an airplane all around the jungle and tell people about Jesus. That was just what he had done. When he was fourteen years big Virgil had gone to the States for pilot's training, and come back with a license and an ultralight kit, which had been bought for him by Larry and Libby Brandenburg and their church in Maryland. Virgil had assembled that ultralight with Miguel, and the two of them had had more fun playing with (and even crashing) that thing than was even right! Virgil had also used that little ultralight to do just what he'd always dreamed of doing: spread the word of God. He'd strapped a little television and a VCR to it, and off he'd fly to villages and even into the army bases to show movies about Jesus. There it was now on the airstrip in flames.

"Rosita!" Lisa suddenly remembered her pet parrot, who was kept in a cage just outside the kitchen door of their house.

The family had been hoping since the gas cans appeared that this was all just to scare them, that the buildings were not going to be burned, but now as they stood before the burning airplanes they knew that the gasoline was no scare tactic.

"Please, don't let her burn!" Lisa begged the guard to go get her parrot.

He gave no reply. What could he say? The military could show up at any moment and retaliate, they were in the middle of a raid, and this little girl was worried about her pet parrot!

Finally, her urgent pleas worked, and he agreed to let her go. "Look," he said, "if we all start shooting, you need to lie on the ground or, if possible, get back in the room."

With that he let something show that he'd been trying to hide. He wasn't a heartless and cold-blooded warrior. He was a person, and he cared. He didn't want to see her get hurt. They were the guerrillas, yes.

They were the bad guys in this situation, yes. But they weren't all bad guys. Some of them were good guys fighting a bad war.

· · · · ·

By now, the Maule was also completely engulfed in flames. The family stood there watching the flames licking around the fabric fuselage. One of the wings broke loose and fell to the ground. Everyone was speechless as their hearts broke for Virgil.

Then the flames started behind them. Their home was on fire. It didn't take long until their wooden house was burning hot enough that the propane tanks outside the kitchen got hot enough to go, and they went with a very loud "Boom!"

Lisa held Rosita close to her, watching alongside her sisters. Everything she owned in the entire world, every special thing that she had and treasured, was now being burned right before her eyes, and there was nothing she could do about it. A tear ran down her cheek.

Anita reached her arms around her mother as tears also streamed down her face.

Maria stood by watching as her own people destroyed the work of the man who had been her father for all these years. These men who were doing this weren't from some foreign country. These men were people who had been born just a few miles away, people who had benefited from this clinic. Now they were destroying it. This just did not make sense!

Elam put his arm around Jean, who stood there sobbing. Although it felt like it was just a bad dream, it wasn't. This was real.

Chapter 28

The Choice

"It shall be when these signs come to you, do for yourself
what the occasion requires, for God is with you."
1 Samuel 10:7

This was not what Virgil should be doing at this time of night. This time of night was for sleeping, and here he was dressed for bed and driving a boatload of his own stuff and some armed guerrillas to who knows where to do who knows what to him. He'd felt that he and his dad were in danger tonight in a way he'd never felt before, and he thought constantly about what his plan of action should be.

He imagined somehow getting the men to all stand up so he could turn the boat sharply and send them flying into the water and head back to La Anchura. Or, he could simply drop silently off the back of the boat and take the fuel line with him. By the time they noticed he was gone, he'd be under the dark water, and they wouldn't be able to find him or shoot him as their boat continued to float downriver, because they wouldn't be able to restart it or fix it.

Either plan led him back to La Anchura alone, and he knew that they would catch up to him eventually and then he'd really be in trouble. He slipped off his boots anyway and had the fuel line in his hand in case he needed the quick escape.

They passed by Mario Mendez and reached a small tributary which Virgil was instructed to enter. It was a tight fit, but he weaved the boat in, cut the motor, and began slowly moving farther into the jungle, while the three guerrillas called out and waited. No reply came, so they finally decided on a place to dock and unload. The river was high, so docking the boat was difficult, and everyone had to get out in the water to get to shore.

The guy that looked like he was a sub-commander swung his gun around to his back and hopped out of the boat into the water. He began pulling the boat in toward the trees and tied it off. One of the other men also swung his gun around onto his back and began grabbing boxes and unloading them.

Virgil sat in the boat wondering what in the world was going on. How was this happening? Why was God allowing this? As he sat wondering, he heard the sound of the propane tanks as they exploded just four miles or so up the river. He looked and could see the sky light up over La Anchura. "God, no!" he thought.

He had lived his whole life in the middle of this war and had seen and heard about many awful things. He had known of many homes that had been destroyed and burned by the guerrillas, and he knew that most of the time the family being attacked was burned inside—if not the whole family, at least the father was.

"God, I have to save my family!" Virgil prayed with desperation building up inside him. He'd also seen and heard of things that the guerrillas had done to young girls in situations like this. What about his little sisters? "God! Show me what to do!"

He found his attention being drawn toward the guerrillas' guns. There were only three guards with him, as no one had yet come out of the jungle to meet them, and all of them were busy unloading their new stuff from the boat. What if he could get one of their guns? The three of them all had high-powered M16s. The guerrillas normally carried either those or Israeli Galils, which they were commanded never to put down. They played soccer and swam in the rivers with their guns strapped to their backs.

Virgil had never held an M16 before and had never held anyone at gunpoint before; it had never even entered his mind. There was nothing in the world that he owned that he would have ever defended at the expense of someone's life. But there was something strong inside him now that was urgently drawing him to take a gun from one of these guys.

"God, give me a peace about this. If it's Your will that I escape, make one of these guys put his gun down."

Almost immediately, one of the guerrillas who was only about fourteen years old took his gun off of his shoulder and leaned it up against a tree.

"Oh God!" Virgil's heart raced. "He set the gun down!"

His adrenaline was pumping a million miles an hour. He knew this was an answer to his prayer, but he also knew that as soon as he made a move he could be shot by both of the other guys. He hadn't even really thought of what he could do when he finally got a gun in his hand, and he wasn't sure if he could even figure out how to use the gun if he got it in his hand. He just felt like this was what he was supposed to do. "God I trust in you! Give me wisdom now!"

Then, all their backs were to him, and he just sprang out of the boat, grabbed the gun, and held it up at the three. "Put up your hands! Put up your hands!"

The three of them turned around. "Oh, no!" the young boy thought, seeing his gun in the hands of their enemy. If the gringo didn't shoot him, he knew that for this mistake his commander might.

"Put down your guns!" Virgil aimed at the guy who was in charge.

He put his gun down right away and got down on his hands and knees; the others followed his lead. Virgil could see their hands trembling as they fumbled with the gun straps to get them off of their shoulders.

"Down! Down on the ground! Now!"

The two young men with their commander lay there on the ground, terrified. If the three of them were military guys and the man with the gun a revolutionary, the three men on the ground would only have a few seconds left till the lights would go out. It was the way the guerrillas operated. They had no mercy.

For what seemed like ten minutes there was silence. As the seconds went by, Virgil thought about hell. Just tonight he'd been talking to God about hell, and now here he was faced with a dilemma. He looked at the young men on the ground before him, waiting for what he would decide to do with them. Did any of these three know Jesus? If these guys were to die right now, where would they go? If they weren't Christians, which wasn't likely, he would be the one sending them to hell. No matter what they were doing to him and his family, were the lives of his Christian sisters and parents worth sending anyone to hell to save?

He could see their hands shaking and knew the fear they were feeling. They were just kids. They were people, his neighbors. In another circumstance, they could be his friends. They had been indoctrinated and brainwashed by the communist propaganda, and possibly had been involuntarily drafted into the guerrilla movement. They weren't his enemy. Satan was. Hell was.

Virgil started talking to them. "Listen, we are not mercenaries. I don't know why you guys are treating us this way. We came down here to give new life. We didn't come to Guatemala to kill anybody." He paused for a moment. "If you guys shoot me I'll go to heaven because I know Jesus and have Him in my heart, but I don't know where you would go."

In that moment, more than ever, Virgil knew what life was all about. He knew what mattered and what didn't. He thought in his heart, "I would rather die and go to heaven than shoot somebody and send them to hell." It was so clear.

He spoke again to the three men who were still waiting to find out if they were going to live or die. Now, the desperation was gone from his voice, and there was peace. "When I was five years old I came here to this jungle with my parents as missionaries. We came here to *give* life, not to take life. I want you to know that! I am going to show you that I'm not that kind of person. I could kill you, but I'm going to spare your lives."

He then did the unthinkable in their minds. He threw the gun down at their feet right in the mud. Now it was Virgil's turn to wait to see if he would live or die.

Flustered, the three guerrillas scrambled to their feet and regained control of the situation. They half-heartedly held their guns on him, but felt almost silly doing so. Virgil made eye contact for a moment with the boy whose gun he'd held. Now, in place of coldness and hatred in those eyes was a bit of humility, confusion, and fear. Virgil realized that he recognized him. He'd been delivered by Barbara, born in the clinic that was now being burned back at La Anchura.

No one said anything else as they continued unloading the boat. Once it was unloaded they all got back in to make another trip back to La Anchura for more things. About a quarter of a mile off, Virgil could see his home in flames in the distance.

When they reached the shore, he informed the guerrillas in the boat, "I'm going to see how my family is," and took off for where he had last seen the family.

He heard one of them say without much conviction in his voice, "If you leave the boat, we are going to kill you."

Virgil knew he didn't mean it, and even as the words left his mouth, the man knew he didn't mean it, either. It was the programmed response to a situation like this, but Virgil was not fitting in with the program. The uncomfortable feeling that had started when they were given their guns back had not left, and they simply watched Virgil run up toward his family as the empty threat fell to the ground.

No sooner had Virgil leapt from the boat than the roof of his home caved in. He stopped for a second to take it in. He was horrified to see his home crashing to the ground, but his real horror was in not knowing if his family was inside the house or not. Once he reached the place where his family had been, he saw that everyone was still there.

"Dad, is everyone OK?" Virgil asked, out of breath.

Elam had been watching his son as he ran up from the river. "Yes, Virgil, we're all fine. Where did they take you?"

Virgil quickly told Elam where they had gone and all that had happened back at the camp. As he spoke to his father, he could see in the darkness off in the distance the glow of the remaining fire on his airplanes. As soon as what he was seeing registered, he tried to put it out of his mind. He would have time to grieve over that later. Just then, a guerrilla came looking for Virgil and told him roughly he needed to drive the boat again, and he was off.

Elam watched his son head back down to the boat. Elam had never felt as though anyone in his family had even come close to being harmed in this war, but tonight seemed so much more serious, especially now that he knew Virgil had actually held the guerrillas at gunpoint. Elam had no idea what was about to take place just four miles away, but what he did know was that God was good. Instead of choosing to be afraid, he chose to trust Him and wait.

· · · · ·

Virgil got in the boat and started it up. The commander with the thick glasses and three other leaders hopped in the boat with the original three passengers from the first trip and ordered Virgil to set off. He started the motor and headed off again into the night. He was taking another trip down the river with boxes of things his family had worked for for so many years. So much donation money was represented by these boxes, so many years of so many people giving to the work here.

There was another thing that was taking a trip down the river in this boat tonight that was not in a box. It was what was inside of Virgil. It was worth more than anything these boxes held, and it was going to save his life.

Chapter 29

Fire

But Jesus was saying, "Father, forgive them; for they do not know what they are doing." *Luke 23:34*

Elam sat down for a bit in the grass and just tried to take it all in. He looked around at all the men, strangers, walking around treating his life's work as though it were nothing. Here he was the head authority on this property—his wife and children's protector—and he was powerless to stop this.

So many missions teams from so many churches over the years had come and sweat in the Petén heat to build this clinic. So many missionaries in the U.S. had sent funds to make it all possible. It had taken so many years to build this place up to what it was, and now in one night it was all being undone.

The irony of the situation was overwhelming. Ever since that first trip he'd taken to Guatemala so many years ago, Elam had loved the Indian people. It was the Indian people whom Elam felt almost "akin" to. It was his love for these people that had brought him to Guatemala and had driven him day after day working and doing without things just to help these people who needed Jesus.

While he could have been back in Lancaster County earning a highly skilled cabinetmaker's wages, and living a "good life," eating turkey on Thanksgiving instead of iguana as he sweated in the jungle, he spent evenings he could have been home with his wife watching TV in a nice, cozy living room outside in the rain in a boat, in the dark, going to muddy villages and giving unauthorized blood donations to the local mosquito population while helping the churches he'd planted.

He'd never resented the loss of the good life in the U.S. In fact, he'd loved every minute of his time in Guatemala. He had loved helping the people, living off the land, and hearing screeching parrots and howler monkeys greet him in the morning. It was ironic then that the very people that had inspired Elam come to serve were the very same people who were the main supporters of the URNG—the guerrillas who were now trying to chase Elam back out of the country.

Elam had just watched the commanders head down to the boat that his son was leaving in. This part was a little nerve rending. The guerrillas seemed to be finishing up, and the leaders were leaving, so why had they taken Virgil with them again?

Elam wondered just how this was all going to end and how they would pick up these pieces. The last raid had not been this intense, and it had been almost fun pursuing the guerrillas through the jungle to get things back. This was very different. Elam had watched them all night long raiding each and every building on the property. It wasn't just what a few dozen guys could carry on their backs that had left the compound this time; it was everything. What hadn't been looted out of their house had burned. Everything they had was gone. The only thing that the guerrillas had not found was the secret room where the expensive and hard-to-replace ham radios Elam had used for surgical procedures and contacting family back in the States were hidden. All of them had burned inside the house.

Barbara tapped Elam on the shoulder quietly and pointed. The gas cans appeared again. What were they going to burn now? There were three buildings left; the apartment, the clinic, and the canning center.

Jean saw they were about to burn the apartment building where she was living and headed straight for one of the guerrillas. "Hey! If you are going to burn that building, may I please go in and get a jacket for my mom? You just burned everything my mom and sisters owned in this world. We have no clothing except what we have on our backs."

The guard gave an emphatic, "No."

Jean was good, though, and politely kept on giving him reasons why he should say yes. Next thing you know, Jean was being escorted down to the building by the guard, who really didn't know why he even cared if this girl's mom had a jacket or not. These people were the enemy!

Once inside, she saw that they had taken everything and piled it in the middle of the room, probably to make it burn easier. She went through her things quickly and grabbed some warm clothing and one very important item: her wedding dress. She'd found that guitar-playing prince charming whom she'd always dreamed of, and she was engaged to be married. That done, she dashed back out to where her family was.

"Did you get your papers?" Barbara asked. She knew they were going to have to leave the country soon. Everyone else's papers were now gone, but Jean's things were still in the apartment.

Jean smiled, still holding her dress. "No! I totally forgot!" She went over to one of the guerrillas again. "Can I go back to my house and get some more things?"

Why they felt like doing anything for this young woman in the middle of the raid they didn't know, but she was pretty and had a nice smile, so off Jean went again to her room in the guesthouse. She moved quickly, grabbing clothing for the girls, too, and this time dug into her secret hiding place and found her passport and some money. Then she saw something else she needed to grab and returned to her family again.

"Hey, you got Chico!" Lisa exclaimed, beaming when Jean returned with her pet coatimundi in her arms. Anita reached out and took him from Jean and gave him a hug.

"Where was he?" Maria asked.

"He was hiding. I would have thought that when the guerrillas went in there he would have run away, but he hid instead!" Jean was now glad she had gone back that second time, or else Chico would have been burned inside!

Elam's eyes glanced at what Jean brought back with her but was focused on what was still behind her. The building she'd just left had flames starting in it. Once that fire was started, the guerrillas moved to the clinic, setting some fires inside. By now, most of the guerrillas had left, and it seemed that they were in a hurry to get going. The family became bolder, as they could see by now that it wasn't their physical lives they'd set out to destroy tonight. All the girls ran across the yard and inside the clinic and began stomping on whatever fires the guerrillas lit.

"Get out of here!" The guerrillas ordered the girls back outside, but the girls didn't budge.

Lisa was standing next to one of the guerrillas when he lit a paper on fire and was ready to toss it onto a large pile of papers, and she just smacked it out of his hand. His eyes got large for a second, and he looked at this crazy little gringa. What was she thinking? He held his gun up at her and ordered her to leave the building at once. He expected her to cower a little and turn tail and run, but she looked at him in the eye, gave a little "Hmph" that said more than she had time to say, stomped her foot, and turned and grabbed a trash can and started grabbing things to salvage from the building.

· · · · ·

The sun was just edging up over the horizon toward Mario Mendez, leaving a familiar red glow on the river. Give a child crayons and let him color the sun and he will color it yellow, but the sun is actually white, because it is all the colors of the rainbow combined to make white light. It is the sun that gives light and color to everything on earth, which reflects its light—like the Son of God who gives light to the earth, without whom there would be nothing beautiful to see on this earth.

Normally the light rays reflected by the surroundings at La Anchura were a pleasure to Elam's eyes every morning. But this morning, the light reflecting off the remains of Elam's life work held no beauty. What a newsletter this was going to make. What a mess this was going to be to clean up. How would they rebuild? Then, he noticed smoke coming out of the canning center. "What is the *matter* with these guys?!" Elam thought. "This canning center is to help their own people!" It was all just so insane.

On two separate occasions the family had been forced to attend one of the guerrillas' pep rallies in Mario Mendez. The first night, they'd just arrived in the village and had just hopped out of their boat. Virgil had gone around the side of a big barrel to "use the restroom" when he was greeted by a weapon aimed on him and an angry guerrilla who was almost peed on.

The second time, they'd already been in the middle of the church service there when the guerrillas surrounded the church and began banging on the sides of the building and yelling. They then entered the church, went straight up to the podium, and informed everyone that church was now over and that everyone was to go to the soccer field.

On both occasions, the guerrillas held the entire village there for an hour and gave them their pep talk. They told them how they were the poor people's army and all about the evils of capitalism and their greatest enemy, the United States. They pointed at the Stoltzfus family and said, "They are the enemy!"

But no matter how many times they said they were the poor people's army, the Bible says you will know people by their fruits, and as long as Elam had been in Guatemala he had never seen any of the guerrillas do anything to help end the suffering that he saw daily in the villages. He never saw the guerrillas help educate the people who lived their lives in ignorance and fear. He never saw them put food on anyone's table or clothing on anyone's back. When they came into a village, it was not to help anyone but themselves. They would come into poor people's homes and take the little food they had, no matter how poor or needy that family was. They would take the food and the supplies they needed by force and head back out into the jungle, not caring if that family had enough left for themselves and their children or not. It was all in the name of the revolution. That was the fruit of the guerrillas' revolution.

Elam had worked with the Heifer Project to help introduce other ways of getting food to the people, and had introduced cattle to the area. Then, he had seen the local people working all year investing in and fattening up a pig or a cow, only to see that animal gone in a few days after butchering. Without refrigeration or canning, the whole animal had to be used up and sold before it rotted. Such a waste!

Growing up Amish and Mennonite, Elam and Barbara knew the value of canning. It was what had helped them get by so long here in the jungle. Just how many cans of iguana and howler monkey meat had the family—and their guests—eaten by now? Who knew? Who wanted to know? So, Elam had gotten the idea to create a commercial-sized canning facility. It would make it possible for those families who worked all year to fatten up an animal to bring in their animal, and then after butchering it can the meat so that they would have meat all year—not just for a few days. Then, they would have more than beans and tortillas to eat each night! The idea of the communities along the river changing and seeing so much of the suffering of the malnourished children becoming a thing of the past was exciting!

The center had been in the planning stages for a while, but was finally now almost ready to be used. It had only recently been fully equipped by a Christian from the U.S., who had sold the equipment to Elam at practically half price and was allowing him to have years to pay it off. The center was going to help feed everyone in this whole area! It was supposed to help end some of the suffering of the poor, and now the poor people's army, the guerrillas, were trying to destroy it! Elam didn't imagine that the guerrillas mentioned things like this on their fund-raising tours in the U.S.

Elam couldn't just let it go without a fight. Earlier that night, after the fire had been put out on the one tractor, the guerrillas hadn't gone back to restart it. Maybe if he could get the fire out in the canning center they would leave it alone! He slipped over there to see what he could do. Jean saw her dad head that way and followed close behind to help.

When they got to the center, Virgil's dirt bike was on fire inside. They found buckets and started running back and forth from the river and tried to put the fire out, but it was useless. Each time they returned with another bucket, the fire was bigger. Finally, the fire got into the wood and up into the rafters, and from there it was out of control. It was clear that it was futile; the canning center was lost.

Elam dropped the bucket in his hand to the ground in exasperation and just stood there and watched, disbelieving, heartbroken. "Why? Why? Why?" He hung his head, feeling as though all of the strength had gone out of his body. Then his attention was turned back toward the clinic.

After the guerrillas had chased the girls outside, they lit more fires, and once satisfied that it was well on its way to burning, they left the clinic and headed down to the airstrip. The last thing on their to-do list complete, they were now to head back to their camp.

Barbara, Lisa, Maria, and Anita stood there outside the building, determined that they were not burning the clinic down. They all raised their hands toward the building and commanded the fire "in the name of Jesus, stop!" and that fire actually stopped.

The guerrillas who'd left the building as good as burnt looked back from halfway down the airstrip and noticed a distinct lack of flames in the building, so they turned around and came back.

"The fires went out!" one guerrilla who had just exited the clinic after relighting several fires said to the guard who was stationed near the family. "Did these girls go back in?"

"No sir, they've been right here the entire time!" the guard insisted.

"Well, don't let them back in there," he said and headed with his small group down the airstrip again.

The small army of four looked at each other and prayed again. The fires went out again. Four times they did this until finally the guerrillas got radical inside the house and made sure it was burning before they walked away.

The girls had done their best and knew God was on their side and that His desire was to save the clinic, but when people insist on doing bad things, there's not a lot anyone can do. If God stepped in every time someone chose to do something bad, then there would be no virtue in doing good things, because there would be no other option. The fact that God leaves us free to choose is why good things sometimes happen to bad people, and vice versa. Tonight, something bad was happening to some good people, but God is the master at turning everything for good for them who love the Lord, and the family knew that. They fought as hard as they could against what was happening, but ultimately they trusted God to bring good from the situation, and that gave them peace.

Once it was clear that they could not save the clinic building, they all ran back in and started running around, dumping whatever bottles of medicines and other materials they could salvage into trash cans and buckets and ran outside with them. They made several trips. They kept making trips until the last time their exit had them running through sparks as pieces of the ceiling were giving way on their way out of the building. After that they just stood back and watched, with tears streaming down their faces.

Their mission completed, the remaining guerrillas began to disappear into the jungle, and the family was left to wander around, looking at what was left of their home and ministry.

Chapter 30

The Walk

For to me, to live is Christ and to die is gain. *Philippians 1:21*

It was almost time for Virgil to be getting up in the morning, and he hadn't even gone to bed yet as he pulled the boat up to shore just below Mario Mendez with the second and final boatload of his family's belongings. While they were unloading the boat, a man who seemed to be the head commander finally showed up. The sub-commander, who had been one of the three on the boat when Virgil had snatched the gun, approached the head commander and they talked for quite some time. Virgil could not hear what they were saying, but he figured that the commander was telling the head commander about what had happened earlier.

Virgil was ordered again to help unload the boat, and then he was told to "stay over there" under guard. It seemed to him like he sat there forever in a long boring and losing battle with the local mosquitoes, who had taken notice to the fact that Virgil had been "caught with his pants down" tonight…or at least in a pair of cut-offs and nothing more. He sat there in the jungle with no shirt on and his legs sticking out. Such a tasty treat for so many hungry insects! Finally, he couldn't take it any more and got some gasoline and wiped it all over himself to keep them away.

The head commander and the commander with the thick glasses spent most of their time on the radio, talking and making plans. From what Virgil could hear it sounded as though they were on the radio with the higher-up commanders who were just across the border in Mexico. He could hear only fragments of the conversation, which was mostly in code, but he heard that there were murciélagos (bats) in the air looking for the grillo (cricket) and that they needed to clear out and move right away. Virgil figured since he could hear helicopters off in the distance that the bats were helicopters, and since he was the only hostage he knew of right now, and he was a gringo, the grillo must be him.

Finally, the commander with the thick glasses moved away from the radio and came over and stood by Virgil. The look that he'd had in his eye earlier at La Anchura was gone, and now he seemed to want to talk.

"You realize we had to do this tonight, as we have information that your family works for the CIA," he said matter-of-factly.

Virgil almost smiled. "No one in our family works for any government. Trust me."

For some reason, maybe because the only people the poor ever saw who had money were government people, it was not uncommon for Americans to be suspected as being spies working for whatever acronym they knew of in the U.S. government: the DEA, the CIA, or the FBI. It was something that had been believed for years and something that would still be believed even after the war was over.

Virgil added, "Do you suppose that if I were CIA I would have put that gun down?"

The commander looked at him for a moment but made no reply. That was a good point.

Virgil continued, "My family is just missionaries, sir, not mercenaries. We don't work for anybody. We've tried to maintain a neutral stand through everything, but I have to admit that after this that would be a little harder."

The commander still didn't reply, as though he had something on his mind. Then someone hollered out for him, and he turned and walked back to the radio, leaving Virgil alone sniffing his gas fumes again.

After a while, everyone started looking and acting very agitated. They had their orders that they needed to move out. They'd been up all night, and now the sun was up. They were starting to feel nervous that the army was going to soon be on their trail. They had to get moving.

The commander again approached Virgil. Now he looked very upset. Mad even. As he walked over toward Virgil, he was throwing all kinds of profanity back and forth with the other men. "There's got to be some kind of honor in this war!" he said almost to himself.

Virgil stood silently and waited.

He said to Virgil, "I don't know why you didn't kill those men. You're a smart person. Why didn't you use that gun? If I had been in your shoes after what we did to your family I'd have had no mercy. I don't know why you didn't kill them."

Virgil said, "I'm a Christian. I couldn't kill them. I knew I would have been sending them to hell."

He shook his head and said, "Virgil, I don't understand that. I'm a Christian. Jesus was the first revolutionary, and we are still fighting the war He started nearly 2,000 years ago! A war for equality! Take from the rich and give to the poor!" He paced a little more and again speaking almost to himself he said, "There's just got to be some kind of honor in this war! There just has to be!"

Virgil asked him, "Are you saved?"

The commander stopped and looked at him.

Virgil continued, "Are you born again? Do you know where you're going when you die?"

He'd just claimed he was a Christian, which is easy to do. Most people do not want to totally deny God in their life, and when you ask them about *religion* they will say that they are a Presbyterian or a Methodist or a Catholic and claim some sort of connection with a church whether or not they go to church. They will tell you, "Well I was raised Presbyterian," or "My grandmother was Catholic," but only a person who knows Jesus and has become His friend will admit to being saved and born again and all that religious-sounding stuff.

"Do I know where I'm going when I die? No." He thought for a second about that. "No, I do not know where I would go." He paced some more and swatted a few mosquitoes away from his face, then quietly he added, "But I do know that I definitely don't have my life right with God."

There. He'd said it. A Christian is a person who has their life right with God. He'd said he was a Christian, but when it came down to it, the truth was that he was not God's friend. He knew the truth, but the truth hadn't set him free yet.

Virgil added, "So, if I were to shoot you, you would go to hell, right?"

Then, his teaching took over again. "Well, I don't know. We're not supposed to believe in heaven and hell. The revolution is what we believe in.

Jesus Christ started the revolution over 2,000 years ago, and we follow His command."

These were the things he was trained to say whenever someone started talking to him about Jesus, especially if they had struck a nerve. Once his mind was back on autopilot he could get back to business. No more of this religious discussion.

The radio interrupted again. Something about the bats again and moving the grillo. The commander ordered some of the men to take what they could and get going, ordered a few men to stand guard, and ordered the radio operator to stand by. They all growled and grumbled at each other and started moving.

The commander, still operating in autopilot, began to follow his orders. He set his machine gun down and pulled a 9mm out of his belt and cocked it. He looked up at Virgil, motioned toward the jungle away from the camp, and said, "We need to take a walk. Let's go."

Virgil was filled immediately with fear that only a person who has actually looked death in the face can know; he knew what this meant. He had seen this happen to other men. Men who took this walk didn't return. He was going to die. Like, for real. He was about to be executed.

He turned and began walking in the direction the commander had indicated. He no longer felt the heat or the itch of a million mosquito bites or the burning in his nose from the gasoline he'd rubbed himself down with. Now, he just felt fear.

In a few short moments so much went through Virgil's mind, and he wanted to panic, he wanted to run, he wanted to fight for his life! But in a few more moments he caught himself, and remembered that fear is the opposite of faith. Fear is sin. So, he began praying for peace: "God, help me not to be afraid right now. Please, take the fear away!"

As he walked, his thoughts turned from running to save his life here on earth to what his life was about to turn into. He realized that within a few short minutes, he would not be in the middle of this horrible war anymore but in the most awesome place in the universe. In a few minutes he was about to meet his greatest hero: Jesus. He'd been dreaming of the day he'd meet Him all his life, and today was the day. Today, he would be standing before Almighty God in heaven.

Just as much as he hated hell, he loved heaven, and he was about to get to go there. The fear of dying was gone. Now, instead of feeling like, "I'm going to *die*!" he was filled with an exhilarating anticipation. "I'm going to die! I'm going to heaven!"

They had walked far enough into the jungle to be out of sight of the other men. "Stop here," the commander told Virgil.

Virgil stopped and turned around to face the man who would send him into eternity. His gun, held in the grip of a shaky hand, was raised and pointed at Virgil's forehead. This was it. Virgil thought as he watched the commander's hand shaking just two feet from his face about how he had heard before that you can tell when someone is really about to shoot someone because no matter how many times they've killed before their hand will shake. His hand was shaking, that was for sure. This was really it!

Moments passed, and Virgil noticed that there was no long tunnel with a light at the end of it, no angels singing. He was still standing in the jungle in a pair of old cut-offs with the commander. It suddenly occurred to Virgil that he wasn't dressed properly to go to heaven, and he almost smiled.

The commander started talking. "Look, I know what your family has been doing here in this country. I posed as a tourist once and came to the clinic to check you out. I believe your family did a lot of good for this country." He almost looked apologetic.

He continued, "But you see, I have my orders." He yelled something back to the radio operator with a string of expletives attached.

The radio operator replied in like fashion but did as his commander ordered and brought him a little piece of paper, which almost had the appearance of a newspaper clipping. He showed it to Virgil. It was the orders for tonight's events, bearing the signatures of the three top guerrilla commanders of the URNG.

"You see, it says that the pilot is to be eliminated. That's you." He gave Virgil a few moments to look at it and then, following another trail of choice words, he ordered the radio operator to return to his post. "I have a lot of respect for you personally, Virgil, but if I fail to follow my orders, I will be executed."

Their eyes were locked. This was to be the last face that Virgil would see on earth—the face of the man who killed him. Then he would see

Jesus. Or would he? He wondered if, when he opened his eyes in heaven, Jesus would be right there immediately, or if Moses or Joshua would meet him and take him to Jesus.

The commander had looked men in the eye many times before and pulled the trigger. He knew what men looked like when they knew they were about to die. Virgil didn't have that look.

"Aren't you afraid?" He couldn't understand what he was seeing in Virgil's eyes, and that was because what he was seeing was the peace that is beyond all understanding that only comes from God.

"No," Virgil replied.

A moment passed as the commander processed the reply. It was an honest reply. He was about to die, and he was not afraid at all.

"Why aren't you afraid?"

"All my life, Jesus has been my greatest hero, and I'm about to meet Him! You can only kill my body, but my soul is about to go home," Virgil told him.

The commander had heard the words about Jesus that Virgil had spoken earlier, and like so many words they had gone in one ear and out the other. "Yeah yeah, sure. Jesus is my commander, too," he had thought, but what he was seeing right now wasn't something he could ignore. There was nothing in his training to tell him what to do with this.

Death was part of this commander's life, and more than once he'd been in combat situations where he feared that he might not make it out alive. Every day he lived in fear that the army would find them and blow them up or shoot them. He feared death with his every breath. This man was about to die, yet he was not afraid.

Virgil spoke again. "We are missionaries. We came to give new life, not to take life. I did the best I knew how to do as a missionary, and I figure you are doing your job the best you know how as well."

The commander's mind was in turmoil. This man he was about to kill had shown his true colors tonight. He was hearing what this missionary was saying, and unlike so many of the church people they had drafted into the revolution who killed with zeal and went right along with anything they did, this man had had the opportunity tonight to kill to save his own family, and he had put the gun down. This man was not just a man of words; he was for real.

"There's got to be some kind of honor!" the commander said, throwing up his hands in agitation as another string of expletives flew from his mouth. "There's just got to be some kind of honor; there's got to be some kind of respect in this revolution. This isn't right." He paced a little. "I have a lot of clout with the head commanders. Somehow I should be able to get you off."

The commander had killed many people. People he knew. People he even had once called, "friend." Why was this so different? He struggled and just stood there, shaking his head. His eyes welled up with tears as he said, "I can't shoot you." He shook his head again and said, "I don't understand."

A battle was being waged inside his mind and heart. If he failed to carry out his orders, he would almost certainly be executed, but he couldn't kill this man. Finally, he made his decision and said, "I can't!" He dropped his gun to his side, turned his back on Virgil, and walked away.

Almost as though God was answering the un-prayed prayer of the guerrilla commander to be able to spare Virgil's life, back at the camp the guerillas started making a lot of commotion. The sound of an oar hitting the side of a boat could be heard coming in closer and closer to their campsite. Finally, visible through the trees was a small boat with eight men from Mario Mendez, armed with a rope.

The guerrillas challenged them: "What do you want out here?"

The men had assembled back in Mario Mendez a few hours before when they'd heard that the guerrillas had taken Virgil hostage. They had one machete between all of them, but they knew they had to do something, and they were willing to give their lives trying.

Here they stood, unarmed, surrounded by men with machine guns, and they bravely said, "We lost a cow. We're looking for it." It was the best they could think of, and because they had a rope with them, it almost looked true.

The guerrillas put the men to work for a little while and then told them to leave.

The eight men looked at one another. It was now or never. "We aren't leaving without Virgil," one of them said.

"What? You can't take him! Leave now at once!" the commander replied, but inside he knew he had his ticket to letting Virgil go.

"No, really, that's the real reason we're out here. We weren't looking for our cow," one of the men admitted. "We came to take back Virgil. He's our friend, and we're not leaving without him."

Another guerrilla shouted, "Who are you to demand his release? You're crazy. You don't have any guns. We have the guns! We are in charge!"

The guerrillas were always in charge! But the eight men armed with the rope looked at each other and boldly declared, "We're going to take him back; he's our friend."

Virgil watched this in utter amazement. One of the men was a man who, whenever he got drunk, used to make fun of Virgil for preaching in the villages. But there that guy was right up in the commander's face, so close he couldn't get his gun between them. "I demand the release of Virgil Stoltzfus. Virgil is my friend, and if it hadn't been for Virgil and his airplane that you guys just burned, my younger brother would be dead now." He told the commander about how his brother had been bitten by a snake and how Virgil had flown him out to a hospital and saved his brother's life.

Another man added, "Virgil's father and mother have treated us all in their clinic, our friends, our families. Most of our brothers and sisters were born in their hospital. Virgil's a true friend of ours, and we're going to save him."

Right away another guy said, "If it hadn't been for his mom, my wife and my child wouldn't be alive."

Virgil watched as one by one, every one of them came and gave testimony of something the Stoltzfus family had done for them, some way that their clinic had touched their lives. Finally, one of them had an idea. "Listen, we have 300 men right now out in the jungle, and if you don't release Virgil we are going to storm you and there is no way you can kill us all. You might kill twenty or thirty of us—and I'll be the first one to take two or three bullets from your gun—but we are going to help our friend to escape."

The guerrillas really didn't know what to do. No one ever dared to stand up to them for one thing, and for another, if they had 300 men ready to storm their camp, they knew he was right that they wouldn't be able to kill all of them.

When in doubt, just do nothing and hope the problem goes away! But a couple of hours passed, and the eight guys were not going anywhere. In fact, now they were starting to feel a little hungry, so they went to the guerrillas' backpacks looking for food—food that had been stolen from La Anchura.

The guerrillas had enough of them and tried ordering them away again saying, "Get out of here! Beat it! Scram! Go home!" But nothing worked.

"Nope." They sat down and said, "We are not going home without Virgil." These men were not budging.

The commander got on his radio and talked with his commander again, and then he motioned for Virgil to come to the radio.

"Virgil," the man over the radio began, "you may have won the battle, but you cannot win the war. I'm releasing you to these men, but we'll get their names. They will be shot for what they did. And Virgil, if you do not turn yourself in voluntarily within seventy-two hours and support our revolution, we will find you wherever you go in this world, and we will execute you. We are going to put out a death warrant on your life."

Virgil smiled and handed the radio back to the commander. God had so clearly stepped in and spared Virgil's life. He wouldn't have done that for no reason.

The eight men and Virgil went to the river's edge and got into their boat. They quickly pushed off, made their way out of the creek into the river again, and headed for Mario Mendez as fast as their rowing arms could get them there. For a while no one spoke. The only sound was of paddling and the distant howling of monkeys.

The stillness, serenity, and beauty of the water before him in light of the reality of what had just happened was surreal to Virgil. While everything in the world around him looked perfectly normal, just as it had every other time he'd traveled the river, the reality was that nothing was normal right now. Virgil thought about what he had just gone through and was overwhelmed by a feeling of utter futility. Just like in Ecclesiastes, "Vanity! Vanity! All is vanity!"

He started talking to God. "God, I have just lost everything I've worked for my entire life, the last twenty years of my life, in one night. Gone!" he began. "It's like my whole life and all that work was for nothing!"

He felt in his heart that God said, "In the end, you're going to lose all of that stuff anyway and leave it all behind when Jesus returns."

"So then, what point is there? What use is it to work another twenty years of my life and have the same thing happen again?"

"Virgil, the only thing worth living and dying for is people. That's what Jesus died for: people."

Virgil sighed. "God, if only I could just have a bank account in heaven where I could keep everything safe!"

Then, as clear as anything he had ever heard, he heard God speak to his heart, "The only thing you can bring to heaven with you, Virgil, is people."

Suddenly, the light of the sun was not the only light shining on Virgil. Suddenly he *got it*. His whole life he had been working as hard as he could doing everything he could, but in the end, nothing he built with his hands would stand. The only things he'd bring to heaven with him were people.

With this realization, total peace washed over Virgil, and he believed that he had never been in danger that night. In all of his time in Guatemala during the war, he'd never known of a time when the guerrillas did a raid like this where the family was not killed. The men were always killed and the women and girls always raped, yet tonight no one had been touched. Not even Virgil, with the written orders for his death signed by three guerrilla leaders, had been harmed. It was as though God had established boundaries, and satan could only destroy the temporal things, the material. The eternal things, the things that really mattered, were off limits.

Virgil had asked God that night just before the guerrillas arrived what it was that He wanted Virgil to do with his life. Now he knew.

As they approached the village, one of the guys looked at Virgil and started taking his pants off. Virgil smiled and put up his hand and said, "That's alright; you don't have to give me your pants!"

Another guy thought about it and quickly took off his shirt and gave it to him.

"Hey, what about you?" Virgil asked. "You don't have a shirt now; what are you going to wear?"

He said, "Don't worry about me. The whole village is waiting for us, and everybody's going to be looking at you."

When they arrived at Mario Mendez, it was true: the whole village was there. They wanted to know everything that had happened. There was a lot of crying and people thanking God for his safe return.

Virgil thought about how at times his family had wondered if the people appreciated what they were doing. He looked around at all the crying faces as everyone hugged him and thought about what God had just shown him. He had been feeling as though he'd lost everything he had in the world, but he hadn't. Everyone wanted to hug him. He thought about the eight brave, *or possibly crazy*, guys who had come out to the jungle to rescue him, and he finally broke down and wept.

Chapter 31

Tested

*Each man's work will become evident; for the day will show it
because it is to be revealed with fire, and the fire itself will
test the quality of each man's work. If any man's work
which he has built on it remains, he will receive a reward.*
1 Corinthians 3:13-14

Not too many people get a chance to see just who really cared about them before they die, because those people usually pop up and have all sorts of kind things to say once it's too late—at your funeral. Today as Elam went through the ashes of what he had thought had been his life's work, the work he'd really done was shining as boatload after boatload of people he never would have expected came to the shore carrying gifts, with tears in their eyes.

Elam, Lisa, Maria, and Anita had all gone down to the river's edge to wash up and were talking to the people who were arriving. It was then that Elam was able to see another of the fruits of his labor.

"Oh, what are you going to do?" one neighbor cried as she gave Lisa a big hug.

"Will you be going back to the United States?" asked another person.

Lisa, replied with conviction, "No way! We're not leaving! This is our home!"

Maria agreed, "We definitely do not want to go back and live in the States."

Lisa added, "We love it here. We're going to rebuild. You'll see!"

The person they were talking to looked around and said, "But you've lost everything!"

"No." Anita smiled and gave them a hug, "We haven't *lost* everything. We *have* everything."

Elam's children were not afraid or angry. He felt proud of his girls and agreed wholeheartedly with everything they had said. No, they weren't leaving! This was their home, and they did not want to go back to the United States. There was too much work to be done here. Even now, he thought of all the people who had gotten up before the sun this morning and had started walking for miles through the jungle from their hut or village to the river to catch a boat to come to La Anchura for one thing or another because they didn't know that it had been destroyed. He decided where he could put a makeshift clinic in the kitchen pavilion and thought there would be a chance they could find some medical supplies and have them ready for when people came.

Already he was figuring out how and where they could start rebuilding the clinic. He thought also of the churches that were planted all along the river. Although he'd done what he could to release them to local pastors, they still needed his constant love and attention. Especially in Mario Mendez, where at this time he was their pastor, he couldn't just up and leave them. Maybe the guerrillas hadn't really meant that they had to leave the country.

Barbara was busy looking through the remains of the clinic for medical supplies. Her husband, who was too busy worrying about taking care of visitors and figuring out how he was going to set up another clinic if people came today, had not noticed his badly burned hand. She found some bandages, found Elam, and made the jungle doctor sit down for a bit and get doctored up.

Elam looked down at his hand and finally had time to realize that it did actually hurt quite a bit. When the yellow tractor had been set on fire, two wires melted together, starting the motor, and it had started rolling down the hill toward the river. Elam had jumped on it to try to stop it and instinctively grabbed the steering wheel, not thinking that it would be hot from the fire. It had burned his hands. The satellite dish ended up in the tractor's way, and that's where it stopped.

After she got Elam's hands fixed up, Barbara called out, "Lisa! Go get some other supplies, and let's head over to see if the neighbor lady has had her baby yet." The husband had stopped by the clinic last evening to let Barbara know that his wife was in labor and would likely be showing up sometime that night. If she had started walking over that night, she had likely noticed that Barbara was *busy* and had gone back home to her hut to have her baby.

Then, just as expected, many people started showing up for medical care, among them a lady who was waiting for Elam to make a set of dentures for her.

"Oh, I don't suppose today is such a good day to ask you if you have my dentures finished yet, is it?" a tear even came to her eye as she looked around.

Elam looked at this sweet lady who was very poor and had no teeth left in her mouth, and he thought again about the poor people's army and the irony of the whole situation.

"No, it isn't the best day for that!" Elam held back a smile as he walked over to a box of miscellaneous items and pulled out her teeth and held them up to her.

Her eyes widened as she looked at them.

"God must really want you to have these, because we actually found them in the ashes this morning." He handed her the undamaged set of new dentures that he had made for her, and more tears came to her eyes.

Later, Barbara and Lisa prepared to go check on the neighbor and her baby and headed down the airstrip toward their hut when they saw Elam standing by the airstrip talking to a bush. Since the bush wasn't burning, they didn't figure that he was talking to God.

"Elam, what are you doing?" Barbara laughed as she spoke.

Elam had been told that he had been given seventy-two hours to leave the country and he would be allowed to live. But they'd also taken the family's boat along with them (the one that Virgil had driven), so they had no way to leave. They had been told that when the guerrillas were done with the boat they would release it, and since it was upriver from them it would make its way back to them. It hadn't shown up yet. Elam knew that though the guerrillas had left, there were still some posted in the dense jungle that surrounded the compound to watch and make sure they were leaving.

"I'm trying to explain to this bush here that unless our boat is returned we can't leave, but that we intend to leave Monday morning!" he smiled back.

But right now, the bushes weren't talking.

Barbara and Lisa both laughed and continued on their way toward the neighbor's house. "I can't believe we're actually leaving," Barbara said, thinking of all the people who would not have a doctor anymore.

"I know, Mom!" Lisa smiled. "But it won't be forever. We'll be back!"

Barbara looked at her daughter, who was growing up into a very godly woman. "You're right! The Lord will provide for us, and we will be back soon."

· · · · ·

A boat arrived that was going downriver, and seeing what had happened they stopped at the dock. Since there were no phone lines and no 911 to call anyway, someone needed to go to Sayaxché to report what had happened to the authorities. When the boat that had arrived was ready to leave again, Jean got them to take her to Mario Mendez so that she could borrow a boat there to go to Sayaxché.

At this time there was no actual police force in the Petén, only the military. When Jean reported at the base in Sayaxché, they hadn't heard anything about it and told her she needed to make her report out at the main army base in Flores. So, she hopped on the back of a pickup, crossed the ferry, and headed toward Flores, which was about thirty miles away.

She got as far as Subín, only a few miles out of town, where the truck had to stop at the standard military checkpoint. The army lieutenant who was stationed there recognized Jean and after greeting her with, "Buenos días! Como estás?" (Good morning, how are you?) he did not get the standard, "Muy bien" (Just fine) response from her in return. She chuckled a little and told him how she was.

The lieutenant then took her into the base to use their phone to make a few important calls. She called the U.S. Embassy in Guatemala City, her fiancé Kevin, and Miguel.

They fed her lunch, and then she set off again on the rough dirt road for Flores. By the time she got there, it was already getting dark. She went to the army base and was received again with kindness and given a meal. They told her they would take her back home, but that they would have to wait till morning. After lunch the next day, they would be off in a helicopter to La Anchura.

. . . . .

Then, another boat pulled ashore, and a clothed Virgil stood there on the dock, helping others out of the boat.

Elam looked up and saw his son, and a flush of relief washed over him. He had trusted that God would keep him safe, but sometimes safe can mean in the arms of the Savior home in heaven, and Elam was glad to see that Virgil was still with him.

"Hi, Dad," Virgil said as he approached. "Is everyone OK?"

"Yup. We're all OK. No one was hurt," Elam replied with a faint smile.

Virgil looked around the property, which he was now seeing for the first time in the daylight. "Wow," he said.

"Yeah, wow. We've been sifting through the ashes all morning, but there's not much that is salvageable," Elam said almost glumly. He pointed over to the pavilion. "I want to set up a makeshift clinic over there."

Virgil processed that for a moment. "What? Why? We have to leave."

Elam shook his head. "All the rest of you, Barbara and the girls, you can all leave, but I need to stay here for the churches and for all the sick people who are probably walking through the jungle right now to come here because they don't know we've been burned out!"

Virgil shook his head. "Dad, you don't understand. These guys mean business. We have to leave whether we like it or not!"

Virgil knew the threats were serious. Elam did, too, but didn't want to accept it. Yes, Pennsylvania was his home, but Guatemala was also his home now. And Pennsylvania didn't *need* him. Guatemala did! The kids had all grown up here, and to them it was home so they didn't want to leave either! It was no easy thing to think of pulling out and leaving. How could they just turn their backs on the last twenty years of their lives and just go?

. . . . .

The next day, in the afternoon, Virgil was standing near the end of the airstrip with about 150 people when he heard a military helicopter coming from far off. It sounded like it was headed right for them, but Virgil thought that certainly the helicopter wasn't coming there to land. They had to know the place was infested with guerrillas!

The helicopter flew over the property low to the ground and then flew the length of the airstrip as though checking to see if everything was safe and clear for landing. Then the bushes that had not had anything to say to Elam the day before came to life. Dozens of guerrillas popped out of the tall weeds on either side of the airstrip and ran and dropped back into the weeds at twenty-foot intervals and hid. Two of them were carrying what Virgil recognized as Chinese Bastions, or rocket launchers, on their shoulders.

Virgil knew what this meant. The tactic was to wait until the helicopter landed and then open fire, and the helicopter would likely explode. All occupants inside would be killed. Virgil thought for sure that the helicopter would not land, they *had* to know the guerrillas were still around, but the helicopter turned and came back toward them, definitely coming in for a landing. Something inside him screamed out that Jean was inside that helicopter, and he took off running.

"¡No aterricen! ¡No aterricen! Don't land! Don't land!" Virgil took off and screamed, waving his arms and running toward the helicopter.

The 150 visiting people had lived for all these years in this war zone, too, so they also knew what this meant, and they all took off running toward the river in a panic. Elam saw what was going on. "God, help!" he prayed. He knew the guerrillas might shoot Virgil now for warning their target. Virgil knew it, too, but he just felt like his sister was in that helicopter.

The pilot saw Virgil and knew that something must be wrong, so he stopped his descent, pulled back up, and immediately radioed for help.

The guerrillas, seeing that their target was no longer coming to land and sit there to be shot at, chose plan B and all came out onto the airstrip and began firing on the helicopter. One of the rocket launchers fired but missed its target, and it came back down and blew up on the ground in the weeds.

The sound level inside the helicopter drowned out anything Jean could have heard going on, but all of a sudden the gunner, who had sat motionless the entire ride, came to life. The helicopter took several bullets as it made its escape, and that Jean did notice. One bullet came flying in right past the gunner and embedded itself in the interior of the helicopter.

Just then, everyone could hear a loud, powerful whirring sound as the turbocharged engines of some nearby PC7s came flying in to defend the helicopter. The sound was incredible as the engines wound up and came directly toward them at full speed. The guerrillas also heard the sound and immediately turned and ran in all directions. The PC7s came in at about 5,000 feet and turned and dove straight down toward the property, unloading bullets and rockets onto either side of the airstrip.

Jean didn't realize how close she had just come to being blown up, nor that it was her missing brother who had just saved her life.

When the helicopter finally landed at the army base in Pipiles, Jean was greeted by almost everyone in the village. Everyone wanted to know what had happened at La Anchura. Even as the words left her mouth she wondered, "Did all that really happen?" It was all too incredible to believe. Had the guerrillas really come in and burned twenty years of their life and work to the ground?

• • • • •

Having been told they had seventy-two hours to leave the country, they looked through the remains of their buildings for whatever could be salvaged and prepared to head home to Pennsylvania. Although the buildings had been destroyed, much of their equipment was untouched and needed to be prepared for a long period of non-use. And, of great importance to the girls were their pets, who needed to have people to care for them while they were gone.

Sometime that afternoon, Lisa took notice of how much food was there. There was a Mayan temple-sized pile of bread; enough to feed an army! There was no way their family would be able to eat it all by the time they left. She had an idea. "There are lots of hungry people out in the jungle, Dad. How about let's take it out to the guerrillas." Why not?

"Sure, go ahead!" Elam encouraged. "How many men have kids like these?" he wondered to himself, "kids who will show kindness to people who have just hurt them so deeply?"

Lisa drafted Virgil, and the two of them, armed with bags and bags of bread, set off in the direction where they all believed the guerrillas were camped. They had seen glimpses of them several times during the day and at night had seen the red embers of cigarettes through the darkness, so they had a pretty good idea where at least one of their camps was on the property.

Once they reached where they thought they were, they weren't, of course. They were hiding. So they called out and let them know what they were doing. "We have food for you!" Lisa called out.

"It's a trick! Shhh!" one man shushed the others as they all hid in the thick underbrush, guns poised.

Virgil thought about the people in Lancaster County who had also been feeding the guerrillas throughout this war. Sometimes, when Miguel and Virgil were out hunting they would find intriguing things at the abandoned guerrilla campsites. More than once they even found empty cans of food that had been canned, ironically, in Lancaster County, Pennsylvania, by well-meaning people who had been visited by people promoting the war as though the guerrillas were the persecuted underground church in Guatemala. What group of Christians would *not* want to help a cause like that? Because they lived in the United States, thousands of miles away from Guatemala, they didn't know what was really happening in Guatemala. Believing the spokesmen of the war, they did what they could to help. Sweet little old ladies canned food they grew in their gardens and donated it to misguided charities that supported the guerrillas.

Lisa called out to the guerrillas a few more times to let them know what they were doing, and then they left the food there in their camp and headed back.

· · · · ·

Elam visited with the Nueva Vida (New Life) church at Mario Mendez to ordain new leaders to take over while he was gone. It's too bad that one has to get their house burned down and their kid kidnapped to pack out a church, but that's what it did alright. The entire village was packed into and all around the church as Elam tearfully said good-bye to his congregation.

· · · · ·

Monday came around, and Elam, Virgil, Lisa, Maria, and Anita all got into their boat and headed out to Sayaxché. They'd left before the seventy-two hours were up. Barbara and Jean decided to stay behind to get some more things ready. The family knew they'd return, and their groundskeeper, Efrain, would be staying on the property with his family. They wanted to leave things as in order as possible for him while they were gone.

Wednesday, Elam sent a boat down for his wife and oldest daughter, and the whole family reunited in Sayaxché. They had paperwork to take care of and people to say good-bye to. All of them needed to settle up accounts with stores and get new IDs made up at the local municipal building.

The next day, the family headed out to the airport in Flores, and the U.S. Embassy sent a Guatemalan air-force DC9 plane out to get them. On their way through the airport they met up with some people they knew.

Jean threw her arms around her husband-to-be, Kevin, and smiled like she hadn't in days. Miguel took his hand out of his wife-to-be's and reached his arms around his mom for a hug.

"Hi, Virg. I see you're still with us." Miguel smiled at his little brother.

"Yup. You're all going to have to put up with me for a few more years, it seems," he agreed.

"It's good to see you, Dad," Miguel said.

"Yeah. It's good to see you, too, Miguel," Elam smiled.

They were all together. Everyone was safe. After a brief time, they all headed their separate directions again. Jean, Kevin, Miguel, and Dwyanna headed back to Sayaxché and then on to La Anchura. Virgil had wanted to go back with them to salvage the motor in the Maule, because someone had heard about what had happened and was offering $4,000 for the motor. The Embassy had a fit when they heard that suggestion. The military had satellite pictures of the area, and they could see that the guerrillas had little camps all over La Anchura and had the military surrounded at this point.

Finally agreeing that he could not go back, Virgil made some calls and found someone who would be willing to salvage the motor for him. The person who wanted to buy it sent a truck out for it and hauled the whole thing back to Guatemala City and took out the motor. (Today that engine flies a small aircraft around for one of Guatemala's senators.)

$$\cdot\ \cdot\ \cdot\ \cdot\ \cdot$$

When the family arrived in Guatemala City, they were met at the airport by the press and some officials from the Embassy. They were taken to the U.S. Embassy to the basement, where they held a press conference and told the story of what had happened. The ambassador was there as well as most of the people who worked in the Embassy—most of whom sat listening in tears.

Elam lived through the war every day and saw on the news on occasion some stories about it. It was sad how twisted and wrong most things came out. Traps the guerrillas laid for the army would make the national headlines somehow as massacres by the army. One in particular happened in the village where Efrain, their groundskeeper's mother, had lived. The guerrillas had come in and basically taken the whole village captive and had hidden out in all the homes. When the military convoy came through town, the guerrillas opened fire from the huts, and the military returned fire at the huts, so innocent men, women, and children in the village got hurt and killed in their own homes during the gun battle.

Finally, the military fled to get reinforcements, and the guerrillas simply fled. When the military returned there were no guerrillas, just dead and traumatized civilians…and the press. When it was all said and done, it came out in the news that it was the military who were the bad guys. The national news said that the military had shown up and mowed down the villagers in a horrible human rights-crushing massacre.

Much of the world had never heard the truth about what was going on in Guatemala. Most of the time, it's not what you're selling but how. Package something up just the right way and give it the right jingle, and it will sell. The guerrillas had been good at selling themselves—good enough to keep them supplied with enough food and money to keep the war ravaging the country for over thirty years.

After the compound was burned, there were some headlines that ran in publications supporting the guerrillas, and even today doing a

Google search on Elam Stoltzfus will bring up this article (campesinos are villagers or farmers):

Further Action Against U.S. Citizen Elam Stoltzfus as reported in the CERIGUA. The Guatemalan National Revolutionary Unity (URNG) released new information this week in the case of U.S. citizen Elam Stoltzfus. In early September the insurgency charged Stoltzfus, who had lived in Guatemala for 19 years, of collaborating with the army. On September 1, rebel units took over his property in western Petén and found weapons, military communications equipment and written information related to army operations. They destroyed buildings, aircraft and the landing strip on his property, and ordered Stoltzfus and his family to leave the country. The U.S. citizen claims to be a missionary whose only goal was to assist the people living in western Petén. In the latest report on Tuesday the URNG charges Stoltzfus with turning over to the army two campesinos whom he accused of being guerrillas, who were then detained and tortured on his property. The insurgents report that Stoltzfus later transported the campesinos to the Sayaxché military base in his private plane. One of the men suffered severe head injuries as a result of the torture and the other is being held in prison in Santa Elena, Petén, according to the guerrillas.

So much for believing it if you see it in writing!

Chapter 32

The Bump

Therefore, since we have so great a cloud of witnesses
surrounding us, let us also lay aside every encumbrance and
the sin which so easily entangles us, and let us run with
endurance the race that is set before us,
fixing our eyes on Jesus.... *Hebrews 12:1-2*

"You watch your back! Alright?" Elam smiled and hugged his son.

"I'll be fine, Dad." Virgil assured him.

"Bye," Barbara said, also giving her son a hug.

"I still think you should just fly out with us today," Elam said.

"I know, but I really want my car while I'm in Pennsylvania. Everything will be fine!" Virgil reassured him.

And then they were gone. The whole family got onto the airplane, and Virgil stayed long enough to watch as it took off for the States.

Virgil was trying to think *practically*. Even though the property and all of their earthly possessions had been burned up, just picking up and pulling out of the country wasn't so easy. He had a lot of loose ends to tie up first. He had to make the arrangements for the Maule to be salvaged. There were people who owed him money and people he owed money, too. And, since he knew he'd be in Pennsylvania for a while, he wanted to drive his car up so he would have something to drive while he was there. His car, however, was not in any condition for driving up through Mexico, so he took it to the repair shop he always used and dropped it off.

When he arrived to pick up the car, the mechanic asked him if he knew anyone with a yellow Mercedes-Benz.

"No. Why?"

"Well, there has been a yellow Mercedes driving past here. They seem to be watching your car."

Virgil paid for the work and headed toward the U.S. Embassy, keeping a watchful eye on his rearview mirror. Sure enough, it wasn't long until there was a yellow car following him. He made a few turns to see if the car really was following him or not, and no matter where he turned the car stayed behind him, tight on his trail. Once he was convinced they were really following him, he started doing his best to lose them, and after about fifteen minutes he lost sight of them.

"Good, I lost them!" he said to himself.

The guerrillas in the yellow car had decided to hang back a little, to give Virgil the idea that he'd gotten away. They followed him from a distance, waiting for their chance. Their chance came when he stopped at an intersection with heavy traffic going both directions. The driver of the Mercedes weaved around traffic until he got right up behind Virgil and gently bumped up against the back of his car. Then he floored it to push Virgil out into traffic.

Virgil felt the bump, looked behind him, and could not believe it. His pushed on his brakes, but the Mercedes was pushing him out into the intersection whether he liked it or not. He looked up into the oncoming traffic and saw an opening, so he tried to floor it to escape. His plan didn't work, and he instead managed to get himself right in the path of an oncoming car. It smashed into his rear quarter panel and spun around, stopping on the other side of him.

The driver of the car that was following that car slammed on his brakes, which sent him spinning around several times in front of Virgil's car, finally stopping right in front of him. Then the driver of the car behind that one lost control and ended up skidding sideways almost into the side of Virgil's car. Other cars skidded around and slid everywhere. He was completely boxed in. The driver of the first car jumped out of his car right away and was trying to figure out what was going on. Virgil opened his door and got out of his car right away and tried to figure out if he had to run. He was surrounded. This did not look good.

But what at first seemed like a disaster turned out to be a miracle. Virgil had just been pushed out into a caravan of vehicles that were transporting one of the vice presidential candidates in the Guatemalan presidential race that year, his son, and nearly a dozen or so heavily armed bodyguards.

"Virgil? What's going on?" A man who had been riding in the second car that had spun around in front of Virgil's car came running up to him. He was the son of the vice presidential candidate and had been at the press conference at the U.S. Embassy, so he recognized Virgil right away. He had reported their whole story in the local news and would someday be a journalist for an international news agency.

"There was a car following me, and it pushed me out into the intersection…" Virgil began.

A man with a blue suit yelled, "They're armed!"

Then, all of the bodyguards who had been getting out of the cars started pulling guns out of their suits. A woman with a machine gun had gotten out of the yellow Mercedes and was coming for Virgil when the accident first happened, but seeing all of the men getting out of the cars she turned and ran back to her the Mercedes, which then backed up and sped away.

"Come on, get in my car!" the man Virgil had been talking to said.

"But what about my car?" Virgil hesitated.

"Don't worry about it!" the man exclaimed and pulled Virgil into his car. He then told one of the bodyguards to get Virgil's car, and they all took off and ended up pulling into a nearby parking lot that had a big mechanic's shop with a wall all the way around the property.

The whole caravan pulled into the shop, and once inside they closed the doors. All the men got out and talked to Virgil. They made arrangements to get all the cars fixed and offered Virgil a ride to his hotel. The vice presidential candidate was a Christian, who also knew the story of what had just happened to Virgil's family. The candidate laughed, "We may not look like angels, but God knew you needed help, and He directed the traffic to protect you today."

The guerrilla commander on the radio that night had said that they would get Virgil no matter where he went, and they meant it. But today Virgil had seen once again that God would protect him.

The U.S. counsel and the government of Guatemala both advised Virgil to leave the country immediately. Virgil finally set practicality aside and agreed that flying to the U.S. alive while he still could would probably be best. But he had no money.

. . . . .

Halfway home up the mountain, Mike and Rocky Beene, missionaries in Guatemala and friends of Virgil's, were driving away from Guatemala City. It had been a long day, and they were eager to be home, but something was troubling them. They didn't understand why, but they felt an urgency to go back to the city, which was actually really low on their want-to-do list. Recognizing that still, small voice of their Shepherd, they turned their car around and headed back to town.

When they arrived in the city, they headed for their favorite hotel, The Hotel Pan American, owned by now-grown-up American missionary kid John and his wife Charlotte Carrette. They walked into the lobby ready to check in and ran into Virgil.

"Well, Hi! How are you doing, Virgil?" they casually asked.

Like Jean and the army lieutenant, Virgil told them "how he was."

The mysterious urgency that had sent them back into town calmed as the light came on in their minds and hearts and goosebumps shot up Rocky's arms.

With their eyes wide and huge smiles across their faces they said, "This is why God sent us back!" Just last week they had received $500 in the mail and were not sure what it was to be used for. Now they knew!

They reached into one of their bags they had with them and pulled out the cash and handed it to Virgil. "Take this money and buy your ticket to get back to the States."

Once again, God had come to the rescue.

. . . . .

The Stoltzfuses spent about a year in the U.S., but all the while their goal was to return to Guatemala and rebuild. A few months after the family returned to Guatemala, the president of Guatemala, Jorge Serrano, invited Elam and Barbara to the Presidential Palace. He apologized for what had happened to Elam and his family in his country, but encouraged Elam that his sacrifice had not been in vain.

The burnout turned out to be one of the guerrillas' biggest mistakes in the whole war. Elam had not been the only one to notice the contradiction between what the guerrillas preached and what they did. The guerrillas thought that Elam worked for the government and because of that he was a threat, but he was no threat. They should have seen him as on their team all along. He was a "rich gringo" from the United States who had given up his right to be rich and had come to spend all his time and money helping the poor. In essence, he had taken from himself (the rich) and was giving it to the poor.

He'd been living out in the jungle doing exactly what the guerrillas preached they were doing, helping the poor Indian villagers. But whatever threat they'd imagined Elam to be turned out to be their own undoing. They were afraid that Elam would somehow give an advantage to their enemy, yet by burning down his clinic that's exactly what they ended up doing to themselves. What they didn't realize was that when they burned the clinic and sent their doctor away, they took something very vital to that whole area full of poor villagers and in so doing lost most of their much-needed support in the area.

Since Elam had lived in the midst of the war-torn area of the Petén, it had been one of his greatest desires to see the war end. (Delight yourself in the Lord, and He will give you the desires of your heart. Psalm 37:4) Elam had delighted himself in the Lord, and the desires of his heart had been given to him. La Anchura had become a fountain of new life for everyone it touched. Now, its destruction had been an important link in the chain that led to the end of a bloody and brutal war that was taking the lives of so many. Its destruction had helped bring new life to a whole country.

· · · · ·

Years after the war officially ended in 1996, the country is a whole different world. Where the war has been pruned away there is new growth. Businesses have flourished, cell towers have gone up, roads, bridges, and schools have been built. A twenty-eight-mile road now winds through all the villages that Elam first visited along the Passion River from Sayaxché all the way to Mario Mendez, trailed by electrical lines. In this world where often the family had to go all the way to Flores to use the phone (one or two day's journey, depending on the roads), now, just twelve years later in 2008, they just whip out their cell phones and talk. Every day it seems that something is changing, something is progressing. Steadily, the country keeps moving out of poverty toward prosperity.

Elam hadn't been the most skilled laborer that Jesus ever had. He hadn't been the richest. He hadn't been the most educated. He hadn't been the most anything, really. What set Elam apart to do great things for God was that he was willing because he had the faith to follow God. If Hebrews chapter eleven were to be written today, it would include Elam's name. He took what he was born with, what he had, and he took it wherever Jesus said to go in faith that God would do whatever he couldn't do, trusting that even in the bad circumstances God would work that situation together for good.

Where Elam was weak, he knew his God to be strong. He did what he could, and Jesus did the rest. Because of this one man's faith, a whole country was blessed. Because of this one man who was willing to hold God's hand and go somewhere that the rest of the Christian world said was unwise to go, literally thousands upon thousands of people are alive today. Family trees that would have been cut off are still alive today because of this one man and his wife and children. Even today, the ripple effects of his life are still rippling.

Any of you who look in awe at this man's life, be encouraged! Missionary families are often looked at as though they are super-Christians, because they dare to take their faith where others fear to go. But the image you have in your mind of what a super-Christian does is not something only other people can achieve. It's not a matter of *can* but *will*. It's a matter of choice. "The righteous will live by faith."

The safest, most successful, most meaningful, and most fun place in the whole world to be is in the center of God's will. No matter who you are or what skills you have or don't have or where you live, God is calling you. He has a special place for you that no one else can fill.

Missions work is not about places; it's about people, and there are brokenhearted people everywhere who need good news. There are people everywhere who are mourning, who need encouragement, or who are prisoners to things like drug or alcohol abuse who need to be freed. You can thank God that all those people are not in the jungle. Some places that need missionaries have Starbucks and Wal-Mart, and to change your world all you have to do is go to those places and put Him first in all you do.

So many people think that if there is a person down the street who has a hard life, what he really needs is a Democrat president in the White House or a Republican president in the White House. What your hurting neighbor really needs is a neighbor who cares. God can use you to change your world no matter where you are if you just hold His hand, allow Him to lead you, and have faith that He can and will do miracles. "New Life" can be the theme of your own life, too.

Chapter 33

And Then

"His master said to him, 'Well done, good and faithful slave.
You were faithful with a few things, I will put you in charge
of many things; enter into the joy of your master.'"
Matthew 25:21

So what happened then, after all this? About a year after the fire, with the help of many family and friends from many different churches, the family came back and cleaned up and rebuilt. Some of the buildings that had been destroyed like the guesthouse and canning center were simply cleaned up; neither were rebuilt. But a new, bigger clinic was built, which included housing for the family on the second floor. The family's house was never cleared away or rebuilt. The remains of it, the foundation and some walls, are still where they were and how they were the night it was burned down.

A new, bigger, and better airplane was purchased within a few years, and many more hundreds of hours were logged on it flying people to hospitals. There were many stories of things that happened that could add many more chapters to this book. Some of the stories had happy endings with people arriving at the hospital just in time for all to go well. Some stories had unhappy endings, and the airplane would simply fly the person right back from Guatemala City to the Petén for their funeral and burial. Some stories—like the night the man showed up with his head nearly cut off—had unreal endings.

It was a bar fight, of course, between two best friends with machetes. (Is it any mystery why none of the Stoltzfus children ever found alcohol a temptation?) After the fight, other friends brought the man to the clinic, barely alive. It was nighttime, but they got the airplane ready to go anyway. Flying at night is dangerous, because unlike in a car where you're on the ground and have headlights to guide your path, in an airplane you can't see the ground so you have no headlights. The only guide you have is your instruments.

Not only is the actual flying dangerous, but in the Petén it's also illegal. Guatemala lies coast-to-coast across Central America. It lies geographically between the manufacturers of many illegal drugs and the customers in the U.S., and so sees a lot of drug trafficking, especially in the Petén. Because of that, flying a single-engine aircraft at night in the Petén is illegal.

But, just like speeding to the hospital in the States, there are things you have to do when someone's dying. The machete whack had severed the man's windpipe, so he was no longer breathing from his mouth or nose. Rather, Barbara kept her fingers in the man's open trachea so he could breathe, while Elam was there working with the IVs and keeping track of the man's vital signs, ready to resuscitate him if necessary.

While some things slip by the DEA and reach the States, this plane wasn't going to! No sir! Although one would imagine that no intelligent drug trafficker would be flying his drugs *south* into a major international airport, when Virgil came on radar and Guatemala City knew he was coming, the authorities were alerted and waiting at the airport.

Virgil will always remember when they landed; a big, burly, long-haired tough guy with a big machine gun thrust open the passenger's door of the airplane to inspect what was inside, only to quickly turn and run off to toss his cookies in a nearby bush. Definitely not drugs in that airplane that night!

Although once Virgil had landed it was very obvious that this was an emergency flight of the gravest sort and there was definitely nothing illegal going on, Virgil was still reprimanded sharply by the authorities and nearly lost his license.

The doctor who arrived with the ambulance asked them why they'd bothered flying this man in. The man was nearly dead! He obviously was not going to make it.

The next day when Elam, Barbara, and Virgil went to the hospital and talked to the guy, who was sitting up in bed, eating, and watching TV, they decided that that had been why they had bothered, and that it had been worth Virgil almost losing his license.

At La Anchura, Elam had new plans to build a surgical wing so that doctors could be brought in to be able to perform emergency C-sections and other emergency surgeries so that flights in the middle of the night wouldn't be needed. Teams came from the U.S. and built the foundation and main structure of the building, and supplies to equip the facility were donated.

Virgil spent some time in Lancaster County working and sending money to his parents to help with the building. Meanwhile, one of his prayers the night of the burning was answered. Being of Amish descent, his testimony was of particular interest to a particular group who didn't get out much in the world. He was able to share his testimony with his own relatives all over Lancaster County for a year and realized that some of his favorite people in the world were Amish.

One thing he learned was that the Amish youth were really not that much different from youth everywhere, in that they have a lot of energy and like to play, but for teens and young adults there really are no places to go play—at least no place good. So, he and Sam King, also of Amish descent, built a youth center with friends. The Chicken House was a simple game room in an old chicken house where mostly Amish kids came and hung out and played or watched football on a big-screen TV. It was nothing complex, but it was a safe and productive place for the kids to hang out, and the results were really awesome.

Kids started coming on a regular basis and were really enjoying having fun without partying. The Chicken House was so successful that when it was time to return to Guatemala, Virgil decided that he wanted to do something similar in Mario Mendez for the Guatemalan youth. He even had a little piece of property he thought would be perfect for it.

Elam caught on to this idea right away and got really excited about it. He was getting older, but not too old to remember being a young guy looking for things to do on the weekends! And, in Guatemala, the church was ultra-religious and frowned upon basically anything fun. The Christian kids in the villages were expected to show up at church every night or else they were backslidden and needed disciplining. Nothing fun was allowed. Especially not the Guatemalan national pastime, soccer! Christian Guatemalan kids could do nothing but go to church, which obviously often led kids to totally leave the church. A Christian youth center would be so awesome!

What had started off in his son's mind as a small thing grew in Elam's mind to a huge structure with a skating rink, popcorn machines, and a movie theater, and he moved forward on getting folks excited to build it! At the same time, he also dreamed of buying a concrete truck and pouring floors for village houses to help stop some of the sickness that came from the people just being too dirty with their dirt floors! He made pamphlets and talked to churches and was excitedly and actively working toward these new things.

But, then, this unstoppable energetic guy seemed to be slowing down a bit. He was very tired all the time. He was getting forgetful. After finally being talked into seeing a doctor, in the fall of 1997 he was diagnosed with Non-Hodgkin's Lymphoma. Cancer. Not a problem. He was confident he'd be cured.

Ultimately he was cured, but not the way he'd expected. In a hospital in Houston, in October of 1999, while surrounded by his family and leaving instructions as to what projects needed to be completed yet, he took his last breath and left this planet for heaven.

At the graveyard behind Spring Garden Church in Lancaster County, Elam's sons Miguel and Virgil stood side by side with shovels in their hands and buried their father. His departure from the clinic happened only a few years after the road was finally built from Mario Mendez to Sayaxché. So, the doctor leaving the clinic and the fact that the hospital was now only an hour away by truck sent most people out to the hospital right away. Slowly, over the next few years, the clinic became unnecessary.

· · · · ·

So, what did the kids do then? What about them?

Jean got to use that wedding dress that she had saved from the guerrillas' fires less than a year after the compound was burned and married Kevin Boehmer at Petra Christian Fellowship in Pennsylvania. Kevin and Jean began their married life in Guatemala, but then settled in Belize where they reside today with a few hundred geckos and their four children: Kayla, Jon, Kareem, and Joy.

Miguel married the fiancée whom he had brought with him to Guatemala right after the fire: Dwyanna Pearce from Houston, Texas. They moved to Guatemala and lived in a tent during the time of rebuilding. Dwyanna was soon pregnant and a year after arriving in Guatemala went into labor on the property at La Anchura. After some time, it was apparent that the baby was not coming, so an army helicopter came and whisked her off to the (scary) hospital in San Benito.

She delivered Jonathan by C-section, and hey, the power only went off once during her operation. It was OK, though, because the doctors had some flashlights to use to finish sewing her up. (Yes, it is appropriate to be gasping in horror at this moment!)

A few years later, Miguel and Dwyanna built their own home across the river from the clinic. They added to their family several years later, in 1997, but this time it was another lady who had the chance to go to the scary hospital. After little Guatemalan Armando was a few days old, Miguel and Dwyanna adopted him. Then, ten years after that they adopted another child, this time a daughter named Briandy Gabriella. Today they reside in the village of Mario Mendez.

Virgil, the third child, who waited patiently and chastely for a wife, was the last to marry at age thirty-three. He married Dara Shelton Kachel, a crazy widow-lady from Pennsylvania who already had four children: Casey, Sean, Josiah, and Alisson. They moved the whole family down to Guatemala, where they lived first at La Anchura in a thirty-seven-foot camper. All six of them. (Yes, they did go a little crazy.)

On their one-year anniversary, their first child, Joshua, was born in the camper with Grandma (Barbara) wearing the catcher's mitt and Casey cutting the cord. Two and a half years after moving to Guatemala, their house in Sayaxché was finally ready, and they moved in. Within a month of the move to town, Evelyn was delivered via C-section in the (also scary) government hospital with two Cuban doctors and two local doctors attending. Two years later, Elisa was born in a nice, clean, private hospital in Guatemala City. Then, two years later in 2008 came Victoria Grace, bringing the family total up to ten.

Their ministry in Sayaxché involved a bulldozer, a Hummer that turned into a police station, a café, a bookstore, a hardware store, and a tourist trap. Some of their own adventures include crazed mobs, fleeing town, corrupt government officials, and guys with big guns, but that is another book. Today their family is making plans to move to British Columbia, Canada.

Soon after the fire, Anita went to a Bible school in a town west of Guatemala City called Xela (Sheh-la). There she met and married Edgar Cosiguá. They had two wedding ceremonies, and one of them was held in Edgar's hometown, Xela, the first town that Elam and Barbara had stopped in so many years ago as boyfriend and girlfriend on the singing tour. They started off their married life serving as pastors of a church that Elam had started in Pipiles (where the military base along the border is located). Later, they, too, built a house at La Anchura and lived there for several years with their three children, Alex, Sara, and Barbie.

One of Anita's adventures was being kidnapped along with Barbara and two other people who were at the clinic at the time and having to walk miles through the jungle just a few months after having a C-section. Virgil was given a mere four hours to come up with two million dollars in ransom. Instead, the military came in and had a shoot-out with the captors, who went running away without their money. Everyone was safe in the end. That adventure, too, is another book.

For the first few years after Elam's death, Anita dedicated herself to doing whatever she could do to help her mom around the clinic. Eventually, Edgar and Anita moved to Sayaxché and got involved with the New Life church that was started by Richard Hood and his wife Mirna. They then joined up with some missionaries from Lancaster County, Arlen and Keturah King, who work with Missionary Ventures and are living in Sayaxché. Today they were working also under Missionary Ventures with Arlen and Keturah and are building a youth center in Sayaxché.

Once Lisa was grown, she went to the States for a time to study for her pilot's license, with the intention of going back to Guatemala and joining up with Virgil in the flying ministry. She started going to Petra Christian Fellowship in New Holland, Pennsylvania. There her plans changed when she met and then married Mahlon Smucker.

Mahlon is a man with a great love of horses, and great skill working with them. His skill and love for horses led them on a number of different adventures including the owning and operating of a tourist business in

Lancaster County called Abe's Buggy Rides for a few years. Their greatest accomplishments came in 1997 and 1998 and were named Sarena and Sean. In 2006, Nicholas came on the scene, bringing their family to a total of five. Today, they are living in Lancaster County, Pennsylvania.

Maria married Walter Fuentes from Mario Mendez. She and Walter lived in the village for a while with his parents, and only after much prodding and coaxing by Elam did they go to La Anchura to live. Elam did not like the environment provided by life in the village and so offered Walter full-time work on the property. Before Elam died, their family was up to six with Dinny, Omar, Wesley, and Ivy.

In 2000, just a few months after Elam's death, Walter and Maria's fifth child, Ashley, was born at La Anchura, delivered by one of the family's most trusted nurses and best friends, Zoila. When Ashley was about three months old it was discovered that there was something wrong with her heart. Barbara took Walter, Maria, and Ashley into Guatemala City where she would be for a month in the hospital. Unfortunately, on July 25, 2000, Ashley became the first of Elam and Barbara's grandchildren to meet up with Grandpa in heaven. Today Walter and Maria are still living on the property at La Anchura and planning to move to Mario Mendez.

Barbara continued to offer medical help to the people who had come to trust her as the most able midwife in the area. The clinic ministry that had once seen boatloads of forty people at a time showing up at the clinic on a daily basis eventually trickled down to a few patients a day and sometimes none at all. But, although people with other medical emergencies were heading straight out to the hospital, the ladies in labor kept coming.

Over the years, trapped out in the middle of nowhere far from a hospital, Barbara was forced to pray and just learn to do things that would frighten any stateside midwife into the ER with her patient. Barbara had to do all kinds of things to get babies out of their moms that are considered big no-nos, like when just a hand or just a foot would present during birth. She would just have to stuff that body part back up and try to turn that baby around to get into the right position. God was there with her, and she had very few babies die under her care. God greatly blessed her in that regard, and the people trusted her because of it.

But, when the clinic ministry was lessening, Barbara did not just sit around and learn to knit (not that there is anything wrong with knitting!

I even know how to knit!). It wasn't only Elam who'd been the Energizer Bunny. One thing she really enjoyed and has now been doing for years is taking crippled people to see a doctor near Guatemala City who has committed to helping anyone she brings to him free of charge. Every few months she takes a new vanload of people to see this caring Christian doctor. In Guatemala, the disabled often receive no help from the government or any organizations and are simply left to deal with their disability on their own, and in many cases, their disabilities can be fixed with surgery. All they need is someone who knows and someone who cares, and Barbara has become that person for many people.

She helps with other ministries around Guatemala with translation and in service. She helps whomever she runs across whenever she can to the point that she is hardly ever at home. The property that the clinic is on is a big piece of land, which requires a lot of mowing. It has offered full-time employment to more than one person just to maintain. It also has required a lot of fuel for the tractors and for the generator, about $2,000 worth every month or month and a half. So, just as one puts a hammer down once the house is built, the tool that this mission compound was for Elam as he reached out with Christ's love to the sick and needy has also seen the end of its need.

While a hammer is a lot easier thing to put down than an entire piece of property you've lived on and built up for years, a home where you've raised your family and served God faithfully, it still reached a stage where it was time to put it down. Time to find another tool and build something new. In 2007, the property was put up for sale.

While all of the children have had their own struggles, obviously, Elam could be proud that none of them ever turned their backs on God as can be so common with pastors' kids and missionary kids. These kids grew up working alongside their parents in everything and all left home with a great love for their parents and a longing to go back home whenever they could. The property may have become a thing of the past, and Elam may have moved on to heaven, but the real reason for Elam's mission in Guatemala still lives on in his wife and children, and now his grandchildren.

"Though he is dead, he still speaks."

Elam and Barbara with Jean, Miguel, and Virgil on the houseboat just before leaving the U.S.

Virgil, Jean, Barbara, Miguel, Elam, Lisa, Maria, and Anita at La Anchura.

Elam with Miguel, Virgil, and Jean and "Christmas Dinner" their first year in Guatemala in 1972.

1973–Baptismal service held in the Passion River at the village of La Flor (The Flower).

1974–Virgil, Miguel, Jean, Anita and a few of their jungle pets. Some of the fun the kids had in Guatemala.

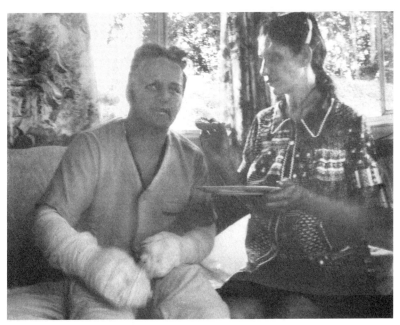

1975–Elam with Barbara after the houseboat explosion.

1976–Elam in the jungle with Virgil and Miguel cutting lumber.

1980–Elam talking on the ham radio.

1976–Julia all better with her husband and baby.

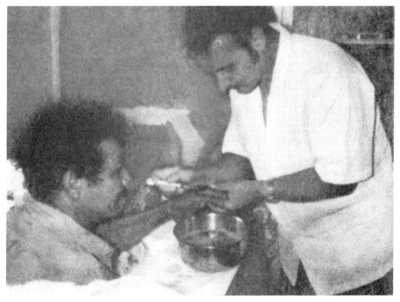

Elam working on a patient with a nasty machete cut on his hand.

1976–Baptismal at the village of La Flor de la Esperanza (The Flower of Hope).

1976–Elam removing part of and fixing up the rest of a mangled toe.

The family's house which was destroyed by the guerrillas in 1990.

April Gore (friend of the family), Lisa, Maria, Elam, and Barbara with Guatemalan President Jorge Serrano and his wife.

1977–28 baptisms during a convention held at La Anchura.

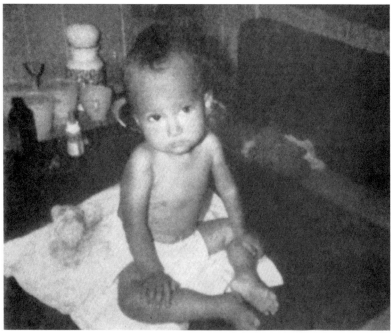

1977–Sweet malnourished baby Elida, brought to the clinic at age 19 months weighing only 12 pounds.

1977–Baptismal service for the church at the village of La Bella (The Beauty).

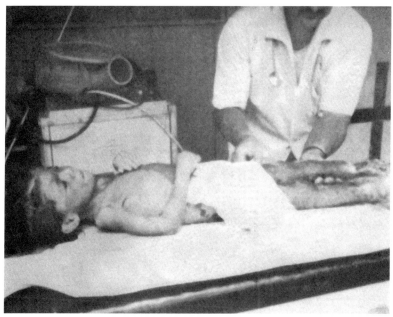
Maria being examined by Elam when she first arrived at La Anchura.

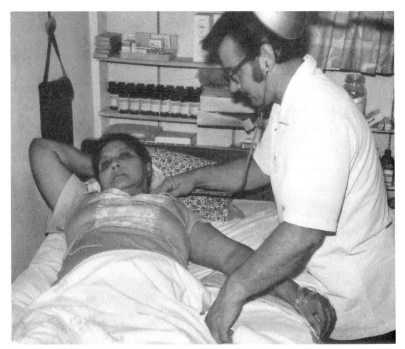

Elam examining a patient.

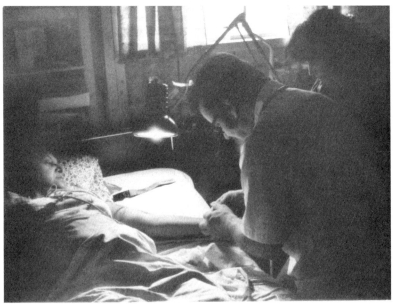

Elam examining a patient.

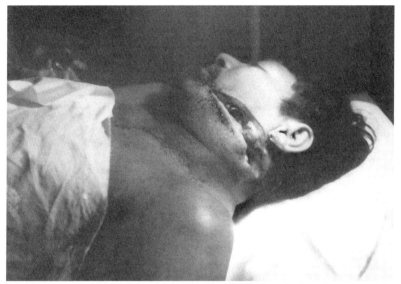

A man who was cut in a bar fight by a friend's machete before Elam sutured him up.

After Elam sutured him up.

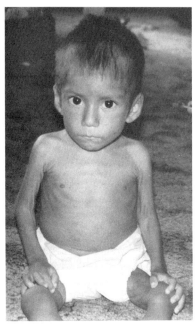

Herson, a little malnourished boy who was brought to the clinic for help.

Herson just a few months after being cared for by Barbara round the clock.

A view of La Anchura from the air in 1980.

Jean, Lisa, Anita, Maria, Barbara, Elam, Miguel, and Virgil at Lakewood Church in Houston, Texas.

Virgil in his ultralight with TV mounted for showing evangelistic videos.

The Maule which clocked over 800 hours of emergency flights.

The Maule after it was burned.

The Maule after it was burned.

1990 –The recently finished cannery less than a month before it was destroyed.

The canning center after it was burned.

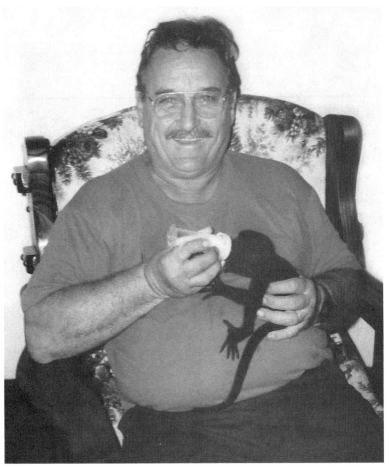

1990s–Elam in the 90s with a baby howler monkey.

2000–The new clinic.